9:02 a.m.

APRIL 19, 1995

The OFFICIAL RECORD of the OKLAHOMA CITY BOMBING

D1568435

Oklahoma Today *Magazine*

Oklahoma Today (ISSN 0030-1892) is published six times a year, in January, March, May, July, September, and November by the State of Oklahoma, Oklahoma Tourism and Recreation Department, 15 North Robinson, Suite 100, P.O. Box 1468, Oklahoma City, Oklahoma 73101, (800) 777-1793 or (405) 521-2496. U.S. copyright 2005 by *Oklahoma Today*. All rights reserved. Reproduction in whole or in part without written permission is prohibited. Visit *Oklahoma Today* at oklahomatoday.com.

Editor's Note: Oklahoma Today *originally published* The Official Record of the Oklahoma City Bombing *in January 1996. Two subsequent editions were published in January 2001 and January 2005. All content appears in its original form.*

CONTENTS

This American elm came to be known as the Survivor Tree because it was one of the few things in the vicinity to survive the blast. Here, it stands against the backdrop of the damaged Journal Record Building, prior to the creation of the Oklahoma City National Memorial.

THE FORK IN THE ROAD

Our task is to ensure they did not die in vain.

January 1996

IT IS IMPOSSIBLE to overstate the significance of the bombing of the Alfred P. Murrah Federal Building in downtown Oklahoma City—to America or to Americans. We are a people whose forefathers fought so that we might each have the freedom to speak our mind, air our disagreements (even with our leaders), and follow the God of our choice. We have traditionally valued noble ideals and ideas over simplistic icons and dogmas. We have been a two hundred-and-nineteen-year experiment in democracy that has managed to survive depression, war, cold war, racial and social unrest, Vietnam, and the toppling of a presidency.

April 19, 1995, however, recalled the darkness of the Civil War and the assassinations of presidents Abraham Lincoln and John F. Kennedy.

In Oklahoma, where we saw the horror firsthand, it was impossible to comprehend that another human being could believe blowing up innocent men, women, and children was a solution to anything. Was the human condition in a tailspin? Or was America herself?

It will always be a matter of conjecture whether what happened next was a factor of the place the bombers chose to explode or simply a true reading of the American character. But beginning in the very seconds that followed the explosion, aye, before the black clouds rose above the downtown tree line, Oklahomans exhibited the acts of heroism, devotion, and hope that—when brought together—have always moved our nation forward. More hopeful yet, this response was mirrored by that of our fellow countrymen, suggesting that the same heroism, devotion, and hope remain lodged in the hearts of innumerable Americans.

Our reaction would not have surprised the writer Bruce Catton, who observed after the death of JFK: "Americans are always uneasy when we find ourselves keeping our noblest ideals in moth balls, carefully shielded from contact with the workaday world; deep in our hearts we know that we are supposed to take them out and work for them even if contact with harsh reality occasionally knocks chips off of them here and there."

What happens next in America is indeed up to us. We ask only this: Read the memorials of the men, women, and children who died that day and in the days that followed. But before you do, cover up the photographs. In the stories of their lives lies the ultimate evidence that goodness and kindness and courage and godliness know no color, no economic, no age, no social barriers. Then turn and look at your neighbor—or better yet the next stranger you meet. And remember, we are all Americans. And our country needs each and every one of us. And mourn the 168 we lost.

Jeanne M. Devlin

Downtown Oklahoma City before the bombing, looking southeast from St. Anthony Hospital

From Braced Against the Wind, a literary tribute

to the victims of the Oklahoma City bombing.

Nothing gentles down from
A mild Heaven here.
We are always braced
Against the wild wind.
We were ever hand in hand
As far as the eye can see.

Cataclysms are the story.
Our cities sprang up overnight,
Are flattened at a tongue-lashing
By clouds, and bush-whackers and
Bonnies and Clydes
Struck fast and hid against
The land, stretched and pegged
Flat to the Four Corners
Of the Earth. We do not cower
At disaster.

We join hands, sing hymns.
We share tears, and
Bend our backs, raising
A neighbor's barn.
Do not think your
Abrupt terror will
Destroy us.

Wide horizons stretch our
Vision. We do not believe in limits.
We shift with the red dust,
Dance golden like the wheatfields.
We believe. We move on.
We bend and dance
On the tallgrass.

The prairie sings our pain.
The land shouts our praise.
The wind calls us together.

—*Carol Hamilton*
Oklahoma Poet Laureate

TO A[...]
WE WILL FOREVER
REMEMBER YOUR LOVE, COURAGE & TEARS.
MAY GOD BLESS
YOU ALL.

CITY OF NEW YORK
AMBULANCE

NYC EMS
AMBULANCE
75   75

IN LOVE,
CHRISTINE
SALIBA #3385
NYC·EMS

APRIL 19, 1995

THE STORY OF THE OKLAHOMA CITY BOMBING

'This isn't supposed to happen here.'

View from Integris/Baptist Medical Center parking garage about ten minutes after the blast

COY/DAWSON/SIPA

Above, Three minutes after the explosion, a local worker helps an injured man thrown by the blast. Some six hundred people were said to have been injured in the bombing. Right, Sergeant Ted Mapes clears spectators from the site; far right, Oklahoma City Police Chief Sam Gonzales.

T HE IMPACT WAS felt first. In Guthrie and Chandler it was mistaken for a sonic boom. At Gethsemane Lutheran School in northwest Oklahoma City, Miranda Wardeman and her fellow students joked that lightning had struck on a clear April day. Eight miles north of downtown on Britton Road, television reporters jumped into their cars in anticipation of a natural gas accident. At the Will Rogers Building on Lincoln Boulevard—two miles northeast as the crow flies—workers felt their building buckle and thought something had exploded on a lower floor. As the windows blew out of the third floor of the Bricktown Brewery just blocks away from Robinson and 5th, Jim Cowan's thoughts turned immediately to an earthquake. Down the street at the Journal Record Building, occupants at a meeting were blown from their chairs; outside, cars exploded in flames.

Inside the Alfred P. Murrah Federal Building, it was as if someone had simply turned out a light.

It was 9:02 a.m., April 19, 1995.

And for the rest of our lives we Americans will remember where we were that Wednesday morning. Could any one of us forget the relentless horror of watching families torn asunder and innocent children orphaned, maimed, or buried in what would come to be known as the worst act of terrorism ever committed

Team 5
4-19-95
We Search for the truth
We seek Justice.
The Courts Require it.
The Victims Cry for it.
And GOD Demands it!

Clockwise from top right, Timothy James McVeigh exits the Perry County Courthouse; Terry Nichols turns himself in in Wichita after hearing his name on television; the Perry courthouse; the Mercury Grand Marquis McVeigh was driving when an Oklahoma highway patrolman pulled him over for not having a car tag (he was subsequently detained for transporting a concealed weapon). McVeigh was almost released before police realized he was "John Doe No. 1," the subject of the greatest manhunt in United States history. Everyday police work brought the suspect in just ninety minutes after the bombing.

on U.S. soil? But in that first hour on April 19, only the men, women, and children left alive in the Alfred P. Murrah Federal Building and the rescuers and officials who ventured into its bowels knew the degree of devastation wrought by 4,800 pounds of ammonium nitrate and fuel oil.

Experts would later determine that the first wave of super hot gas moved at 7,000 miles an hour—fast enough that someone ten feet away would have been hit with a force equal to thirty-seven tons. In about half a second, the gas dissipated, only to be

Facing page, clockwise from top left: Rescue scenes; rescue team flags; message spraypainted on the Journal Record Building wall; burial of Salaam Ahmed (his mother miscarried after her home was terrorized in the wake of reports linking Islamics to the bombing); rescue scenes

replaced by an equally violent vacuum. The resulting pressure wave moved outward, lifting the building up and causing beams, floor slabs, and connections to weaken or collapse. When the pressure wave passed, gravity took over. Nine stories on the north side of the Alfred P. Murrah Federal Building pancaked, creating a crater some thirty feet deep. People who had begun on the ninth floor ended up at the bottom of the building. Had the force of the explosion all been directed at the ground, it would have been equivalent to a Magnitude 4 earthquake; as it was the pressure wave itself was a Magnitude 1.

In a matter of seconds downtown Oklahoma City had been rearranged to resemble any other war zone. As gas tanks and tires exploded in the shadow of a nine-story building ripped open to

KWTV 9/FITZGERALD ASSOCIATES

Sergeant Mark Mollman guides Dr. Brian Espe from the fifth floor of the Murrah building; Espe, a USDA veterinarian, lost seven coworkers in the blast. Right, Oklahoma City firefighters work in the area known as "the pit." When recovering the victims, the work was done a brick at a time.

the sunlight, one couldn't help but recall similar scenes from Beirut or Belfast—places that had always seemed worlds away.

It took sixty seconds for the first person to open his eyes, stagger to a working telephone in the YMCA, and dial 911. By then the rescue had already begun. The first official report of an explosion came from a police patrol car in the area, and the first paramedics that arrived on site at 9:02:18 actually used the hazy cloud of debris hovering over the Murrah building as a lodestar to guide their ambulance to the injured. "In an awful way," recalls EMSA emergency medical technician Jana Knox of the sight she and her partner saw as they drove up the street, "It was breathtaking. There was glass shimmering on the streets and scrap metal everywhere." Eventually law enforcement officials would find a piece of the Ryder truck—believed to have carried the bomb—a few blocks away; it would become one more piece of evidence culled from the rubble.

Within seconds after the explosion, police and fire department radio channels erupted with reports, and EMSA dispatchers began fielding hundreds of calls. Eventually all firefighters—both on and off duty—were called in, a first in Oklahoma City's history.

At the site, it was still, as if the world, for a moment, had simply stopped turning. And then the survivors did something that captured America's heart as much as anything that came out of this tragedy: They started running. Not away from the

building, but toward it, as if each person had heard someone call their name for help.

It was about 9:07 a.m., and the sky over downtown Oklahoma City was still raining glass, the shards making a delicate tinkle as they hit the concrete. In front of the Murrah building, the rows of burning cars had begun to give off a dark, billowing smoke. And the atmosphere on the street was fast becoming one of organized chaos. Rescue and emergency workers and law enforcement officials—from the sheriff's department to the Oklahoma City police—shifted into automatic pilot. They had been trained for a major disaster, and they knew what they had to do.

In the minutes that followed, some survivors simply got up and walked down the staircase of the Murrah building; others trapped on ledges where the floor had fallen away or buried under piles of rubble, waited for Oklahoma City firefighters to find them. On the street, a few survivors picked themselves up and limped off in a daze; others drove themselves to the nearest hospital. Many more sat on curbs, staring into space or comforting others. The seriously injured were loaded—often bleeding, broken, and with shards of glass protruding from their bodies—into the beds of pickups, cars, or ambulances and driven to nearby hospitals.

A triage and treatment area was set up nearby to handle the hundreds of injured people expected to need help after the rescue was complete. That second wave never came.

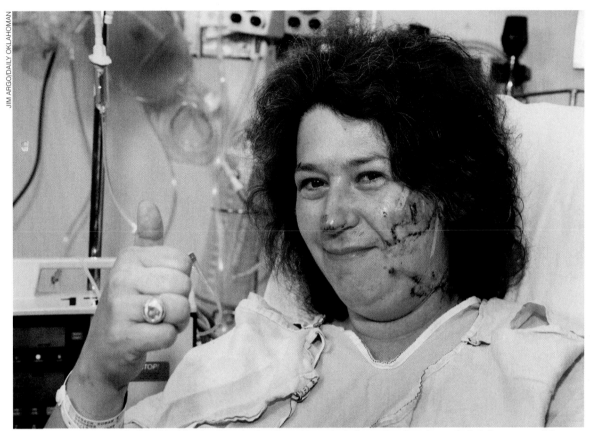

JIM ARGO/DAILY OKLAHOMAN

Susan Urbach, wounded in the federal building bombing, displays the positive attitude that endeared survivors to both their rescuers and the world. Six months after the bombing, many had yet to regain all their hearing.

For those outside the two miles of destruction that radiated from the Murrah building, the clue that all was not right was the sight of that dense, dark cloud rising ominously above the tree line on our television sets. For what seemed like an eternity (but in actuality was only a matter of minutes), that image was the only link most of us had with what was happening to our friends and loved ones downtown.

Initial news reports were sketchy and inaccurate. The first Associated Press bulletin read: COURT EXPLOSION URGENT. Television and radio announcers ran with that story, placing the explosion at the Federal Courthouse (two buildings farther south) and speculating that the cause was a natural gas accident.

Facing page, clockwise from top left: Free supplies for rescue workers; scene after the May 5, 1995, memorial service; Melanie Ames after Regency Tower residents were briefly allowed in the high-rise apartment complex to retrieve possessions; boarded-up windows Oklahoma-style; a fallen sign on I-235; the Journal Record Building; inside an office destroyed in the bombing; the media circus

As a stream of reporters barreled down I-35 to the site, the TV choppers took to the air. By 9:16 a.m., most stations had confirmed that the building was in actuality the circa 1977 federal office building named for the late Federal Judge Alfred P. Murrah. It was also about this time that someone mentioned the possibility of children being in the building.

The news that indeed a daycare was located on the second floor of the Murrah building knocked the air out of everyone, and it coincided with some of the first pictures from what would come to be known as Ground Zero. If the first televised pictures from the air of the building's gaping face had been heart-stopping, the ones from ground-level cameras at the base of the building were even worse: people wrapped in white gauze bandages, bloody faces, screaming children, weeping women, backs of men slashed red as if they had been whipped.

Inside the Murrah building, where the TV cameras could not go, debris was falling, people were dying, and others were trapped—choking on smoke and, in some instances, petrified of

Top, Oklahoma City Mayor Ron Norick joins Lieutenant Governor Mary Fallin and Governor and Mrs. Keating in a moment of silence at the base of the Alfred P. Murrah Federal Building. Left, Hundreds of people turned out for a May 5 memorial service at the site of the Murrah building. Second from top, rescue workers console each other after the memorial service held at the building's base (afterwards rescuers threw long-stemmed roses on the remaining rubble pile). The building ultimately became so unstable that efforts to recover the last two people believed to be entombed were ceased. Their bodies, along with another, were recovered after the building was imploded.

drowning. Oklahoma City Police Sergeant Jerry Flowers found one woman imprisoned under a huge slab of concrete and rebar, yelling to rescue workers not to leave her. Knox and another paramedic found a group of adult survivors, only to stumble next upon a pocket of children, all of them dead. Firefighters freed survivors trapped in the debris by listening for their moans, digging them out brick by brick, and handing them one by one with tender hands to others, who passed them down a human chain to the street. "In about fifteen minutes," recalls Knox, "our ambulance was almost stripped of supplies. People needing help were everywhere. I would just finish with one and turn around to find twenty more. It was like a scene out of hell, and it would be like this for hours."

FALLEN ANGEL OF MERCY
Rebecca Anderson

As *Newsweek* observed when it named her among its five heroes for 1995: "She was the kind of person who took in stray animals and, against her husband's wishes, picked up hitchhikers." No one who knew Rebecca Anderson was surprised to hear the 37-year-old nurse had rushed to help in the aftermath of the Murrah bombing. In trying to save others, however, she lost her own life. Found dazed and confused on site, she died from head injuries four days later. (Her heart and kidney went immediately to help two people waiting for transplants.) Friends recall her thoughtfulness and her practical jokes. Her husband and four children remember her as a woman of great compassion. "Rebecca gave her life," said Fred Anderson, "doing what she wanted to do."

Almost as if they were dazed themselves, television reporters filed reports that in the days to come Oklahomans could only wish could have been true. Estimated injured: twenty or thirty. Estimated serious building damage other than the Murrah building: none. Estimated death toll: a few. When Channel 9 reporter Randy Renner emotionally observed, "This is something that happens someplace else...This is not supposed to happen in places like Oklahoma. It's not something that's supposed to happen at home," the cameras quickly cut away. No one wanted to panic anyone unnecessarily—those were people's loved ones inside and hurting on the street. But in the weeks to come, as the death toll grew higher and higher, we knew what he was trying to say in those early minutes of the disaster. And we weren't surprised when ultimately other seasoned reporters —from Barbara Walters of *20/20* to Tom Brokaw—also candidly admitted on air that this was an American tragedy of unprecedented proportion in their experience.

In those first frantic hours, no law enforcement officials were saying what or who was suspected of causing the explosion, but many on site had seen the crater and the carnage. And those with military experience recognized the work of explosives when they saw it. Whispers began to circulate about foreign terrorists. But others had noticed an uncanny coincidence: April 19, 1995, was the anniversary of the showdown in Waco. And indeed before the sun set that day, an American was being held as the government's main suspect.

That night Oklahomans went to sleep with the hope that the morning would bring news of more survivors, knowing full well that each passing hour made that less likely.

Thursday morning dawned, and Oklahomans headed back to work. But our thoughts were elsewhere. As we drove down the streets and highways of Oklahoma City, one by one we turned our headlights on in the full day's light.

Thanks to the Academic Broadcasting Services of the University of Central Oklahoma, KEBC Radio, KWTV 9, KOCO 5, WKY Radio, the Oklahoma City Fire Department, EMSA, and the Dallas Morning News *for providing transcripts and tapes for this story.*

Oklahoma City firefighters head to the command center at the Alfred P. Murrah Federal Building site on April 30, 1995.

LEAN ON ME

If Oklahoma thought it would have to suffer the bombing alone, it soon learned otherwise. The entire country—indeed much of the world—seemed determined to help us carry on.

The morning of the statewide prayer service, the president and first lady planted a dogwood in honor of the victims on the White House lawn before heading for Oklahoma. Right, United States flags are lowered on April 20.

THE JAPANESE PRIME minister sent a message of sympathy on behalf of the people of Japan (their consul general sent $10,000). Turkey's ambassador donated $10,000 to the American Red Cross, while people from Australia to Scotland to Slovakia sent their prayers.

From a single county in New Jersey came $100,000. Olympic figure skater Nancy Kerrigan and Dallas Cowboy Troy Aikman contributed $10,000 each. The Los Angeles Hard Rock Café sent $25,000, New York financier Henry Kravis (like Aikman a former Oklahoman) gave $200,000, and the *Boston Globe* raised $37,000 (from sales of Dan Wasserman's cartoon of a dejected teddy bear).

Meanwhile firefighters and rescue workers from across the United States flew, or drove, in to help—many on their own initiative. AT&T provided phone lines so out-of-state rescue workers could stay in touch with their families, florists sent tens of thousands of flowers by the stem for the services, and Peruvian artist Mario Torero mounted his mural, "The Child," on the north wall of the Myriad for inspiration.

Individuals the world over—from Switzerland to New Zealand to Puerto Rico to Maui—sent cards, toys, teddy bears, books, and flowers (many also included donations). The Oklahoma City school system alone received 400,000 letters (the governor, 10,000 in a single day). Indeed, the outpouring was so great, the *Daily Oklahoman* took to publishing a regular column on "Acts of Kindness," and we all felt reassured about the inherent goodness of human beings.

AP/WIDE WORLD PHOTOS/SANCETTA

Judy Hoffman of Oklahoma City tours a maze of cards sent from out of state (Simon Property Group gathered some 50,000 signatures and messages of support from patrons of its sixty-two malls).

FITZGERALD & ASSOCIATES

The Duchess of York raised funds.

AP/WIDE WORLD PHOTOS/LENNIHAN

A lone flag flew in New York's Rockefeller Plaza.

AP/WIDE WORLD PHOTOS/WIDEMAN

Indy car drivers paused on April 23, 1995.

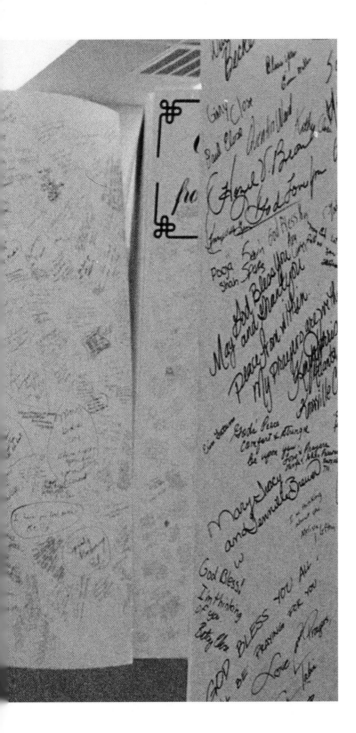

A moment of silence on Capitol Hill

'WE SHOULD ALL PLANT A TREE.'

T HE SUGGESTION CAME first from a little girl to the President of the United States of America. By year's end, like the proverbial fish and loaves, it had multiplied tenfold. President Clinton and his wife planted a small dogwood on the White House lawn on April 23, 1995. Oklahoma City Mayor Ron Norick declared the week of May 19, 1995, "Plant a Memorial Tree Week," and schools, churches, and families across Oklahoma took up the challenge, planting redbuds, dogwoods, and red oaks. In Oklahoma City, Governor and Mrs. Keating planted nine trees (three with white blossoms for the 19 children killed in the blast, three with red blossoms for the rescue workers, and three with pink blossoms for the adult victims) at the governor's mansion on the one-month anniversary of the bombing.

Yet the most touching gesture of all may well have come from Iowa. Dan Cooper, then state horticulturalist for Iowa, was recuperating from surgery when he heard about the Oklahoma City bombing. His first reaction, says Camille Valley of the Iowa State Horticultural Society, was, "Geez, we've got to do something."

Cooper suggested a formal bosk, and Valley and others selected the trees: a hundred and fifty fragrant Littleleaf Lindens (one for each adult believed to be lost to the bombing) and nineteen Prairifire Crab Apples (one for each child who died). As envisioned, the Lindens would grow taller than the colorful crab apples, their crowns and branches eventually interlocking in a tight embrace, forming a thick canopy. "[The very idea] just sent chills through your body," recalls Valley.

Cooper mentioned it to Iowa's governor, who mentioned it to Governor Keating, and by early November, Valley was meeting with Keating's staff and the Murrah building memorial commission to select a site. Ultimately, the bosk was laid out on the north lawn of the capitol by some two hundred Iowans during the week of November 12 (they brought four semi-loads of trees, sand, and equipment and enough donations to also install an irrigation system). At week's end, a few workers were making plans to return in spring to see the crab apples in bloom.

Dan Cooper, however, did not live to see his idea to fruition; he died from complications in September.

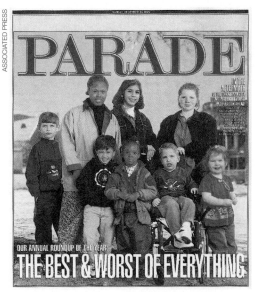

After the bombing, publications from People Magazine *to* Parade *tracked the progress of the youngest survivors as well as the children of those who died. Thanks to people like Chris Gross, most will at least look forward to a free college education. Opposite page, left to right, Keith Harris, Gary Thurman, and Scott White.*

The Reverend Jesse Jackson taking notes at the bomb site.

The Reverend Billy Graham encouraged rescuers.

SETTING AN EXAMPLE

O N THE EVENING of April 23, 1995, Chris Gross sat on the floor of his Santa Clara home composing a voice-mail message to the executives of the $3 billion company for which he works. In it, he informed them that he had decided to give up a year of his salary and donate it to the children who had lost parents in the Oklahoma City bombing. And oh yes, he added, he hoped his company would match his pledge.

Not only did the powers that be at Applied Materials agree to the match (a few days after getting the message), but soon other companies and individuals also chipped in. Reasoned Gross: "When it's a millionaire, everybody says, 'Oh, that's nice, but he's worth $100 million. Big deal.' With me, people say, 'Oh my God, if this guy can do it...at least I can throw in fifty or a hundred bucks.'"

The twenty-seven-year-old's sacrifice of $53,874.08 had in late fall become $650,000—all of it going to college scholarships for the victim's children, and all of it safely in a special fund at the twenty-five-year-old Oklahoma City Foundation. Gross's main motivation? "I kept thinking, 'What would it have been like if I'd lost my parents at that age?'"

Now living on $12,000 in savings in an area with one of the nation's highest costs of living ("I just stopped spending money in general," he says), he has no regrets: "It's brought me a lot. You can't put a price tag on the feeling that I have."

Prayers in Seattle

A COMMUNITY SEEKS CONSOLATION

Oklahomans joined a president, a preacher, and
their countrymen in a day of national mourning.

THE IDEA WAS conceived before the clock struck twelve on April 19, 1995, by First Lady Cathy Keating and a few choice aides and family members. Not one of them doubted that their fellow Oklahomans would come—the naked need was obvious by looking into the eyes of any Oklahoman. What no one expected was the nation to show up as well.

They drove in from Colorado, New Mexico, and Texas. They flew in from New York, Washington, D.C., and points in between (the First Lady of Illinois, Brenda Edgars, sent six hundred teddy bears for the bereaved families). Some arrived before dawn; by noon, radio stations broadcasted gentle warnings cautioning people that if they were not already in line, they would most likely not get in. At three o'clock in the afternoon when the doors opened, nineteen thousand were waiting. And still they came.

Tens of thousands of people filled first the State Fair Arena, then the Made in Oklahoma Building, and finally All Sports Stadium. Yet even more Americans eavesdropped over car radios or watched the finale—Ernestine Dillard's rendition of "God Bless America"—at home. Against a backdrop of song, prayer, and poetry, the nation took a collective moment to share its grief and to gain encouragement from the words of the Reverend Billy Graham. The day was April 23, 1995, and the death toll stood at 73 dead, 154 unaccounted for, and at least 460 injured. There was worse to come, but there was also, finally, some comfort.

Left, Hundreds line up for the memorial service. Above, The President and First Lady of the United States and the Governor and First Lady of Oklahoma flank Jason Smith and Dan McKinney, son and husband of Secret Service employee Linda McKinney.

Oklahoma State Fair Arena

United States Attorney General Janet Reno received a standing ovation as she entered the prayer service.

Some twelve thousand people filled the State Fair arena to capacity; another eight to ten thousand watched on big-screen televisions or listened over loudspeakers at All-Sports Stadium.

Dust to Dust

'I just go home at night and cry for awhile so I can come back the next day.

I can't cry with them. I need to be strong for them.' —funeral director

E VEN PEOPLE WHO consider death a part of their daily schedule were shaken by the enormity of the Oklahoma City death toll. In early May, a chance visitor to Arlington Memorial Gardens outside Oklahoma City could not look in any direction without seeing a fresh, flower-festooned grave. Indeed more than one morning dawned with survivors facing more funerals than they could possibly attend in a single day. "We cried with the families," one funeral director told the *Daily Oklahoman*. "We cried with each other." Children were laid to rest with teddy bears and favorite toys, veterans received military burials, and more than one church was filled to overflowing as friends, relatives, and coworkers came to pay their last respects to the men, women, and children who were taken too early from us.

Above, Luther and LaRue Treanor were buried as they lived—side by side—on April 28, 1995, at Summit View Cemetery in Guthrie. Right, An Oklahoma City Fire Department honor guard accompanies the casket containing Carrie Ann Lenz and her unborn son, Michael Lenz III.

Master Sergeant Vickey Sohn, a mother of five, received a soldier's burial on April 29, 1995, in Midwest City.

PICTURES WE WON'T FORGET

Photographers were among the first on site April 19, 1995. They came initially in a trickle and then in droves—amateur, corporate, newspaper, wire service, magazine, tabloid. By sunset that first day, they were everywhere and seemingly from everywhere else: Muskogee, Tulsa, Fort Worth, New York City, Los Angeles, Europe. Though television piped the story directly into our living rooms, it was still—even in this age of twenty-four-hour broadcasts—a few particular photographs that captured the world's imagination, summing up the horror—and the hope—as no amount of footage seemed capable of doing.

Medical assistants Janet Froehlich, Wilma Jackson, and Kerri Albright run from the Murrah building Wednesday, April 19, 1995, after a call was sounded that another bomb device had been found. Rescuers were ordered to leave the site—and those trapped in the rubble. The report proved unfounded; it was one of two false alarms that day.

Taken moments after police sergeant John Avera sought help for Baylee Almon from Oklahoma City firefighter Chris Fields, the image was captured by two local photographers. This Pulitzer Prize winning image, taken by Charles Porter IV, went on to grace the covers of Newsweek, Time, Life, *and* The Economist, *and for many, it came to symbolize the senseless tragedy. Baylee was pronounced dead at 9:45 a.m. at St. Anthony Hospital.*

View from Ground Zero

Skip Fernandez and his golden retriever Aspen of Dade County, Florida, were among more than forty-two FEMA man-dog teams. Observed one team member: "When [my dog] finds someone alive, he barks. When he finds a body, he whines...He's done more whining, than barking."

Chad Roy Harris, right, joined his mother and grandmother at a candlelight vigil held April 25, 1995, at Hedge Field on the Oklahoma State University campus in Stillwater, Oklahoma. The vigil drew four hundred to six hundred townspeople, including local officers from the army, navy, air force, and marines. "Every officer in town was there," said one organizer.

Oklahoma
4/95

half-
mast

Pauley 4/95

By Lynn Pauley

The Grahams

FOR SOME REASON on the night of April 19th I wake unable to sleep. On the TV in strong winds is a man reporting on the bombing of the Alfred P. Murrah building in downtown Oklahoma City. Behind him sways a green and white Hanson Sofa Covering sign. Little do I realize that at 3 a.m. on Friday *The New Yorker* will call and ask me to go on site there to draw, paint, and record the tragedy.

It is what I do—chronicling real life events in paint and charcoal—but every bone in my body begs to turn this assignment down. How, I wonder, will I ever stay detached enough to faithfully record what I would witness in the middle of such an emotional fire storm? Yet by 6 a.m. Saturday I am in line to board United flight 95 at John F. Kennedy airport. The ticket agent apologizes: "Have a nice flight. Sorry it couldn't be under nicer circumstances." The passengers' faces on the flight are hardened and defeated, as if they sense the death—the enormity of loss and sadness—we are about to enter. No one speaks to me. I prepare myself emotionally as well. I pray, "Please just let me get visually close enough in three days and help me stay centered myself so I can complete the work."

SATURDAY, APRIL 22, 9 A.M.
Will Rogers Airport
Marianne at Avis Rent-a-Car

"It's a big mess. We tend to be hickish and red neck, but we'll never change. We will always be angry." She hands me my keys and a bright yellow Avis map of Oklahoma City. "I found out it was done by someone domestic. I could understand if somebody from overseas was doing this to retaliate, but one of our own?" She shakes her head in disbelief and with a black pen marks where we are, where the Holiday Inn is located, and, in ink, a line straight to the bomb site. "You're going to the memorial service Sunday, aren't you?" She marks the map black again to indicate the location of the Oklahoma State Fairgrounds.

It is pouring rain. The thunder and low clouds pull in deep black, and lightning cracks close to the ground. God is grieving his loss by raining torrential tears. "Bomb Suspect Charged" in huge block letters covers the front page of the day's *Daily Oklahoman*.

SATURDAY, 2 P.M.
One-Hour Developing Counter, Wal-Mart on MacArthur Boulevard
Reverend M.C. Graham and his wife, Rachel

"Don't look at my pictures!" Words from the first people I meet. The Grahams were part of the first relief efforts to arrive on site Wednesday. They arrived at 9:20 a.m. "I thought it was a sonic boom," the minister tells me. "Rachel and I live three miles from the site. We went right down there, and for some reason we got right in there without press passes

Albuquerque firefighter

"My bad habit paid off; my Pepsi habit paid off today. I've cleaned out sixty two-liter bottles and put in good ol' well water for the guys."

"We listened to the list on the radio—wash rags, gum, kitchen towels. We decided to bring things."

"We felt helpless watching all week."

SATURDAY, 5:30 P.M.
My voice on hand-held tape recorder.

This entire section is cordoned off. All the windows are blown out. It kind of looks like Beirut or a war zone. There is nobody here. It is desolate. But there is still that small-town feel. Even though it is a major city, you feel like you can find parking anywhere.

SATURDAY, FIREMEN COMING OFF THEIR SHIFTS
Jeff Herod from Elmo, Texas, and Django Belote and Paul Duval from Albuquerque, New Mexico

Q. Did it change things for you now that you know it's American terrorists as opposed to a Middle Eastern attack?

Jeff. Oh, yeah, definitely. It makes you angry. It's hard to believe someone in the U.S. would do this to their own people...when you find out, from what I understand, people from our own armed services were involved, you think how could they stoop so low?

Q. When did you get here?

Django. Last night around midnight. We drove all night.

Paul. We don't know where we're staying yet.

SATURDAY NIGHT
Room 113, Holiday Inn, Route 66

My voice is shot from interviewing people in the pouring rain. I am back from picking up photos from Wal-Mart and working on six paintings at a time. I don't have time to think; I don't have time to cry. I can cry when I get home. I order tea from room service. "I'm sorry, we can only deliver items that total more than five dollars."

"What do you have on the dessert menu?"

"Sherbet, ice cream, apple pie."

"Okay, sherbet and tea."

"I'm sorry, that still only comes to $3.50."

I forget. Here in America's heartland, things are cheaper. I order apple pie, lime sherbet, ice cream, and tea. The lime sherbet goes untouched and melts in its dish next to the apple pie on the tray. *Forrest Gump* plays over and over on pay-per-view.

SUNDAY, APRIL 23, 3 P.M.
Statewide Prayer Service
Oklahoma State Fairgrounds
Cathy Keating, First Lady, State of Oklahoma

"Whenever you see a firefighter, a policeman, a volunteer, a nurse, remember to say thank you."

SUNDAY, AFTERNOON
Statewide Prayer Service, Oklahoma State Fairgrounds
Waiting in line

Retired volunteers from The Sundowners Club stand at the door with cardboard boxes of purple ribbons. There are so many people waiting we are moved to an alternate site. No one complains; everyone moves politely to their seats. Brady Wright, sixteen, sits next to me as I draw. "What are they going to do?" he asks me. "Ban fertilizer here in Oklahoma?" What impresses me are the proud silences, personal Bibles, kids dressed in their

or anything. We spent three days giving the firemen pop, sunglasses, food—whatever they needed—as they searched through the rubble." He describes people walking about with shards of glass protruding from their faces, bleeding onto the street; he saw one policeman holding two tow-headed boys bleeding profusely, not crying, just stunned. In their three days there were two other bomb scares. "We had to vacate and literally run across the street."

"The worst was when they brought out the dead military guys. When those bodies were pulled out of the wreckage, they didn't use body bags; they actually put them on gurneys and brought them out on stretchers. The volunteers would stop, stand, and salute as the gurneys went by."

"Did you cry?" I asked.

"Yes."

SATURDAY, LATE AFTERNOON
On site
Tina Goforth and six-year-old Derrik Sponemore

"Does it bother you that Americans are suspected of doing it?" I ask Tina.

"It makes me sick to my stomach."

Sandi Sheppard Dailey and her daughter Kelly

"We had to come see it. When you see it on television, you think it could have happened anywhere."

Overflow site at Statewide prayer service

Sunday best. They are all here, present for the service. More concerned with how you are doing, their guest, a stranger, than themselves. They wait for hours in line, willing to sit in a poorly lit, overheated hall because they want to be together. To sit together, sing together, share their overwhelming grief. For most it is the only thing they can do.

I leave early. The sway of 9,000 people singing, "Amazing Grace" is too much to bear.

MONDAY, APRIL 24, 8:15 A.M.
Downtown Oklahoma City
Kiffa Shirley, National Guard

"We were brought here to protect the perimeter," Kiffa tells me, then asks to see my press credentials. "The PRESS," he sneers. "What's with you media people anyway? Already we've had *Hard Copy* reporters sneaking into the site in fake fireman equipment."

They are so desperate to fill pages and air time with anything, and anyone is fair game. Carmen, my waitress, confides when I return later to the Holiday Inn for breakfast: "They're loud, aren't they?" She motions her head to the reporters at the next table. They seem sure of themselves, talking about the blast site, the sixty-eighth victim: "Yeah, I heard McVeigh bought the Mercury so many days before," one of them speculates. Carmen confesses she overheard a group of reporters joking about how "soft" the local media has been. "It's hard not to say anything." She leans over me with a big white and purple handmade ribbon attached to her uniform with an angel pin, the homemade corsage so big it all but covers her name tag. "We're not going to change. We were all friends before," she says, refilling my cup with coffee. "This won't defeat us," nods again at the next table. "This will only make us stronger."

A Sundowner volunteer

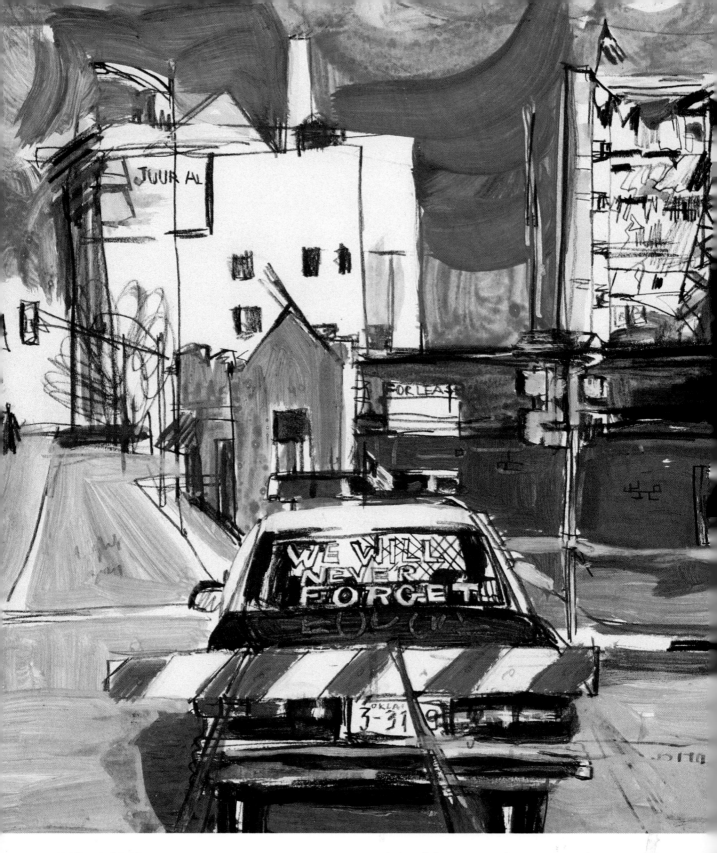

MONDAY, 2 P.M.

At the site

Two young guys from Kansas come up to me as I am drawing on a knoll several blocks away from the site. Gabe Garcia and Jeremy DuBois. Gabe says to me, "Geez, we know a better place, closer, that you can draw. Follow us." They lead me to a clearing, and to my amazement, it is the exact site I first witnessed on my own television at 3 a.m. on April 20th.

"We will forgive, we will never forget," neatly written in white shoe polish on the windshield of a police car at the scene. The phone rings and rings in the boarded up Hanson Sofa Covering store, but no one answers. People come with their kids, their cameras, their camcorders, their prayers, their flowers, but no one says a word. They just stand there for hours, looking The eye of the storm, ground zero.

TUESDAY, APRIL 25, 8:25 A.M.

Will Rogers Airport, Gate C9, United

Now I understand post-stress trauma, and I was only here for three days Finally leaving, I note that the death toll reads: 71, injured 400, missing

150—it will only grow worse in the days to come. I pick up *Newsweek* and look at the photos and go to read it, but there is no way—it's too much. I know these people now.

Maybe this is the wake up all America needed. Maybe this tragedy will remind us that, yes, there is evil, but goodness, and good-hearted people can overcome anything by banding together. These Oklahomans proved that to me—that being open, enthusiastic, and kind is still the way to go. I feel like I was led here. What I feel personally is as intense as any feelings I have ever had being on site. It jumbles together my undying pride at being an American and renews my own unabashed faith in God and humanity. I feel respect and awe for these people, these Oklahomans—slapped brutally in the face, angry, oh so angry, who still retain the ability to forgive, vowing never to forget.

This is worse than any site I have ever been on.

Maybe now I can cry.

. . . .

Lynn Pauley of New York City has documented stories on site for the New York Times, Sports Illustrated, *and* Ladies' Home Journal.

FROM AROUND THE CORNER, AND AROUND THE WORLD, THEY CAME.

By Ralph Marsh

IT WAS THE oddest of pilgrimages. People from everywhere hurrying into downtown Oklahoma City on a warm weekend in late spring. Massing into traffic jams. Parking cars anywhere this side of the yellow police tape and quickly loading children into strollers. Rushing with worried brows as if late to a doctor's appointment. A man with a plastic hose in his nose pulled a wheeled oxygen container with fatalistic determination. A middle-aged black couple, solemn in dark Sunday best even on a Saturday, strode resolutely, steeling themselves. Fathers carried sons on their shoulders so someday they could tell them they saw this historically horrible thing.

"Children, we better start looking for Jesus." An immaculate reed of an old woman said it quietly and walked away.

There is a tiny walled courtyard on the paved grounds of St. Paul's Episcopal Cathedral, no bigger than a room, and inside it is cooler even than the rose garden. In the circular flower bed beneath the tree that air-conditions the little room, a sign gently admonishes that "Thou Shalt Not Walk." Jonquils flower there in spring, or did before April 19, blooms arching from little ruffled cuffs like wrists of refined ladies. People retreat there, in normal times, from the hot and angry streets of Oklahoma City. But on this day there was danger the roof might fall. And a man with fear in his eyes paced the sidewalk outside and pointed at the church and talked with too much authority to any who would listen.

"It broke the baby Jesus from the arms of Mary," he cried. And his voice drew heads from rolled-down windows of passing mini-vans, and the fact that what he said happened had not happened at all did nothing to diminish the awful feeling that it had.

"Oh, my God," he said suddenly. And he pointed in panic to the highest point of the old gray wall. "The cross has been broken."

Thus it was, thirty-three days after an explosion of hate and agricultural fertilizer tore through a weak point in the American fabric and let terror through. They still came to downtown Oklahoma City to look at the wound, wearing Bermuda shorts and flowered shirts and out-of-town license plates. Fulfilling in agonizing irony the dream of a city for just such crowds as this in its downtown on just such a warm weekend in late spring. "I wish I had my camera and 14,000 rolls of film," one onlooker said.

A stolid workman swung by a rope from the roof of the Southwestern Bell building, tapping glass shards from a hundred broken windows, maybe more. In one of the unbroken panes a sign read, "Thank you, America," and you realized with a touch of wonder that no dry Okie sarcasm was there.

"Still here," another window read. "Staying here."

Nearing the shrine, only loosely strung plastic mesh protected the once-precious inner sanctum of a money-to-loan shop. Spectators touched the yellow police tape, bent to look through the broken glass with the awed thrill of a child looking in windows where people do not live anymore.

Tents of the television crews were gaily colored, carnival-like. A tired newspaper reporter stared into the debris, looking for a scrap somebody overlooked. Signs no longer new offered parking up close for $2. Outside Walker Stamp & Seal Co., a workman's head and shoulders disappeared behind a sign that said, "A Time to Heal, God Bless the Families and the Volunteers." Replacing masonry that was ripped away.

And in and around it all, they swirled.

Tourists?

They bumped elbows and shoulders, stepped around baby carriages and big leashed dogs. They smiled sometimes, turning aside to watch a pretty redhead in shorts and tattoos. Instant merchants scurried behind

Left, Onlookers visited the chain link fence in the days following the bombing.
Above, Momentos left behind

temporary tables to wait on customers eager to buy memorial prints. $20. "All funds will go to disaster relief education funds."

A tired-looking man scooped runny coleslaw from a paper carton over a sign: "Pins, $5. Proceeds to YMCA kids."

Sheriff's deputies rode horseback trying to keep people and cars apart as the fluctuating mass squeezed a four-lane street down to three. Sometimes two. A purple truck passed, its bed packed with children. A woman plunged out to the waist from the passenger window and clung by her elbows, trying to get one quick picture. A television camera taped a tourist taping people taking pictures. But something more was happening.

You saw it first in the faces of those coming away. A new softness on the streets of downtown Oklahoma City. A strange, saving sadness. An old man with sun-reddened cheeks, jaw set, keeping his eyes down. A pretty young mother crying and wiping her nose with a fast-food napkin saved from the children's lunch. Motorists driving carefully, unusual patience disguising their faces.

And then you knew why.

Cameras lie. Or do not tell the whole truth. Can't. To a man sitting in a rocker in the cool breeze off Blackfork and Rich Mountains it hadn't looked like this on TV. It was not like this. Sitting there.

The building hurts. A scary childhood ache in the belly, crowding the breath away. Hurts firsthand. And in that there is some strange sense of relief. The blacktop is hot. Air smothery. Hanging concrete rough enough to shear the skin away. The crowd goes quiet. Holding hands. Big men step strangely back from each other's path.

"Pardon me, sir. You come on."

A former rescuer tries to tell his mother gently where they found the most bodies. The most parts. There is movement the size of an ant in the middle of the building, halfway up, and a gasp as if some of the evil has stayed behind. It is two men standing on a ledge suspended over air. Still working.

An old man strokes his throat as if it hurts and looks at the sky and says "My God" without speaking. A silver-haired woman breaks suddenly from the crowd, clutching at her lapel. She hurries to the pile of toys left for babies who will never hold them. Kneels quickly before a long-eared rabbit doll. "It could have been my baby, my grandbaby!" And she quickly pins her gold angel pin to the rabbit's floppy ear and disappears into the crowd.

And a tiny girl who has misunderstood about the children to whom the toys belong pulls fiercely at her mother's dress. "Where are the babies, Mama?" she demands. "Where are the babies?" Getting, here at the shrine, her first brutal lesson in life. Mother has no answer.

Fleeing out through the historical district of Oklahoma City where ancient elms still touch fingers across wide streets and barefoot children still stretch blissfully on cool brick banisters, you know, finally, what has been so odd about the day. It was the quiet. Over all that rushing crowd. The incongruous honk of a single horn scaring people a block away. New softness on the streets of downtown Oklahoma City. Strange, saving sadness.

Nobody wanting even a nodding acquaintance with anger.

After seeing firsthand what hate does.

Above left, Edward and Mary Ellis of Pauls Valley survey the site on April 22, 1995. Above center, Members of the Christian Life Missionary Baptist Church in Oklahoma City hold a prayer vigil on April 28, 1995. Above right, Lynn Rupe of Oklahoma City looks at the destruction for the first time since the bombing.

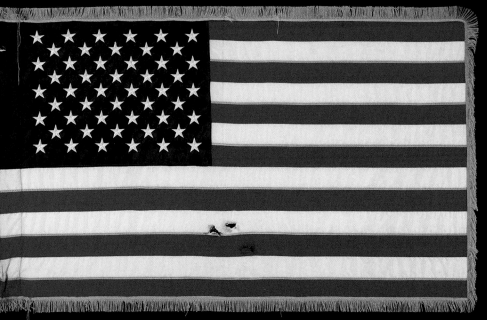

First American flag removed from the Alfred P. Murrah Federal Building on April 19, 1995, displayed atop the crane used in the rescue and recovery efforts. Later presented to the State of Oklahoma by the Bureau of Alcohol, Tobacco, and Firearms, who recovered it from the building.

In Memory

LUCIO ALEMAN

Lucio Aleman Jr. , 33, of Oklahoma City; husband of Gabriella Aleman; father of Alynna and Lucio; son of Lucio R. and Ofelia Aleman; safety coordinator and civil rights officer, Federal Highway Administration.

Lucio Aleman appreciated children, especially his own two. Indeed his future plans all had a family twist: building a swing set, starting a peewee T-ball league, being a Cub Scout troop leader. "He was very family-oriented," said his wife Gabriella. "He loved the kids, and he wanted more. He was very proud when the boy was born." Gabriella and Lucio attended college together at Texas A&I in Kingsville, Texas. Lucio graduated with a bachelor's degree in civil engineering in 1989, and the couple was married in 1990. Right after graduation, Lucio began work at the Federal Highway Administration.

Lucio enjoyed drawing and listening to jazz (his favorite was Stevie Ray Vaughan). He attended St. Eugene Catholic Church. Said Gabriella, "He was very concerned about homeless people and anything to do with children. When we were still living in Washington, D.C., he once dragged me out looking for one guy he often saw who was homeless; he wanted to give the man a jacket and some money. We looked and looked and couldn't find him, and that bothered Lucio so much."

TERESA ALEXANDER

Teresa A. Alexander, 33, of Oklahoma City; wife of Martin Alexander and mother of Michael, LaTress, and Sean, all of Oklahoma City; nurse's assistant, Baptist Medical Center, and pool supervisor, Marriott Hotel; died while obtaining a Social Security card for her son.

Teresa Alexander worked two full-time jobs, led her daughter LaTress' Girl Scout troop, cared for a family of five, and worked Sunday mornings in the nursery at St. Eugene Catholic Church in northwest Oklahoma City, where she was a member. "She had a full plate," said colleague and friend Cathy Hickman. Yet Teresa was never one to complain. Her workday usually began at 7 a.m. at the Marriott; she left at 5 p.m. to tend to her family. After a few hours of sleep, she arrived at 11 p.m. at Baptist Medical Center for a shift that lasted until early the next morning.

As a nurse's assistant in the intensive care ward at Baptist, she enjoyed doing the little extras for patients. "She'd braid their hair, wash their hair, or shave their legs," said Hickman. "She didn't overlook those things." "She liked helping people whether they were sick or not sick," said husband Martin Alexander.

Teresa worked two jobs so her children could attend Catholic school, but she was also involved in their lives. If she could not attend a child's sporting event, she made sure they had a ride. And she called to check on them, making sure homework was done or that they didn't chat too long on the phone. "It wasn't about her," Martin said. "It was always about her family."

RICHARD A. ALLEN

Richard A. Allen, 46, of Oklahoma City; father of Melissa Sutterfield of Kansas City, KS; son of Lena Allen of Topeka, KS; claims representative, Social Security Administration.

He was the ultimate sports fan. Richard Allen could recite the score of an NFL game played fifteen years ago and name the team that won the 1963 World Series. "He would have the TV on one game—the volume turned off—and be listening on the radio to a different game," said his daughter. Friends, family, and coworkers all knew his favorite team was the Redskins and his least favorite the Dallas Cowboys. (A Barry Switzer fan, he warmed a little to the latter after Switzer became head coach.) Many believed coaching was his real calling. Yet he was also a meticulous twenty-two-year employee at Social Security, one of the few who could quote information upon request. "He knew it," marveled coworker Barbara West. "He didn't have to go look it up." "He was a perfectionist living in an imperfect world," observed coworker Richard Dean.

Beloved by colleagues, Richard bowled, snow skied, and collected Roseville pottery. On weekends (when not watching sports) he cooked Chinese food, watched cooking shows, and antiqued. In 1966, he received a full scholarship to Panhandle State in Goodwell, where he was co-captain and center of the football team; he graduated with a bachelor's degree in social studies and physical education. A Vietnam-era veteran, he served with the Sixty-fifth Military Police Platoon at Dugway, Utah.

TED ALLEN

Ted L. Allen, 48, of Norman; husband of Caye Allen; father of Jill, Spencer, Gretchen, Meghan, and Austin Allen and Rachel Goodloe; economic development specialist, Community Planning and Development Division, HUD.

At six foot six inches and 260 pounds, Ted Allen was a big man with a bigger heart. He was father of six, yet reached out to those outside his family. A member of the Governor's Council on the Homeless, "He worked for the homeless," said wife Caye, "and he was always there for them." When winter winds blew, Ted and coworkers bundled up and made the rounds of downtown businesses, reminding them to refer the homeless to HUD for information on where to find a warm place to stay.

A devoted University of Tennessee football fan ("Johnny Major was his idol," his wife recalled), Ted was equally involved in his kids' sports. Whether coaching Optimist basketball or a soccer team or cheering with his daughters on spirit squads, Ted nurtured a love for all healthy competition. The only rival for that affection was a white three-quarter-ton Chevy pickup known as The Shrine. "It's a 1991 pickup, and it has 24,000 miles on it. It is a shrine." Caye said she often joked that Ted loved the pickup more than he loved her (though their friends were never fooled).

After the bombing, Ted's wife and children decided to handle their loss by focusing on what they had with Ted. If Ted would want anything, said Caye, it would be for "(us) to pick up and go on."

BAYLEE ALMON

Baylee Almon, 1 year 1 day, of Oklahoma City; daughter of Aren Almon; granddaughter of Debbie and Tommy Almon; niece of Amy Love, Adra Paine, and Abby Baird; cousin of Jake, Joel, Broc, Bianca, Kyrstin, and Kiyana; attended America's Kids.

"She smiled at everyone," said Aren Almon of her daughter Baylee. "She liked everyone and was a happy baby."

Baylee had just started to walk and to say, "Mama." So taken with video recorders was the toddler that when anyone aimed the camera at her, she tried to kiss the screen. She and her mother liked to spend time together, and one of their regular outings was attending the baseball games of Baylee's cousin. The Almon family had gathered the day before the bombing to celebrate Baylee's first birthday.

DIANE ALTHOUSE

Diane E. Althouse, 45, of Edmond; mother of Athena Roy and Aarion Althouse; daughter of James and Dorothy Hollingsworth of Shawnee; grandmother of Stephanie Roy; program support assistant, Office of Housing, HUD.

Diane Althouse was a spiritual woman who spent breaks and lunches praying and listening to religious tapes. Her baby granddaughter, Stephanie, was dear to her, and she happily ran son Aarion to Little League and other activities. She was completing a year as a Benedictine oblate at Saint Gregory's Abbey in Shawnee.

Fun-spirited and outdoorsy, Diane Rollerbladed and cycled at Lake Hefner park. The evening of April 18, she picked up a new Fiat Spider—a departure for a woman whose biggest thrills were usually bargain shopping at Wal-Mart and secondhand stores.

"Diane was a kind-hearted, forgiving soul," said coworker Teresa Cook, "someone who cared and whose eternal generosity did make a difference in the lives of those she touched."

On the second anniversary of the death of Teresa's father (with whom Teresa was very close), Diane happened to mention to her friend that she had dropped by the cemetery. "I thought I'd have a little talk with him," Diane explained. When Teresa went out, she saw a small granite angel perched atop the headstone's flower vase. The angel had a hand-crafted wreath around its neck intertwined with a white rose (for Teresa's dad), a large red rose (for her mom), and five small red roses (for Teresa and her four sisters).

REBECCA ANDERSON

Rebecca Anderson, 37, of Oklahoma City; wife of Fred Anderson; mother of Hilary and Gabe Johnson and Rachel and Britton Harrold; daughter of Bob and Doris Needham of Fort Smith, Arkansas; died while searching for survivors after the bombing.

For some, a profession is just a job. For Rebecca Anderson, nursing was a calling. "Children and the elderly were passions in her life," said her husband, Fred Anderson. "She always wanted to help." As a licensed practical nurse, Rebecca cared for others daily at the Brookwood Nursing Center in southwest Oklahoma City.

When she wasn't working, Rebecca was active in her church, the Reorganized Church of Jesus Christ of Latter-day Saints, Restoration Branch. A confirmed carnivore, Rebecca loved Alaskan king crab, rib-eye steak, and chicken. Rebecca is remembered by family and friends as "very outgoing and friendly." She loved to shop, though not usually for herself. "She liked buying things for kids," said Fred. "Nieces, friends, whoever."

Married only nine months, Fred and Rebecca talked on the phone for hours before meeting for the first time (they were introduced through a mutual friend). "It was almost like we knew what to talk about," said Fred. "We just melded."

PAMELA CLEVELAND ARGO

Pamela D. Cleveland Argo, 36, of Oklahoma City; daughter of Billy and Joyce Cleveland of Stigler; sister of Christi Young of Chicago, IL; data entry specialist, Presbyterian Hospital; moonlighted for a catering service; died while completing paperwork at Social Security concerning the death of her husband just weeks earlier.

Not yet forty, Pam Argo had trekked across Europe, sunned in the Bahamas, and swum in the azure waters of Saint Thomas. With family and friends, she had already seen much of the world.

"We did a lot of family things together," said her mother, Joyce. "It tore our family all to pieces to lose her."

A year ago, Pam purchased her first home and, with her parents, spent many a weekend fixing it up. The morning she died, her ten-year-old second cousin had called just to read a shared memory: "Remember when we had girls' weekend, and we all piled in you and Misty's car and went to Chuck E Cheese's? Remember when we would sneak to Bob's Burger Ranch to eat a cheeseburger and then we acted like we didn't eat?"

Gregarious and fun-loving, Pam befriended everyone—young, old, even two dogs and three cats. She loved black clothes, bright red lipstick, hats, and big jewelry. Some of her friends said she had big-city appeal but small-town charm. Yet she never forgot what mattered most: She delivered meals to the homebound, assisted the AIDS Foundation, and helped Feed the Children.

SANDY AVERY

Saundra G. Avery, 34, of Midwest City; daughter of Dorothy and Vester Avery of Midwest City; sister of Michael Avery of Choctaw; development clerk, Social Security Administration.

Sandy Avery wasn't even a gradeschooler before she began asking for piano lessons. Her mother, having seen how other youngsters had to be harangued to practice, discouraged the idea. But Sandy kept pleading, and at the age of six, she got lessons. She quickly disproved her mother's fears.

"We had a piano," said her mother, Dorothy Avery, "and Sandy just wanted to play it."

She eventually mastered the piano and ten other instruments as well, including mandolin and cello. She graduated from UCO (then CSU) with an accounting degree, but she continued to sing in the choir, play flute in the church orchestra, and direct the hand bell choir at Oklahoma City's Life Christian Center.

Besides her music (she was a gifted sight reader), Sandy took sign language classes three nights a week. She enjoyed cross-stitching, puzzles, sewing, and Agatha Christie mysteries. She collected miniature pianos and for several summers was a counselor at the church's children's camp.

PETER AVILLANOZA

Peter Avillanoza, 56, of Oklahoma City; husband of Darlene Dohi-Avillanoza of Palmdale, CA; father of Derek Avillanoza of Lompoc, CA, and Victor Avillanoza and Michelle Woods of Virginia Beach, VA; grandfather of fourteen; supervisory Equal Opportunity specialist, Fair Housing and Equal Opportunity Division, HUD.

In March 1995, Hawaii native Peter Avillanoza arrived in the Oklahoma City HUD office from California. "He loved the people in Oklahoma," said his wife, Darlene Dohi-Avillanoza. "He also loved his job with HUD. He liked helping people."

Peter was known to champion those who had been discriminated against on the basis of race, religion, or disabilities. His wife and children remember him as a father who would drive six hours to babysit his grandchildren for an evening (he once flew from his home in California to Florida to help a daughter stranded at home with her children and a dead car battery). "That's the kind of person he was," said Darlene.

A former officer with the Honolulu Police Department, Peter was a musician at heart. He played keyboard, drums, and clarinet, sang and composed Hawaiian music, and even played Las Vegas while working for the EEOC in Nevada for five years (his father played tuba with the Royal Hawaiian Band).

A graduate of Kaimuki High School, he earned his bachelor's in criminal justice and his master's in public administration while raising five children and playing music on the weekend. He married Darlene in the early 1990s and became a father to her four children. He was a member of Calvary Chapel. He's buried in Hawaii.

CALVIN & PEOLA BATTLE

Calvin, 62, and Peola, 56, Battle, of Oklahoma City; parents of Gwen Steele, Janet Battle, Doris Smith, and LaDonna Madkins, all of Oklahoma City; Calvin was a machinist for thirty years with Corken Inc. until he suffered a stroke in 1993; Peola, process operator for Seagate Technology; died while checking Calvin's disability benefits at Social Security.

Neighbors of Calvin and Peola Battle never knew how many people actually lived at the Battle residence, since the couple was rarely home without a child or a grandchild dropping by. "We would come and go like it was our house," said LaDonna Madkins, the Battles' youngest daughter.

Most weekends Peola and her four daughters hit the malls on Saturday and the pews on Sunday. Sunday evenings, Peola would cook a roast and bake one of the grandkids' favorite desserts, cherry cheesecake. With their dad rooted on an OU football game, the sisters would settle in their mom's room for girl talk.

Calvin could be found playing back-seat quarterback for OU. Recalled LaDonna, "He'd say [to the TV], 'You're not supposed to make that play' or 'Do the wishbone, do the wishbone.'" Before his stroke in 1993, he attended every OU home game and watched the remainder on television; afterwards, he stopped going to the games, but he wasn't any less a fan. "Those were his boys. Barry [Switzer] was part of God himself," LaDonna said.

Besides an annual trek to Las Vegas, the Battles spent their time at home, where Peola tended a flower garden and sewed (she made all the brides-maid dresses for daughter Doris' wedding). "She sewed until the thread came up," said LaDonna.

DANIELLE BELL

Danielle N. Bell, 15 months, of Oklahoma City; daughter of Deniece Bell and granddaughter of David and Sherita Bell, all of Oklahoma City; attended America's Kids on Mondays, Wednesdays, and Fridays.

Danielle Bell was known to dance jigs to her grand-mother's country music and swim around the family's bathtub with her plastic frog and whale. "Danielle would dance to anything, and she had rhythm, too," recalled Deniece Bell, Danielle's mother.

Fond of her grandmother's black poodle Maynard, Danielle liked birds, swinging on her tree swing, and eating Mazzio's calzones.

In the mornings when Deniece was putting on her makeup, Danielle did, too, using her own makeup basket. Fifteen months old, she already had an appre-ciation for good hygiene. She liked to comb her hair and brush her teeth. "She'd walk around with her toothbrush all day long," said Deniece with a laugh. Known lovingly as "Pooter" by mother and grand-mother, she hobnobbed with the older kids at day care (the three year olds). Children her own age bored her, and she was no crybaby. "She only cried when she was mad," said her mother. Her usual demeanor? "She would hug you all the time and kiss you all the time," said Deniece, "and do stuff to make you laugh."

OLETA BIDDY

Oleta C. Biddy, 53, of Tuttle; wife of Henry Biddy, mother of Daniel, mother-in-law of Jeannean Biddy, and grandmother of Ethan and Lane Biddy, all of Tuttle; service representative, Social Security Administration.

Though she liked to water ski and read Reader's Digest cover to cover, nothing mattered more to Oleta Biddy than nurturing her husband, kids, and grandchildren. According to grandson Ethan, she gave the best baths in town.

Oleta and Henry were married thirty-four years, and their children remem-ber them as affectionate and silly as newlyweds. Once when Henry blocked traffic in three lanes trying to pull out of a bank, Oleta was mortified. Her husband responded with a present—two pairs of Groucho Marx glasses. "When she opened it, I told her she could wear that next time she went to the bank with me," said Henry, recalling how hard they laughed as they tried the glasses on.

Even bad weather couldn't get a rise out of her. "It would be the coldest day—snowing and bad weather and bad roads—and she would carry on about what a beautiful day it was," said Jeannean, who adored her mother-in-law.

In twenty years on the job, Oleta rarely missed a day. "She never called in sick," said Jeannean, who also worked with her. "If it was so bad that she had to stay home, she used her vacation time." Of Oleta, who also helped in the nursery at First Baptist Church of Tuttle, Jeannean observed, "She's got many jewels in her crown. I bet she's having to have help to carry it."

SHELLY BLAND

Shelly D. Turner Bland, 25, of Tuttle; wife of Gary Bland; mother of Jordan Turner; daughter of Mike and Peggy Turner; sister of Kimberly Turner; asset forfeiture specialist, Drug Enforcement Agency.

They all lived in Tuttle: Shelly, her husband Gary, her daughter Jordan Elizabeth, her mother and dad, her sister Kimberly. Such proximity has been known to drive a family apart or bring it together. In the case of Shelly's family, it did the latter.

The Turner daughters sewed, baked, and tole painted together. Birthdays and holidays saw some twenty relatives gather for potluck dinners. Shelly was the oldest of the two sisters, and Kimberly says, "She taught me a lot," encouraging her younger sibling to think and stand up for herself. Shelly set an example by helping others. At her core, however, was her daughter Jordan's needs. Most days, Shelly was home by 6 p. m. , ready to spend a quiet night watching television, coloring, and playing games before Jordan's bedtime. Observed Kimberly, the family lost a kind heart with Shelly's passing.

ANDREA BLANTON

Andrea Blanton; 33, wife of Daniel Blanton; clerk, Office of Housing, HUD.

Friends and HUD co-workers remember Andrea Blanton as a very private woman who nonetheless was fun loving and wonderful to work with. "She was a very, very sweet person," according to coworker Mary Barnett, who said Andrea was like a sister to her.

Andrea took college courses in addition to her full-time job, as well as classes in areas like outdoor yard decorating. Even those who just passed her in the hallway at work remember a woman who always seem self-possessed and nice.

OLEN BLOOMER

Olen B. Bloomer, 61, of Moore; widower of Norma "Tincy" Bloomer; father of Maureen Bloomer of Moore; stepfather of Lucretia Bjorklund and Lee Switzer; grandfather of Jeff Waugh, Amelia Bjorklund, Heather Bjorklund, Sara Switzer, and Christina Switzer; great-grandfather of Dillon Waugh; brother of Esther Willis, Erdene Jones, Elwanda McComas, Muriel Easter, Doyle Bloomer, Dennis Bloomer, and Dean Bloomer; budget assistant, U. S. Department of Agriculture.

At six foot, six inches—and graced with a broad grin and gentle nature—Olen Bloomer was "Big Dad" to his granddaughter Sara. Her favorite perch was on his shoulders, where "From her six-foot-six vantage point," said Olen's stepson Lee Switzer of Texas, "she could see the world."

Family members remember Olen as a happy-go-lucky man whose joyful outlook on life was contagious. "He collected really bad jokes," said daughter Maureen, "and he liked to tell them with this little gleam in his eye and a boyish grin." He spent his free time on his home computer, reading spy novels, working crossword puzzles, and fishing at Lake Eufaula. ("His luck ran to perch," said Maureen.)

A retired air force man on his second career, Olen was admired by his staff for his ability to stay cool under pressure, cut through bureaucratic red tape, and willingness to help his fellow employees. His children remember his devotion to his late wife, "Tincy," and all his children—both natural and not. "We miss you," his family said. "Our tower has fallen, but your light will shine on us, your beacon will shine through all of us, we will carry your spirit forward with us, forevermore."

LOLA BOLDEN

Lola R. Bolden, 40, of Oklahoma City; daughter of Mary Bolden of Newcastle, AL; mother of Pamela Sanders and Ricky and Jonathan Hill; Sergeant, U. S. Army Recruiting Battalion.

Sergeant Lola Bolden, a sixteen-year soldier, had only been stationed in the Oklahoma City Army Recruiting Battalion since January 1995, but coworkers say they had already succumbed to her warm smile.

Her mother, Mary Bolden, described her daughter as a quiet but outgoing person who loved sports. A high school track enthusiast and frequent cyclist, Lola's idea of going to the mall was not to shop—but to walk. She emphasized homework and togetherness to her two sons, Ricky and Jonathan, and the threesome were close. "Wherever she went, they went with her," said Mary. Lola's favorite flower was the yellow rose.

JAMES BOLDEN

James E. Boles, 50, of Oklahoma City; husband of Jennifer Boles; father of Stephen and James; administrative officer, U. S. Department of Agriculture.

The Mississippi native and Army veteran joined the USDA as a temporary assigned to a task force dealing with disease outbreaks among swine in the swamps of North Carolina and Virginia; it attracted some of the nation's finest experts. "They all called on James for counsel, advice, and assistance," said Jack Wooten, a retired USDA area administrative officer who worked with James in Florida. "He became quite a focal point of the task force operation."

James Boles went on to address agricultural problems from Pennsylvania to the Shenandoah Valley, receiving numerous citations and awards for his innovative work.

Colleagues knew him as someone concerned with their well-being, an open and friendly person who was cherished by friends nationwide. Indeed, the day James married Jennifer, he was fixing a friend's (Jack's) plumbing. An hour before the service, the two men realized the time (they still had a forty-five minute drive to the church). "We literally flew to that church," said Jack, going from plumbers to groom and best man in record time. The best description of her husband, said Jennifer, comes from their son Michael, who, when asked in a classroom assignment to describe an outstanding individual, wrote, "An outstanding individual does what my father does: He works hard, takes good care of his family, and is lots of fun."

MARK BOLTE

Mark A. Bolte, 28, of Oklahoma City; son of Don and Joyce Bolte of Bentonville, AR; brother of Matt Bolte; environmental specialist, State of Oklahoma, Federal Highway Administration.

When Mark Bolte was headed from Austin to Oklahoma City, his Texas coworkers had this to say to his future boss: "You're getting a great big teddy bear." Strawberry blond, 250 pounds, and six feet four inches, Mark was always willing to help someone with a problem. "He had a knack for telling if something was wrong [with a person]," said his mother, Joyce Bolte. "We all know he's watching over somebody."

A former altar boy at Saint Vincent de Paul Catholic Church in Rogers, Arkansas, Mark graduated from high school with honors and four years of perfect attendance. An alum of the University of Arkansas, where he was a member of Lambda Chi, he graduated in 1990 with a degree in civil engineering. His hobby was model airplanes, which he hung everywhere in his apartment. Mark played basketball and golf, watched hockey, the Atlanta Braves, and Joe Montana, and remained a loyal Arkansas Razorback. An Eagle Scout, he worked with a troop in the city.

CASANDRA BOOKER

Casandra K. Booker, 25, of Oklahoma City; mother of Ronika, Katina, and twins Rodney and Leroy; daughter of Gloria and stepfather David Graves; sister of Rickey Booker; died while applying for Social Security cards for her twins.

Casandra Kay Booker was outgoing, generous ("She'd take her shirt and shoes and give them to you," said her mother, Gloria Graves), and, as an unmarried mother raising four children on her own, intent on her children having strong marriages someday. She attended business school at Platt College and spent her leisure time playing with her children, shopping at thrift stores and garage sales, and fixing hair (she'd studied cosmetology for awhile and "was good at it," said Gloria).

Casandra remained on good terms with her children's father, Rodney Wilson. "She liked people," said Gloria, "and I didn't know she had so many friends, until after her death. Little things now remind mother of daughter: "The oldest girl looks just like her," she said, "waves just like her." It has fallen to Gloria to play mother to her daughter's four energetic children. A woman accustomed to working two jobs, she has quit both to raise her grandchildren.

CAROL BOWERS

Carol L. Bowers, 53, of Yukon; wife of Jerry Bowers; mother of Joe Bowers of Yukon; operations supervisor, Social Security Administration.

Carol Bowers spent many a sunny afternoon cruising the countryside with her husband, Jerry, in the couple's 1986 metallic red Corvette coupe. The Bowers bought the car in 1992 and were members of the Oklahoma City Corvette Club. Their road trips were a way for the couple to relax together, and Jerry said he didn't mind that every fall meant one excursion to Eureka Springs, Arkansas, where Carol shopped at the War Eagle Arts and Crafts Fair. "I did because that was our time together," he said.

The couple took in movies and dinner on the weekends together, and Carol also found time for doing oil paintings. Once a year, she took off for the Dallas market with some of her nearest girlfriends to shop—a three-day women thing," said Jerry. Carol also liked to help people, he said. She worked thirty-three years at the SSA, and Jerry has taken many calls from across the country from Social Security workers who never met his wife in person but who can't forget how friendly she was on the phone.

PEACHLYN BRADLEY

Peachlyn Bradley, 3 years 11 months, of Oklahoma City; daughter of Daina Bradley and great-granddaughter of Mary Hill, both of Oklahoma City; accompanied her mother Daina Bradley, her aunt Falesha Bradley, her grandmother Cheryl Hammons, and brother Gabreon Bruce to get a Social Security card for Gabreon.

Three-year-old Peachlyn Bradley was a sparkler and a yakker. "Oh Lord, she was a light," said Victoria Slaughter, Peachlyn's great-aunt. "She was such a happy kid. She'd just shine." She brought people together. "She was like a bridge between everyone, and she never shut up," said great-grandmother Mary Hill with a laugh. "We called her motor mouth."

When the preschooler entered a room, she always announced, "I'm here," followed by, "Where's my kids?" (Everyone—from her twenty-three-year-old cousin on down—was Peachlyn's kid.) "She was just a little busybody," said Mary. "She was just a sweet thing." Unable to pronounce "Big Mama," Mary's nickname, Peachlyn dubbed her great-grandmother "Mick Mama." A typical Peachlyn request: "Mick Mama, do you have any shereal (cereal)?" Not surprisingly, her favorite thing when she wasn't gabbing, said Mary, was Cheerios.

WOODROW BRADY

Woodrow "Woody" C. Brady, 41, of Oklahoma City; son of Jeanne Redd, grandson of Janie Redd, and brother of Sarita Redd and Johann Redd, all of Oklahoma City; self-employed publisher of children's books; died while at the credit union.

He made his living tailor-making biographies of other people's children. Parents would bring a story about their child, and from it Woody Brady would make a personal volume. "He loved it," said his mother, Jeanne Redd, of her son's work.

Graduated at the top of his class from Meeker High School in 1972, he was one of three students to receive Meeker's highest student honor (he also won FFA honors). He attended Seminole Junior College, where he earned an associate's degree in biology with an art minor and played varsity basketball. He later attended Oklahoma Christian College.

Golf was his favorite pastime (he also played chess, tennis, basketball, and baseball), and he hit the greens often enough to win several trophies over the years. "He would play golf in the snow," his mother says, laughing. "It didn't get too cold; it didn't get too hot." Her son was always exhorting her to "learn how to play, Jeanne." And yes, he called his mother by her first name. In many ways, Jeanne says, they were more friends than anything else.

On May 16, 1995, the Meeker Student Council, FFA, and Class of 1972 planted a tree in Woody's memory in front of Meeker High School.

CINDY BROWN

Cynthia L. Brown, 26, of Oklahoma City; wife of Ron Brown of Portland, OR; daughter of Gary Campbell of Sherman, TX, and Linda McNew Campbell of Rantoul, IL; sister of Ray Campbell of Bolingbrook, IL, and Kim Gradney of Rantoul; sister-in-law of Andrea Campbell of Bolingbrook, IL; U. S. Special Agent, U. S. Secret Service.

Forty days before the Oklahoma City bombing, Cindy Campbell and Ron Brown—both special agents in the Secret Service—exchanged vows in Sherman, Texas. Then, after a honeymoon in Cancun, Cindy returned to her Oklahoma City office and Ron to Phoenix. Both hoped a future transfer would land them in the same city.

A political science graduate of Baylor University and a former juvenile probation officer, Cindy was recruited by the Secret Service after agents dealt with her on a case involving one of her juvenile charges (the youngster had sent threatening letters to the president). "They saw something in Cindy that [they thought] would make a good Secret Service agent," said her father Gary Campbell.

Uninterested at first, Cindy came around after visiting agency offices in Dallas and hearing more about the job. Once in, she proved a natural. After a night on protection detail for the president in Florida, she confided, "You know, Dad, standing out in front of the governor's mansion in the middle of the night with it pouring down rain probably doesn't sound like much to some people. But you know, it's really exciting."

PAUL BROXTERMAN

Paul G. Broxterman, 42, of Edmond; husband of Cammy Broxterman; father of Aaron, Jared, and Casandra Broxterman of Peoria, AZ; son of David and Peggy Broxterman of Las Vegas, NV; brother of Mark, David, and Janna Broxterman; criminal investigator, Office of Inspector General, HUD.

April 19, 1995, was Paul Broxterman's third day on the job at the Oklahoma City office (his family had been in Edmond just a week), yet Paul, a graduate of the FBI academy, was already enjoying his new post, said his mother, Peggy Broxterman.

A former undercover agent and special investigator with the Bureau of Indian Affairs and the IRS and a one-time private investigator, Paul transferred to HUD shortly after he and his son were approached by a drug dealer in a Phoenix store (Paul's undercover disguises were so authentic, he often had to apologize for his appearance at church, said his mother).

A devout Mormon, Paul was a genealogist who had traced his maternal and paternal roots back to the Deliverance (a ship that pre-dates the Mayflower) on one side and to an Indian princess and a French fur trapper on the other. His Potawatomi and Scottish heritage shaped his life. He had been active in Potawatomi tribal activities in California, Arizona, and Oklahoma; bagpipes played "Amazing Grace" at his funeral.

GABREON BRUCE

Gabreon Bruce, 3 months, of Oklahoma City; son of Daina Bradley and great-grandson of Mary Hill, both of Oklahoma City; accompanied mother Daina Bradley, aunt Falesha Bradley, grandmother Cheryl Hammons, and sister Peachlyn Bradley to get his Social Security card.

Three months old at the time of his death, Gabreon Bruce was already fourteen pounds and busy. "He liked to bounce," said great-grandmother Mary Hill, who held Gabreon just a week before he died. "He was a heavy little something. He had a lot of energy, and he'd take a lot of yours."

KIMBERLY BURGESS

Kimberly R. Burgess, 29, of Oklahoma City; wife of Damon Burgess; daughter of David and Ramona Klaus; administrative assistant to the CEO, Federal Employees Credit Union.

She was known for the friends she had made—from the time she was a three year old who set out each morning from the house on her Big Wheel, arms loaded with fruit, in search of new playmates. "Her lifelong hobby [was] collecting friends," said her father, David W. Klaus.

A 1983 graduate of Evergreen High School outside Denver, Colorado, she spent a year at the University of Northern Colorado before moving to Denver in 1985 and managing a Red Cross shoe store. She married her husband, Damon, in November of 1993, and his air force career took them to Columbia, South Carolina, and finally to Tinker Air Force Base in 1994.

She spoke with her many friends on a weekly basis no matter where she was, vacationing with them and her family in places like Mexico and San Francisco. "She was very happy and outgoing," said Damon. Noted lifetime friend Kim Sell, "She was funny and had a great sense of humor. You could talk to Kim and she would never [judge you]. She had a hundred friends, and she was a best friend to each one."

On July 16, 1995, Kim's birthday, friends and family gathered in Evergreen, Colorado, to hang angels on the branches of a Colorado blue spruce planted beside Evergreen Lake in her

DAVID BURKETT

David N. Burkett, 47, of Oklahoma City; son of Kathryn Burkett of Horntown and the late Walter Burkett; brother of Debi Johnson of Horntown and the late Bradley Burkett; financial analyst, Office of Southern Plains Native American Programs, HUD.

"He was so thoughtful of everyone. He went nowhere without bringing everybody gifts," said Kathryn Burkett of her son, David. "He was a wonderful, wonderful person." Devoted to his mother and unusually close to his sister Debi, David helped put his niece Angela Brooks through junior college (and hoped to do the same for her brother Adam Johnson). Every Mother's Day, he took the family to Krebs for a big Italian meal, and every summer he appeared at the home place in Horntown to pick possum grapes (tiny, tiny grapes you can eat right off the vine or make into jelly, according to Debi).

He was passionate about photography (he used a 35-millimeter Pentax), and his photographs hung in his niece's office and his mother's home. He was to become president of the Oklahoma City Camera Club on July 1, 1995.

A graduate of Moss High School, David supported his alma mater with his money (he helped finance new lights on the school's baseball field) and his time (he regularly attended sporting and alumni events). At his funeral, dozens of Moss athletes came to pay their respects.

DONALD BURNS

Donald E. Burns Sr., 63, of Oklahoma City; husband of Barbara Burns; father of Sharon Ingram of Riverside, CA; Helma Gentry of Washington, D.C.; and Donald E. Burns Jr. of Oklahoma City; grandfather of Amanda Gentry of Pinehurst, NC; and Porsche and Brittany Burns of Oklahoma City; construction analyst, Office of Southern Plains Native American Programs, HUD.

A scholar-athlete while at Oklahoma City's Douglass High School and Maryland State University, Donald E. Burns later returned to Douglass High to teach woodworking and coach football. Among his players was Dallas Cowboys' receiver Thomas "Hollywood" Henderson, who considered Burns a man of character.

At HUD, Burns worked on Indian housing projects and extensively with the Sac and Fox tribe. (On July 7, 1995, the Sac and Fox dedicated their newest HUD facility in Stroud to the memory of Burns and six other HUD employees who died in the bombing.) He was a lifelong member of Fairview Baptist Church, which he designed and on which he served as building manager.

A six-handicap golfer, Burns regularly shot in the seventies and, off the course, cooked a mean barbecue. In a lifetime dedicated to young people, his own children and grandchildren were special favorites. "He adored his grandkids," said Barbara Burns. "They could do no wrong in his eyes." Barbara and Donald were married thirty-two years. "We had a wonderful life together," Barbara said.

KAREN GIST CARR

Karen Gist Carr, 32, of Midwest City; wife of Gregory Carr; daughter of J. L. and Jeannine Gist, and sister of Shirley Goodman, Peggie Pietrowicz, Sandra Poplin, and Lynne Gist, all of Midwest City; advertising assistant, U. S. Army Recruiting Battalion.

Karen Gist Carr believed in making life better for those she knew. When one of her aerobics students was going to quit class because her sick daughter couldn't be left alone, Karen suggested she bring the child with her so they could both watch the girl. When another student couldn't afford to continue, Karen paid the fee herself. "She liked to do for other people," said her husband, Greg Carr. "She was always willing to do what she could."

She sandwiched aerobics between her office hours with the army and her volunteer efforts as a member of Toastmasters International's Mid-Del Club. Her students remember her as a taskmaster who made a hard workout fun. Said Sheryl Campbell, "Karen showed her dedication to, and enjoyment for, her job each day of class. She worked especially hard these past two semesters with deaf students in her aerobics class, learning a way to communicate with them."

MICHAEL CARRILLO

Michael Joe Carrillo, 44, of Oklahoma City; father of Amber, Michael Joe Jr. and James; preceded in death by his wife Cynthia Applegate Carrillo in February of 1994 and son Michael James in 1980; state regional director, Federal Highway Division, Department of Transportation.

Raised in Kansas City, Missouri, Michael Carrillo joined the Navy in 1970 after high school graduation, serving during the Vietnam War era. After his four-year tour of duty, he signed with the army for another four years.

He met his wife, Cindy, at naval yard in Philadelphia. After Michael left the service, the two returned to Kansas City, where Mike went to work for the Department of Transportation. DOT took the couple to Topeka, Kansas; Ames, Iowa; and Raleigh, North Carolina; they relocated to Oklahoma City in the early 1990s. Cindy passed away shortly after they settled in Oklahoma. The couple lost their six-month-old son, Michael James, in 1980.

One of eight children, Michael Carrillo spent his free time drawing and woodcarving. "He would carve eagles out of wood," said his sister-in-law, Connie Carrillo. "It was his favorite pastime." She remembers her brother-in-law as friendly, jolly looking, and happy-go-lucky. "He had a perpetual grin," she said.

RONA CHAFEY

Rona L. Chafey, 35, of Oklahoma City; wife of Raymond Chafey; mother of Misty and Nickolas; daughter of Fred and Retta Kuehner of Bethany; sister of Benny Kuehner of Oklahoma City and Jenny Bechtold of Ponca City; Cleveland County Sheriff's Department, special task force, Drug Enforcement Administration.

Before Rona Chafey was assigned to the DEA, she was a dispatcher and 911 operator for the Cleveland County Sheriff's Department; before that, she worked in the emergency room at Southwest Medical Center. At home, she monitored her own police scanner. "She was always kind of an excitement junkie," said husband Ray Chafey.

When Sheriff DeWayne Beggs needed someone for the DEA post, he immediately thought of Rona, telling her, "This job calls for confidentiality, someone who is very trustworthy, a self-motivated person, and someone who gets along well with other people." The description fit Rona. "She was the one you went to when you needed a little bit of a pickup," said Beggs. "You never caught her in a bad mood," agreed her husband.

She was just as fun loving as a mother, said her mother-in-law Becky Chafey, Rollerblading with her fifteen-year-old daughter Misty while her four year old pedaled his tricycle nearby.

Ray and Rona were high school sweethearts who married six months after graduating from Bethany High School. Rona later attended Oklahoma City Community College and Rose State College.

ZACKARY CHAVEZ

Zackary Chavez, 3 years 1 month, of Oklahoma City; son of Alisha Chavez Hernandez; grandson of Cereaco Hernandez; nephew of Kathy Chavez Hernandez; attended America's Kids.

Zackary Chavez came from a third-generation Mexican-American clan that doted on him. He lived with the love of his single mother and many aunts and uncles. And he returned that love. At the time of his death, said his aunt, Kathy Chavez Hernandez, Zackary was learning a message for his mother's upcoming birthday: "Mommy, I love you. You are beautiful."

Zackary enjoyed his water pistol, Chicken McNuggets, butting heads with his best friend, and quarters (according to his great-grandfather he often turned down dollar bills for the coin).

SHARON CHESNUT

Sharon L. Chesnut, 47, of Oklahoma City; mother of Nikki Chesnut and daughter of Lucille Wood, both of Oklahoma City; sister of Carol Hollan of Midwest City; claims representative, Social Security Administration.

Known for not only answering people's questions but also hooking them up with other services or sources where they might find additional help, Sharon Chesnut worked at SSA for twenty-one years and consistently won its annual Outstanding Performance Award. (Once when the family of a homebound man couldn't find a hospital bed, said coworker Rita Rains, "Sharon got on the phone and called around until she found one.")

Serious about work, she also had a zany sense of humor that kept coworkers and friends in stitches. "She just had a knack of seeing the funny side of things," said Rita. She and her close-knit colleagues worked together, lunched together, and socialized outside of work. Coworker Suzie Welch remembers Sharon as an antiquer, bargain hunter, and "a garage saler deluxe" who collected everything from primitive crocks to graniteware. She was a member of Putnam City Retiree's Travel Club and mall-walked with her mother.

Sharon cooked snacks Wednesday nights for the Christ Lutheran Church's children's Bible lesson and dinner in Mustang, attended Bible study herself on Friday nights, and Sunday mornings taught Sunday school to three and four year olds. In her spare time, she volunteered with the church's Stephen's Ministry for persons dealing with divorce or death in the family.

ROBERT CHIPMAN

Robert N. Chipman, 51, of Edmond; husband of Gloria Chipman; father of Catherine Talbert, Julie Szabolcsi, and Carl Chipman; financial analyst, Oklahoma Water Resources Board (located across the street from the Murrah building).

Born in Nebraska, Robert Chipman was raised in a military family in California. He followed in his father's footsteps, serving in the air force for thirty-one years. He retired in 1992, but not before being stationed in Thailand, Japan, Saudi Arabia, England, and Italy and serving in the Vietnam War, the Panama invasion, and the Gulf War. What he saw of war, said his wife, Gloria, made him wish countries would play a chess game instead. "He was dedicated to his country and state," she said, but "he didn't believe in killing people."

What he did believe in was giving people the benefit of the doubt. He recognized a need for education and was working on his master's in education so he could become a principal and make a difference in children's lives. He had a bachelor's in science and business from Eastern New Mexico, a master's in business administration from the University of Arkansas, and a bachelor's in business education from UCO (he once taught there). Well-traveled and well-educated, he was teased by his family for being a walking encyclopedia. Family outings were always educational: zoos, museums, historic sites (when they traveled in Europe, he insisted everyone learn the history of each country they visited). "Bob was a humanitarian," said Gloria simply. "He could find the beauty in anything." He died April 21 at University Hospital from head trauma.

KIMBERLY CLARK

Kimberly Kay Clark, 39, of Oklahoma City; daughter of Tommie and Agatha Lee Clark of Midwest City; sister of Dale Clark of Olathe, KS, and Donald Clark of Midwest City; fiancée of Namat Moini of Oklahoma City; legal assistant, Legal Division, HUD.

"She was our little China doll," said Lee Clark of her daughter, Kimberly Kay, a native of Hong Kong whom the Clarks adopted at the age of three and a half, "an all-around red-blooded little American girl." She worked full-time at HUD and was an active duty Petty Officer Legalman First Class in the U. S. Naval Reserve. She took evening classes to further her education in the paralegal field, biked ("sometimes little trips up to thirty miles," her mother remembers), traveled, kayaked, and parasailed.

She drove elderly friends to the store and brought her family little treats—Cracker Jacks, candy, baked goods—when visiting. "She parceled them out a little at a time," her mother said, to prolong the pleasure.

Kim had recently acquired a beagle puppy, and she was engaged to Namat Moini. Kim's coworker Susan Ferrell, who also died in the bombing, was planning to host a wedding shower for the couple in her Edgemere Park home on April 21. "Her heart was bigger than she was," said Kim's mother.

PEGGY CLARK

Dr. Margaret L. "Peggy" Clark, 41, of Chickasha; wife of David R. Spencer; mother of Rosslyn, Blayne, and Chelsea; daughter of Mary Spurlin of Chickasha; sister of Susan Winchester of Chickasha and Cindy Clark of Texas; veterinary medical officer, U.S. Department of Agriculture.

Peggy Clark was that rare friend who could tell you were having a bad day just by the sound of your voice. Insightful, fun, and big-hearted, said Dr. Lee Denney, a Cushing veterinarian and friend, "She always laughed until she came to tears." Observed lifelong friend Donna Smith, "When Peggy laughed, her whole face lit up, and her eyes twinkled. She just laughed with her whole face."

And she shared her love of life with her husband and children. A graduate of OSU's veterinary school, Peggy's other passion was big animals (as a vet med student, she lived in a trailer with a Saint Bernard, and she was once the official veterinarian for the Oklahoma Horse Racing Commission at Blue Ribbon Downs). "She loved her horses, and she passed that love on to her children," said Lee. All three of Peggy's daughters began riding at a very young age, and the family was active in Ponies of America (David was a past president), a club for children in competitive riding.

Peggy sewed costumes for the girls' riding competitions, and she supported them in their soccer. "Whatever her kids were interested in, that was what Peggy was interested in," said Lee.

ANTONIO COOPER

Antonio A. Cooper Jr., 6 months, of Midwest City; son of Antonio and Renee Cooper of Midwest City; grandson of Wanda and Allen McNeely of Oklahoma City and Arrilla Cooper of Houston, TX; attended America's Kids.

At six months, Antonio Cooper Jr., was intent on learning to stand. "He was very stubborn," said Renee Cooper, laughing. "He had his own little personality. I'd try to sit him down, and those legs would just be so straight and hard...he'd always have that look on his face like 'Mama, if I don't want to sit down, you can't make me.' "

He liked peas, green beans, carrots, and fruit. He enjoyed baths with his rubber duckies, though "Little Tone," as his parents called him, favored showers with his mom over baths. "He loved that water just spraying in his face," she said. "He tried to reach up and grab the water." His favorite pastime was when his dad tossed him—giggling with glee—into the air. "He'd say 'Da Da' all the time," she said, "but he would never say it until his daddy walked into the room." "He was loved a lot," said Renee. "He had undivided attention from us."

DANA & ANTHONY CHRISTOPHER COOPER II

Dana L., 24, and Anthony Christopher II, 2 years 7 months, Cooper, of Moore; wife and child of A. C. Cooper of Moore; daughter and grandson of Carl and Linda Brown of Choctaw; grandson of Anthony M. and Beth Cooper of Midwest City and Saundra Bauer of Choctaw; director, America's Kids; son Christopher began daycare in early April after a bout with chicken pox.

Dana Cooper was an early childhood education major at UCO, a mother, and a daycare director. "Children were her life," said Linda Brown, Dana's mother. "She just loved the little ones."

Her son, Christopher, attended America's Kids, but Dana treated all the children as her own, bringing home stranded kids because of family emergencies. Dana understood that grownups can ask too much of children, said her mother. "She always preached that you can't expect a kid to stay still forever," said husband A.C.

Christopher liked "Sesame Street's" Ernie and Elmo, chatting on the telephone with his grandmas, playing in his cardboard house, and eating cheese. He could eat an orange in one sitting, and his favorite song was "Jesus Loves the Little Children." The family belonged to First Baptist Church of Nicoma Park, where Dana served on the nursery committee.

HARLEY COTTINGHAM

Harley Cottingham Jr., 46, of Oklahoma City; son of Harley and Fern Cottingham; brother of Sandy Battreall, Sheryl Oviatt, David Cottingham, and Kathy Grimes; special agent, Defense Investigative Service, Department of Defense.

Each year, Harley Cottingham planted five hundred evergreens on his farm. And each fall, the Nebraska native opened a choose-and-cut Christmas tree lot. "He had goals for the future," said sister Sandy Battreall. "He wanted to move back to Nebraska and build a house on his tree farm."

Harley graduated with a degree in criminal justice from the University of Nebraska at Omaha, spent four years in the navy, and served in Vietnam. In 1980 he joined the Veterans Administration as a veterans outreach counselor, and in 1985 he signed on with the Defense Investigative Service, which took him first to Omaha, then Colorado Springs, Colorado, and finally three years ago to Oklahoma City.

He remained, however, a loyal Cornhusker football fan. An avid golfer, he had played at Saint Andrews in Scotland while in Great Britain to visit his ancestral town of Cottingham. Well-rounded, he belonged to a ballroom dance club and did the two-step. "They all wanted to dance with him," said his father, Harley Cottingham Sr. "He got along well with people. That was part of his job...he liked to talk to people and made a lot of friends."

KIM COUSINS

Kim R. Cousins, 33, of Midwest City; wife of Lyle M. Cousins; mother of Corey; daughter of Larry and Janie Dillow of The Colony, TX; program support assistant, Office of Housing, HUD.

Kim Cousins met her husband Lyle the old-fashioned way—at church. South Lindsey Baptist Church Singles Sunday School provided the backdrop both for their courtship and their faith. (Kim was a second grade Sunday school worker at the time of her death.)

A homeroom mother at Steed Elementary, Kim was the proud mother of Corey, a nine year old who never knew his biological father. Said Lyle, "She loved [Corey] immensely. I believe God put Kim and I together so Corey would have a dad." Now, said Lyle, "With God's grace and the help of family and friends, I'm going to raise Corey as my own son."

Affectionate at home, a little shy elsewhere, Kim grew up in Deming, New Mexico, where she graduated from high school. In the mid 1980s, her family moved to Oklahoma City. Although her parents eventually relocated to The Colony, Texas, Kim considered herself an Oklahoman. She and Lyle had been married ten months when she was killed.

AARON & ELIJAH COVERDALE

Aaron M. , 5 years 7 months, and Elijah S., 2 years 7 months, Coverdale, of Oklahoma City; sons of Keith and Pamela Coverdale, grandchildren of Jannie M.Coverdale,and godchildren of John and Sandy Cole, all of Oklahoma City; nephews of Jeff Coverdale of Junction City, KS, Charles Coverdale of Alexandria,VA, Duane Coverdale of Milford, DE, Felicia and Veronica Ballard of Oklahoma City, and Ronnie Ballard of Illinois; attended America's Kids.

Elijah was a big Barney fan. His older brother Aaron favored the Power Rangers. Both boys loved to swim. Aaron was a typical big brother, picking up Elijah's toys and setting out his grandmother's glasses and keys each day so she wouldn't forget them. Before dropping off to sleep each night, Elijah always reminded his granny to say her prayers. "What I failed to see at those times were wings," said Jannie M. Coverdale, the boys' grandmother and guardian (their father worked as a truck driver). "I just saw little boys."

"They were very unique, special little people," said godfather John Cole, who along with his wife helped Jannie care for the boys. The two brothers reminded John of the stars the reverend Jesse Jackson talked about when he visited Oklahoma City after the bombing. "Some stars shine and shine," said John, paraphrasing Jackson's speech, "and then there are others that shine so brightly and are gone so quickly."

JACI RAE COYNE

Jaci Rae Coyne, 14 months, of Moore; daughter of Scott and Sharon Coyne of Moore; granddaughter of Jack and Terri Coyne of Cape Coral, FL, and Collette Kidd of Moore; attended America's Kids about five weeks.

Since she was two days old, Jaci Rae Coyne had heard her mother sing "Itsy Bitsy Spider," which may explain why it was the child's favorite song. "A big ham," said her father Scott Coyne. "If you had her in a crowd of people, she was perfectly happy and content. She had no qualms about giving anybody a hug. She'd hug everybody."

Jaci Rae slipped into every family photograph she could and always carried her bottle on family car trips. "Every time I opened that [car] door to get her out, she threw her bottle down," said mother Sharon. "I don't know how many times I've been in a dress, up underneath my car trying to get her bottle because she threw it out. And every time she just laughed and giggled."

Jaci Rae preferred gadgets that were off-limits (like lamps and tabletops) to toys, and given a newspaper or magazine was in her element ("She'd just shred them into the tiniest pieces," said Scott). Inquisitive, she liked to touch things and enjoyed items of different colors. She ate green beans straight from the can, made grand messes with macaroni and cheese, and, said her father, "really never had a bad day."

KATHY CREGAN

Katherine L. Cregan, 60, of Oklahoma City; mother of William J. Cregan Jr. of Spencer, Mike Cregan of Oklahoma City, and Chris Cregan of Moore; service representative, Social Security Administration.

Before her husband died—nine years before the bombing—Kathy Cregan often trekked through malls and bowled alongside him. Afterwards, plagued by bad health, she settled for working during the week and resting on the weekends—cruising the home shopping channel replaced her mall outings, said son Chris.

Her sons, however, remember her as a mother who hustled them from football and baseball practice and made an effort to attend to their needs. "She was all the time doing for her kids," said son William.

The product of a single-parent home (her father died in a Japanese war camp during World War II), Kathy never forgot the long hours her own mother had to work and how little time she had for her family. "She didn't want that for her kids," said William of his mother. So even though Kathy's health deteriorated while the boys were still young, she managed to take good care of them.

She also found ways to enjoy life. "She read all the time," William said (give her a romance or Stephen King novel, and she was more than content). And she took great pleasure in her five grandchildren and two Yorkshire terriers.

RICHARD CUMMINS

Richard Leroy Cummins, 55, of Mustang; husband of Frances Cummins; father of Courtney Jennings, Nikki Clinton, and Kraig Cummins; son of Christine Cummins of Tucson, AZ; brother of Frank Cummins of Ruidoso, NM, and Wally Cummins of Tucson; father-in-law of Bryan Jennings, Marty Clinton, and Shawn Cummins; grandfather of Chayse Cummins, Austin Jennings, and Collin Jennings; senior investigator, U. S. Department of Agriculture.

Richard Cummins had a well-known soft spot for children and animals. "He let the kids bring animals home," said Frances, his wife of thirty years. "We still have some pets from when they were in the fourth grade." And his concern for animals spilled over into his award-winning work on behalf of the Midwest Stolen Dog Task Force (established to eradicate the theft of animals for resale to research laboratories).

Yet, said Frances, "The main thing about Dick is that he was a loving, caring husband and father. We were what mattered to him."

Though his work required him to travel frequently, Richard tried to visit his children if he was within an hour's drive of their homes. "We saw our kids at least two times a month, and we really supported AT&T," Frances joked.

Fellow investigator and friend Mike Ray remembers Richard as a quiet, fun, easygoing man. The latter was especially true at home, said Frances, where Richard happily took responsibility for many household duties, including grocery shopping and cooking. "He spoiled us all," said Frances.

STEVEN CURRY

Steven Douglas Curry, 44, of Norman; husband of Kathleen Curry; father of Jennifer and Jeremiah; building mechanical inspector, General Services Administration.

The youngest of seven children, Steven Curry graduated from Choctaw High School in 1969. He served in the Navy from 1970-74 and married his wife Kathleen on March 8, 1974. The couple spent their twenty-one-year marriage in Norman, living on five acres near Kathleen's family. "He was a fisherman and a hunter," she said. "He hunted on our land, and he liked to go to Lake Eufaula."

Steven served as a board member on the Robin Hill School Board. He was a deacon for the Calvary Free Will Baptist Church in Norman, where he also coached the church basketball team. "He always wanted to be a coach," said Kathleen. "He loved sports." A licensed electrician, Steven often helped out his friends and family. He had recently moved his parents to the Shawnee area. "He always helped his parents," said Kathleen. "He was a real happy person who enjoyed life. He never met a stranger."

BRENDA DANIELS

Brenda Faye Daniels, 42, of Oklahoma City; fiancée of Arty Marsh; mother of Chasity Pope, Devin Pope, and Stephanie Pope; grandmother of Aarion, Devon, and Brendon Pope; teacher, America's Kids.

The week after she took over the daycare center in the Alfred P. Murrah building, several parents asked Melva Noakes if Brenda Daniels would be back as a teacher. The General Services Admin-istration also had good things to say about Brenda, so Noakes called her in for an interview. Brenda became one of only two former daycare employees rehired by Noakes. The day of the bombing, the other woman called in sick, but Daniels was there taking care of her toddlers. "She was like a big grandma," said Noakes. "She just loved to be around kids," said Deadra Marsh-Buntrock, whose father was planning to marry Brenda.

Brenda hoped to have her own daycare and was working on her certification. Friends, family, and coworkers agree, given a choice of leaving her charges to die alone or being by their side, Brenda would have picked the latter. "That's where she would have wanted to be," Deadra said.

The mother of three collected stuffed animals and Cabbage Patch Kids. She loved indoor plants, and her house was full of ivies. She was also a blues fan and had recently visited Beale Street in Memphis, Tennessee. She was buried with her beloved cassettes of B. B. King and Bobby "Blue" Bland.

BEN DAVIS

Sergeant Benjamin L. Davis, 28, of Edmond; husband of Glory Davis; father of Vandrea; son of Susie Varnes and stepson of Michael Varnes, both of Oklahoma City; operations clerk, U. S. Marine Corps Recruiting Station.

Sergeant Benjamin Davis was awaiting official word April 19, 1995, of an eagerly anticipated promotion to second lieutenant. Just before 9 a. m., his captain tried to put a call through to confirm the news but got a busy line. "He was so excited," said wife Glory Davis. "He just knew he was going to get this promotion. That's all he talked about the last days before this happened."

A marine since 1986, Ben served in North Carolina, Japan, and Hawaii, receiving two good conduct medals, a Sea Service Deployment ribbon, a National Defense Service Medal, and a Meritorious Unit Commendation ribbon. A picture-perfect marine, he never raised his voice nor showed that he was upset.

Married seven years, Ben gave a steady stream of poems and notes to his wife. He read to his daughter Vandrea and cycled with his wife, stayed in shape by running and lifting weights, and attended Wildewood Christian Church in Oklahoma City.

Ben, who had an associate's degree in computer accounting, was attending UCO three nights a week to earn his bachelor's. He had plans to become a CPA to further his career in the marines. He and Glory bought their first home two years before the bombing.

With his schooling almost complete and his promotion imminent, said Glory, "Things were

DIANA DAY

Diana L. Day, 38, of Oklahoma City; mother of Justin; daughter of William and Frankie Day; sister of Bill Day and Dayna King, both of Oklahoma City; public housing revitalization specialist, Office of Public Housing, HUD.

Diana Lynn Day was a long-time metro-area resident who graduated from Grant High School in 1975. Northwest Church of Christ minister Bill Day remembers his sister as a woman with frequent smiles and bubbling laughter who was also a devoted member of his congregation (she served there as Sunday school coordinator).

Diana and her son, Justin, lived with her parents, William and Frankie Day. "She was always so concerned about [Justin's] education and that all his needs be met," said Frankie.

She loved interior decorating, and Diana and her mother spent many hours working together on their favorite pastime, arts and crafts. The mother-daughter team was a regular on the craft show circuit selling their dolls and baskets. Indeed, Diana's death has been particularly difficult for her mother because they were so close. "We did everything together," said Frankie. "She often said, 'You're more than my mom; you're my best friend.'"

PETER DeMASTER

Peter DeMaster, 44, of Oklahoma City; husband of Kay DeMaster; father of Kristin DeMaster and Brian Barry; son of June and Joe DeMaster; special agent, Defense Investigative Service, Defense Department.

Family and friends teased Peter DeMaster about being the perpetual Boy Scout, but they weren't far from the truth. An Eagle Scout, Peter DeMaster never forgot his boyhood creed. "He was a Christian, and he was a nice man," said his wife, Kay. "He was a real good father, husband, and family man," said mother-in-law Melba Massey.

To his Oklahoma City neighbors, he was the man in headphones who paraded his large dalmation and tiny schnauzer through the neighborhood every evening. "Every day that was his job," said Kay, "rain, sleet or snow."

A job as an AWACS instructor at Tinker Air Force Base brought Peter to Oklahoma originally, though he spent the last eleven years of his life at the Department of Defense. He met Kay, also divorced at the time, at a mutual neighbor's swimming party, and within a year, the two (with his daughter Kristin and her son Brian) joined families. They married April 24, 1982.

Raised in Wisconsin, Peter was an avid hockey fan. "He always wanted to be a hockey referee," said fellow hockey enthusiast Cheryl Thiessen. A loyal fan, he never missed a home game of the Oklahoma City Blazers, and when he could, he traveled to see the team play.

CASTINE DEVEROUX

Castine Deveroux, 49, of Oklahoma City; mother of Cathy and Hurtis Deveroux and Timothy, Cedric, Ronald, and Erick Hearn; daughter of the late Ivory and Viola Brooks of Pine Bluff, AR; sister of Minnie Mae Brooks of Oklahoma City, Ivory Tyler, Dorothy Mae Calip, Sylvester Brooks, Curtis Brooks, and Larry Gotrie; program support assistant, Office of Housing, HUD.

Castine Deveroux worked for the U. S. government for twenty-three years and in Oklahoma City for the last seven. She had six children (ages thirteen to twenty-eight) who she chauffeured to judo lessons, basketball games, shopping, and school events.

The youngest in an Arkansas family of eight children, she was close to her sister, Minnie, who also lived in Oklahoma City. Friends and coworkers recall Deveroux as a "lovely person" with expressive eyes and a fondness for All My Children (which Castine always taped).

A longtime member of Saint John Missionary Baptist Church, Castine also belonged to a prayer group with friend Louise Peters. Said Louise, the prayer group will never be the same. "When we get in our circle," said Louise, to join hands to pray, "we miss her so much. Our circle has been broken for the first time."

SHEILA DRIVER

Sheila Gigger Driver, 28, of Oklahoma City; wife of Gregory Driver; mother of Shequandala T. Gigger; daughter of Sharon Williams of Oklahoma City and Curtis Henderson of Antlers; sister of Daron Gigger; student, Langston University; Federal Employees Credit Union customer.

Sheila Driver—newlywed, three months pregnant, mother, and honor student—was deeply religious. Asked to describe his wife, Gregory Driver referred Proverbs 31 and said, "She was a virtuous woman in every sense of the word."

The couple met at church in northeast Oklahoma City three years ago (both attended Greater First Deliverance Temple). They married May 14, 1994. Both Sheila and her husband were homeroom parents at Eisenhower Elementary, where Sheila's daughter Shequandala went to school. According to Sheila's childhood friend Mary Williams, Sheila always stressed the importance of her African-American heritage to her daughter, telling Shequandala, "You're mahogany brown. You're beautiful. Don't ever be ashamed of your color."

A graduate of Capitol Hill High School, Sheila was a full-time student in the physical therapy program at Langston University.

Upon Sheila finishing at Langston, couple planned for Greg to attend Cameron University and pursue an engineering degree. He says the two were "holding onto a vision of our life together," a vision of "being prosperous physically, spiritually, and financially." If his wife taught him any one thing, says Greg, it was if one ventures out by faith, he'll reach victory.

TYLOR EAVES

Tylor S. Eaves, 8 months, of Midwest City; son of Miya Eaves; grandson of Gloria Eaves-Hardin of Midwest City and Victor Eaves Sr. of Oklahoma City; nephew of Victor Eaves Jr. of Midwest City; attended America's Kids.

Give Tylor Eaves bananas, a remote control, and his Lion King or Farmer In the Dell sound book, and he was content. But hold him, said his mother, and he was happy.

"He loved attention," said Miya. "He wanted to know that you were paying attention to him."

"Nanny," as his family nicknamed Tylor, liked to swing in his swing and splash in his bath water. He was notorious for pulling off his right shoe and right sock, over and over again.

Only eight months old, Tylor fit the clothes of a baby three times his age. He had a thick shock of straight black hair that his mother pulled into multiple ponytails. A boy with his own mind, Tylor rarely crawled places ("He wanted to get up and walk," said Miya proudly); however, since technically he wasn't walking yet, he usually settled for traveling backwards in his walker.

Tylor had attended America's Kids for a week and a half.

ASHLEY ECKLES

Ashley M. Eckles, 4 years 9 months, of Guthrie; daughter of Kathleen Treanor of Guthrie and Steve Eckles of Salina; stepchild of Mike Treanor; sister of Zachary Eckles; stepsister of David Treanor; half sister of Stephen and Troy Eckles; accompanied her grandparents Luther and LaRue Treanor to Social Security office.

For Ashley Eckles, keeping up with her older brothers was the focus of her life. "She just followed them everywhere she could," said her mother, Kathleen Treanor, with a laugh. When not playing with the boys, she was usually either showering them with kisses or clobbering them.

Not long before Ashley died, however, her focus had shifted from her brothers to keeping up with the family's pregnant cat. "She'd say, 'I want those kittens to come out so I can play with them,'" Kathleen recalled.

Her mother remembers her as a child who made friends with strangers, loved to color, adored her clan of Barbie dolls, and especially liked chocolate.

SUSAN FERRELL

Susan J. Ferrell, 37, of Oklahoma City; daughter of Donald F. and Sally Ferrell and sister of Cynthia Ferrell Ashwood, all of Chandler; attorney-adviser, Legal Division, HUD.

It began with small-town dance lessons in her hometown of Chandler, but Susan Ferrell ultimately pursued the arts her entire life. Her interest in dance evolved to include jazz and ballet as well as Middle Eastern, Native American, and African dance. "Dance is life, truth, the way of the spirit, passion, the earth," an entry in her dance journal reads.

As sensitive as she was artistic, Susan cared deeply about people, the environment, animals (cats especially), and spirituality.

In the years before her death, she supported—among others—the Jesus House, Peace House, and World Neighbors. Her mother Sally Ferrell suspects nearly half of Susan's salary found its way back into filling community needs.

Her family remembers Susan's passion for life. Observed her brother-in-law, Albert Ashwood, at her memorial service: "If there was a cause that demanded attention, she embraced it. . . She carried its torch with a passion few of us could ever hope to experience. My favorite remembrance of Susan is summed up by one bumper sticker that adorned her car. It simply said, 'Celebrate Diversity. ' To me, it was a bumper sticker. For her, it was a creed."

"She lived life her way," her mother said. "She was, indeed, a complex, passionate, and loving person, concerned about world peace and hopeful of an end to all forms of discrimination."

CARROL FIELDS

Carrol "Chip" Fields, 48, of Guthrie; wife of Ronald L. Fields; mother of Ronald W. Fields; daughter of Rex and Mary Farris of Meeker; sister of Roy and Ella Farris, both of Meeker, Merrilee Wynn and Peggy Rider, both of Shawnee, and Deborah Bradley of Woodward; office assistant, Drug Enforcement Administration.

"Carrol was five foot three, and she wasn't scared of nothing. You didn't mess with her family or friends," recalled her husband Ron Fields wryly.

"Chip," as she was called by family and friends, logged thirty years of government service, was the lead support personnel employee in Oklahoma City's DEA offices, and held the DEA's 1994 Administrator's Award for Distinguished Service. Yet her achievements at work were more than surpassed at home, said Ron: "We weren't married; we were one."

Married twenty-eight years, they were rarely apart and still did little niceties for each other—Ron, for example, served Carrol coffee in bed each morning. He often overheard friends tease his wife about her perfect life. "The girls couldn't believe she was so happy; everything was right in her life," he said. "Carrol always had a smile."

Sentimental about special occasions, it wasn't unusual for Carrol to buy little treasures for her family and skimp when it came to her own wants. "She'd buy expensive presents for other people and then go buy her clothes on sale," Ron said fondly. "She never thought of herself—never."

KATHY FINLEY

Katherine Ann Finley, 44, of Yukon; wife of Riley Finley; mother of Melissa Allen Smith; vice president of operations, Federal Employees Credit Union.

"She taught me, and untold numbers of other people, that laughter and smiles cure more problems than anyone can imagine," said Riley Finley of his wife. And he admired her for raising her daughter (now grown) for many years all alone. "She had an unending love for her only child," said Riley, who married Kathy Finley in 1988.

Kathy worked twenty-one years at the credit union, starting as a teller and rising through the ranks to become vice president. She never, however, quit pitching in when things got busy or assisting long-time customers who felt better dealing with her. "She took their deposits," said Alice Irwin, Kathy's best friend of twenty years and former credit union coworker, "just like it was her job."

Kathy enjoyed books and Elvis movies and Thai food. "All the Thai restaurants knew her by name," said Irwin. Kathy frequented the Philharmonic and sang with her sister at Wilmont Place Baptist Church and for weddings. She and Riley boated, fished for striper at Lake Texoma, and crisscrossed the country from San Diego to Key West, Alaska to Washington, D.C.

JUDY FISHER

Judy J. Fisher, 45, of Oklahoma City; wife of Marlon Fisher; mother of Tara, Kyle, and Zane Cody Fisher; stepmother of Laura Fisher of Nashville, TN; clerk, Office of Housing, HUD.

Laid-back, quiet, Judy Fisher reveled in life's simple pleasures—home, family, friends. She lived a healthy lifestyle: watched what she ate, worked out (more than eight years of water aerobics), walked, and played softball. (Judy always knew the latest vitamin on the market and its health benefits, said friend and coworker Rita Crews.)

Most of all, though, she loved her family. Judy, husband Marlon (they married in 1982), and their children camped and took big summer vacations (Cancun, Disney World) that Judy organized. Since Judy's family lived in Iowa and Marlon's in Minnesota, they took turns visiting their relatives. Eventually, two of Judy's siblings—brother Kurt (now a firefighter) and sister Charlene (who also worked downtown)—followed her to Oklahoma City.

The sisters lunched often and attended '89er baseball games, Lyric Theatre, and the symphony together. "She was always there for me," said Charlene. "She was my mother down here." Observed Rita Crews, "If you met her once in a lifetime, you'd been blessed."

LINDA FLORENCE

Linda L. Florence, 43, of Oklahoma City; wife of David Florence; mother of John David Florence III (Trey); daughter of Lennie Groves McKaskle; secretary, Office of Housing, HUD.

Once Linda Florence married her husband, David, some seventeen years ago, she became a world traveler (previously she had left Oklahoma's borders only twice). Japan, Scandinavia, Europe, much of the United States—she saw them all.

Until, that is, her son, John David III, affectionately called Trey, came along. The Florences had tried for years to have a child; having exhausted the gamut of fertility options, they were just about to try a formal adoption when Linda became pregnant. The couple's last big trip was to Yellowstone Park in early 1993; soon after, they became parents.

David describes Linda's pregnancy as a transforming event in her life: "She was so full of life when she found out she was pregnant. We were older, and she went through it like a teenager." It was, he said, a "labor of love." After Trey's birth, Linda spent much of her spare time reading to, playing with, or just watching her new son. But both son and father feel her absence. "She was my best friend," said David. "We did everything together."

DON & MARY ANNE FRITZLER

Donald L., 64, and Mary Anne, 57, Fritzler, both of Oklahoma City; parents of Lee Anne Fennell of Silver Spring, MD, and Bryan Fritzler of Newark, DE; grandparents of Allyson Lee Fritzler; Don, an architect at Fritzler & Associates, and Mary Anne, a retired schoolteacher who managed the Fritzler business; the couple was at the Social Security office to check on retirement benefits for Don.

"They were just the kind of people you wished everybody could be like," said Mike Bass, a Fritzler family friend and business associate.

Don and Mary Anne Fritzler were people of integrity. "It was always clear [as a child] that the best thing was to go ahead and fess up right away...and be honest about it," recalled Bryan Fritzler, a chemical engineer for DuPont. "Things always went a lot easier for you than if you tried to cover it up." Their parents also taught them to believe in themselves and to always do their best, said Bryan's sister Lee Anne.

Don was a well known church architect who worked in the Southwest. "I really can't go anywhere in Oklahoma or Texas that I don't see a memorial to Don," said Mike Bass of his friend's work. Indeed, architecture was Don's job and his hobby. "A lot of us show up in the morning and put in our eight hours and go home," son Bryan said. "I don't think it was like that for (my dad). It was so much fun, and he enjoyed the whole process."

The Fritzlers were members of Quail Springs Baptist Church, a church Don designed and at which Mary Anne taught Sunday school.

Just weeks before the bombing, the couple learned they were expecting their first grandchild.

TEVIN GARRETT

Tevin D. Garrett, 16 months, of Midwest City; son of Helena Garrett Scott; stepson of Vernon Scott; brother of Sharonda Garrett; attended America's Kids.

Tevin Garrett was partial to his yellow Lion King bike, his sister's hat, and his Snoop Doggy Dogg CD. Always on the go-go," said his mother Helena Garrett, he was never in such a hurry that he left without his hat. "He always had his hat," said Helena. "It didn't match anything. It's his sister's hat, and has big flowers on it."

His activities of choice were zooming headfirst down his plastic slide, eating chicken, and dabbling to big sister Sharonda whom Tevin called "Wanna"). Mischievous, Tevin once upended a display of plastic bowls by pulling one out from the bottom; all passersby heard after the fall was a hearty "Hah, hah, hah, hah, hah" coming from beneath the pile. At home, his favorite prank was the time he stepped into his mother's bath water fully clothed.

Recently, Tevin had been learning how to get his own watermelon Gatorade from the refrigerator. "I would pour him a cup and leave it at the bottom of the refrigerator," said Helena. "I always knew he was in there because I could hear the refrigerator door open, and then I would hear this, 'Ahhhh.'"

Helena, who worked across from the Murrah building in the Journal Record Building, could see into Tevin's room at the daycare from her office's break room. If she didn't see little heads bobbing up and down, she knew it was naptime.

LAURA GARRISON

Laura J. Garrison, 61, of Oklahoma City; wife of Fred Garrison; mother of Tracy Rushing of San Diego, CA, Kerry Hatcher of Los Angeles, CA, and Harold Taylor of Miami, FL; admissions clerk, Oklahoma Memorial Hospital emergency room; was at Social Security making plans for her retirement.

Between taking care of her quadriplegic baby brother and tending to her own three children, Laura Garrison always found time to bake. "It could be a Wednesday night at 3 a.m., and we'd wake up smelling bread," said daughter Tracy Rushing.

Childhood memories for Laura's children include homemade meals every night, fresh cinnamon rolls, homemade jellies and pickles, and her signature German chocolate cake.

For years, Laura was the cook at Children's Hospital but when the job was phased out, the hospital trained her as an admissions clerk. With plans to retire this summer, she was making a list of each of her coworkers' favorite cakes so she could leave each one with something special.

A member of Saint John Missionary Baptist Church in Oklahoma City (a church her grandfather started), Laura's hours away from work and church were spent sewing, doing needlework, decorating, and visiting her children. The twenty-first of twenty-two siblings, Laura spent much of her life caring for a brother paralyzed in the army in the early 1960s while playing football.

JAMIE GENZER

Jamie L. Genzer, 32, of Wellston; mother of Kyle and Krista; daughter of Jay and Nancy Fialkowski; sister of Jef Fialkowski and Anna Marie Perdue; loan officer, Federal Employees Credit Union.

A single mom, Jamie Genzer's life revolved around her two children, Kyle and Krista. She attended Our Lady's of Sorrows Catholic Church in Chandler and was a member of Band Parents and the PTA.

A music lover since her days in the stage band at Mount Saint Mary's High School, Jamie for the last eight years sang bass for the Sweet Adelines and was part of Cameo's quartet. "Jamie lived for the Sweet Adelines," said Zon Kordic-Brinkley, a member of the quartet. "It helped her through some really tough times."

Zon remembers Jamie as "genuine—one of the most real people you'd ever know. When she walked in the room, her presence made it better." Observed her mother, Nancy Fialkowski: "Jamie's most outstanding attribute was her love for people. She had a knack for making people feel welcome and wanted."

MARGARET GOODSON

Margaret E. Goodson, 54, of Oklahoma City; wife of Ron Goodson; mother of Debbie Gomez of Mustang, Keith Betterton of Lawton, and Kevin and Howard Betterton, both of Oklahoma City; claims representative, 20 years, Social Security Administration.

Margaret Goodson always saw herself riding behind her husband on a motorcycle. And when she married her second husband Ron Goodson in 1992, the couple did just that, with one exception: Margaret got her own bike.

Last year, she purchased her fourth bike, a turquoise and cream 1994 Kawasaki Vulcan. "We walked in the motorcycle shop to buy oil, and she walked out with a new motorcycle," said Ron.

The couple began dating in the early 1980s; Margaret was forty-six before she learned how to ride—and then it was a friend's dirt bike. Before too long, however, she and Ron were cruising to Yellowstone Park and Bear Tooth Pass. "We'd load up the saddlebags and strap a tent and a sleeping bag on the back of the seat and take off and be gone nine, ten days," Ron recalled.

In 1993, they joined the Honda Sport Touring Association; weekends became a time to cook out with other members and to back-road tour. Still, Ron says they were happiest at home (where their biggest argument was who got to do the dishes). "Basically, we were homebodies," Ron said. "Together, we didn't need anything or anybody else."

Margaret's other interests were working in the yard, watching birds, and playing the piano—Irish jigs to classical tunes.

KEVIN GOTTSHALL II

Kevin "Lee" Gottshall II, six and a half months, of Norman; son of Kevin and Sheryl Gottshall; grandson of Tony and Sandy Ray of Hemphill, TX, and Earnest and Janice Gottshall of Dalhart, TX; attended America's Kids.

At six and a half months, Lee Gottshall had six teeth and a smile that could knock a person out. He zoomed around in his walker or rolled to and fro ("He wasn't interested in crawling," said his mother, Sheryl Gottshall. "That didn't get him anywhere fast enough").

Capable of rolling across the living room in a matter of seconds, Lee could quickly respond to images of Bugs Bunny or Winnie the Pooh when they appeared on the family's big screen television: "He'd roll over to the TV and get up on his elbows and watch," said Sheryl.

On occasion so intent would her son be on reaching his destination that he was known to roll, or run, right over his beloved dog, a good-natured, ten-year-old Shih Tzu named Baron.

"He knew what he wanted," laughed Sheryl, "and he'd go after it."

Intrigued by water, Lee would "watch the water go down the drain and try to catch it," said Sheryl. "We'd tell it, 'Bye bye' and that we'd see it tomorrow.'"

Lee, who looked just like his father, could handle his own Tommy Tippy Cup. Among his favorite things were sweet potatoes, chicken and rice, and Dr. Seuss' Green Eggs and Ham.

"Lee knew nothing but love, a full belly, a dry bottom, and lots of good times," said Sheryl.

ETHEL GRIFFIN

Ethel L. Griffin, 55, of Edmond; wife of Bruce Griffin; mother of Richard Griffin of Fort Wayne, IN, and Robert Griffin of Independence, MO; service representative, Social Security Administration.

Ethel and husband Bruce were weekend regulars at Jimmy's Egg in Edmond; when not breakfasting, they collaborated on craft projects: Ethel began by first painting sweatshirts, then involved her husband in making ornaments (it snowballed from there). "We did almost everything together," said Bruce.

What the couple made, they sold at three or four shows a year, including Oklahoma City's Affair of the Heart. Ethel named their home business Griffin's Gallery, of which she was both president and CEO. Of his lack of title, Bruce said with a hearty laugh, "I was anything she wanted me to be."

Ethel often took pictures—particularly of her grandchildren. "I don't know if the grandkids would know her without a camera in her hand," quipped Bruce.

She also spent many hours at home reading for pleasure (and always amazed Bruce by being able to simultaneously watch television and read).

COLLEEN GUILES

Colleen Guiles, 59, of Oklahoma City; wife of Gene Guiles; mother of Lanna Peck of Orlando, FL, Matt Gardner and Jay Guiles, both of Oklahoma City, Lorri Montiel of Fort Walton Beach, FL, and Toni Pickard of Norman; underwriter, Single Family Housing, HUD.

If there was any doubt Colleen Guiles touched a great many lives, the matter was settled at her funeral: Some three thousand people attended her memorial service. In life, she had worked as an underwriter, a real estate broker, a mortgage banker, and a vice president at Liberty Mortgage. She had trained her share of realtors and mortgage bankers, too. In the 1980s, Colleen's son Matt and daughter Lorri worked together at a company they founded called Mortgage One.

On the home front, Colleen relaxed with her husband, Gene Guiles, at their house at Lake Texoma (the two planned to retire to the lake soon). Her other great love was her five grandchildren, and Matt observed, "Her love and compassion helped all the grandkids grow up."

Colleen treated both coworkers and kin as family: belting out "Happy Birthday" off-key on their big day (overlooked coworkers used to seek her out and demand she sing it to them), noticing when things weren't quite right, and taking it upon herself to fix them. She was a lot of fun, too, Matt added. And she doted on her children: Until a few years ago, Matt woke every Easter to a surprise Easter basket from his mother at his front door. Said Matt, "She's extra special."

RANDY GUZMAN

Captain Randolph Guzman, 28, of Oklahoma City; common-law husband of Felicia Sims; son of Erlinda B. Guzman of San Leandro, CA, and Rudolph A. Guzman of Sunnyvale, CA; brother of Rudy Guzman Jr. of San Leandro, CA; executive officer, U.S. Marine Corps recruiting station.

Captain Randy Guzman was a die-hard UCLA fan. "I hope God is a UCLA fan," said his close friend and coworker Master Sergeant Top Waters, "because if he ain't, [Randy] will try to convince him he should be."

Avid about sports and his career, Randy was a regular at Blazer hockey games, in the stands at Remington Park, on the fairways (despite a handicap of about 100), and at the gym, where he played many a morning pickup game of basketball with his fellow marines.

At work, Randy Guzman led by example. Observed Top, "If the situation got tough and you needed someone to roll his sleeves up and give you a hand, he'd do it."

He was set to officially marry Felicia Sims in March of 1996 (he had asked her mother for her hand in marriage the Christmas of 1994). His time with Felicia was often spent with her son Jordan; Randy liked to ride the Looney Train with him at Six Flags and make snow angels together. Recalled Felicia, "Here's this big marine out there making snow angels with Jordan."

Randy had a degree in history from California State Hayward; he was a Gulf War veteran and a recipient of the Navy Marine Corps Achievement medal, Kuwait Liberation medal, Southwest Asia Service medal, National Defense medal, Combat Action ribbon, and a Meritorious Unit Commendation ribbon.

CHERYL HAMMONS

Cheryl E. Hammons, 44, of Oklahoma City; mother of Falesha and Daina Bradley and daughter of Mary Hill, all of Oklahoma City; a certified nursing assistant, Four Seasons Nursing Home; with daughters Falesha and Daina and Daina's two children, Peachlyn Bradley and Gabreon Bruce, was at the Social Security office obtaining a social security card for Gabreon.

Since she was a little girl, Cheryl Hammons was always the designated mother hen. She liked to take care of people, and, "She was always trying to be the mother," said sister Victoria Slaughter with a laugh. "As soon as my mom would leave, she'd start running things." Yet Cheryl and her siblings never squealed on each other. "We wouldn't tell on each other, and then we all would get in trouble," Victoria said. Whatever their punishment, once it was over, "We'd all cry together, and then we'd laugh."

As an adult, Cheryl ran a tight ship, sometimes working two jobs. Nursing was her chosen profession. But even it was never as important as her children and grandchildren. Her free time was spent visiting, playing cards or dominoes, shooting pool, or dancing with friends and family. She attended Cathedral of Praise World Outreach Center in Oklahoma City.

RON HARDING

Ronald V. Harding, 55, Oklahoma City; father of Rhonda Harding, Kimberly Harding, and Ronald Harding Jr., all of Oklahoma City; service representative, Social Security Administration.

The Harding household was a musical household. If music wasn't playing—be it clarinet, saxophone, flute, violin, or cello—it usually meant Ron Harding was either not home or asleep. "When we were little girls, the bands would be in our garage," said daughter Rhonda, "and the whole block would just listen. All over the neighborhood everybody would be hearing music."

The Jimi Hendrix fan performed with the Oklahoma City Symphony, a symphony quartet, the Earl Pittman All-Star Jazz Band, the Saint John Orchestra, and the Oklahoma City Community Orchestra. He performed with the choir at Greater Cleaves Memorial CME Church, where he was a member and a regular on holiday programs. As a young soldier, he played with the U. S. Army Band, Second Armored Division and as a young father (Rhonda was only about ten), he toured for two years with the Yellow Sunshine Band.

He worked thirty years at the SSA to support his family, but Ron always dreamed of being a full-time professional musician. He began playing clarinet at age seven, and his interest only intensified through the years. "After work the first thing he did was practice," said Rhonda. "He carried his instruments in his trunk."

Outside music, Ron appreciated the Philadelphia Eagles and Philadelphia Phillies. He was also a steward at his church where he served on its music staff.

TOM HAWTHORNE

Thomas L. Hawthorne Sr. , 52, of Choctaw; husband of Donna Hawthorne; father of Wendy Schoonmaker of Elk City and Bob Hawthorne and Tom Hawthorne Jr. both of Stillwater; twenty-seven year employee, Dayton Tire, and a pension and insurance representative, then United Rubber Workers Union; was at Social Security office to pick up paperwork for a disabled union worker.

The week before Tom Hawthorne died, he left a carefully placed chocolate-covered cherry for his wife to find. It was a gesture that hearkened to their college days, when Tom, a freshman, first presented Donna, a junior, a similar box of candy in the school's union hall. That time, as Tom walked Donna back to her dorm, he confided his plans to marry her. "He didn't ask me; he told me," chuckled Donna.

Two years later, they did marry, and chocolate cherries became an ongoing joke. "I'd find them on my desk or on my dashboard," said Donna, a fifth grade teacher at James Griffith Intermediate School.

The two were inseparable and, after thirty years of marriage, still best friends.

To Tom Jr., one of the couples' three children, his dad was his hero. "He was really Superman to me," he said. "He sold life." Tom Sr. never wore a watch, which may explain, said Donna, why "He always had time for people." During a nine-month strike at Dayton Tire, Tom organized fundraisers and solicited donations to help fellow union members trying to make ends meet. Active in United Way fund raisers, Tom was a member of the United Methodist Church of Harrah. He enjoyed woodcarving and genealogy, and he had just hand-picked wildflowers for Donna in early April.

DORIS HIGGINBOTTOM

Doris "Adele" Higginbottom, 44, of Oklahoma City; wife of David Higginbottom; stepmother of Kelli and David Van; daughter of Melanie Brown Mattox and the late William P. Mattox; sister of Jane Sammons and the late William Mattox Jr.; aunt of James Mattox, Clayton Mattox, and Christian Mattox; purchasing agent, U. S. Department of Agriculture.

Adele Higginbottom was a history buff, a descendant of a colonial sea captain named William Glover and William H. Henry Clayton (a U. S. attorney who served under Judge Isaac Parker—Fort Smith's notorious "hanging judge"—and became a federal judge in Indian Territory). "Adele's roots run deep in the founding of our country," said husband David.

She was deeply involved in the Daughters of the American Revolution and a lifelong collector of antiques. Both she and Karen Holcomb, her old OU roommate and best friend of twenty-six years, collected (and hunted) flow-blue china. "We liked the same things," said Karen, recalling that once Adele got a new rug only to learn Karen had unknowingly purchased the same rug for her own home. Adele enjoyed music and cooking. Friendly, outgoing, Adele was graced with the ability to make people laugh. "She was a big cutup," said David. "She was always trying to make people feel good."

She participated on the USDA's local Safety Committee and belonged to the Greater Oklahoma Chapter of Federally Employed Women. More than once, Adele traveled the country in an effort to protect workers' rights. "I don't care if it was the President of the United States she was talking to," said David. "She never backed off of a challenge of any kind."

ANITA HIGHTOWER

Anita C. Hightower, 27, of Oklahoma City; daughter of Ruth Hightower of Ft. Worth; sister of Joyce Brown, Waymond Brown, and Harry Hightower, all of Fort Worth; mother of Antionette and Ashley Hightower of Fort Worth; secretary, Dynamic Educational Systems, Inc.; killed at her desk in a building across from the Murrah building.

Though Anita Hightower and her mother Ruth Hightower lived a state apart, the two spoke every day, and about once a month Ruth would make the trip to Oklahoma City to visit, shop, and watch a little television with her daughter.

Lovable, loving, and headstrong, "[Anita] didn't meet strangers," her mother said. "Ashley [Anita's youngest daughter] is as friendly as her mother was."

Marsha Cato can remember being impressed the first time she met Anita at an Equipped Ministries retreat. (Marsha founded EM , a multi-denominational field ministry for women.) Soon after, she asked Anita to serve as secretary for Equipped, then helped her secure a secretarial post at DESI, where Anita greeted visitors with her trademark smile and outgoing ways." She had a type of character that really motivated people," said Marsha.

Marsha remembers Anita as someone who loved parties of all kinds and who was a frequent host and guest at Tupperware and home decorating parties.

"You name it, she went," said Marsha with a chuckle.

At the time of Anita's death, her youngest lived with her and the oldest, who had been ill, lived with Anita's mother. Both girls now live with their grandmother.

THOMPSON HODGES

Thompson E. "Gene" Hodges Jr. , 54, of Norman; husband of Deborah S. Hodges; father of C.C. Hodges and Clint Hodges, both of Norman, Angela Hodges of Minneapolis, and Sherrill Hodges of Ellicott City, MD; son of Thompson E. Hodges Sr.; supervisor, Office of Housing, HUD.

A gentle, quiet, kind man, Gene Hodges did what he was supposed to do and did it well, said his wife, Deb Hodges. He worked thirty years for the federal government, belonged to the PTA, and coached his son Clint's soccer team for six years (Gene loved soccer, Deb noted).

Heavily involved with his children's baseball, Scouts, basketball, and judo, Gene devoted a good deal of his time to nudging kids along—athletically and personally.

His approach to coaching— and to sports in general—was that of a teacher. He never pulled a child from a soccer game for making a mistake; instead, Deb recalled, "If kids messed up ... he'd quietly tell them [later] what they did wrong. By the time he was finished explaining, he never made the kids feel like they messed up." Gene understood, said Deb, that everyone makes mistakes.

PEGGY HOLLAND

Peggy L. Holland, 37, of Oklahoma City; wife of Richard Holland; mother of Erica and Kylie; computer specialist, U. S. Army Recruiting Battalion.

Unselfish. That adjective, friends and family agree, most aptly describes Peggy Holland. A Louisville, Kentucky, native, Peggy gave much of her personal time to the Coolidge Eyes and Ears Neighborhood Watch Association and Oklahoma City's Knob Hill Baptist Church.

In recent years, her church had become even more the focus of her life. She taught Sunday school there to third and fourth graders, directed a children's choir, and sang in the adult choir. She spent time each summer teaching vacation Bible school there, too.

COLEEN HOUSLEY

Linda C. Housley, 53, of Oklahoma City; wife of Gary M. Housley; mother of Mark Haggard, Kyma Hopkins, and Ronna Ketner; stepmother of Diana Lewis and Christina Black; grandmother of Michelle Haggard, Amber Blake, Brant Seaton, Courtney Hopkins, Derek Ketner, Tia Ketner, Joshua Lewis, Brandon Lewis, Devin Meyer, and Cheyenne Black; loan officer, Federal Employees Credit Union.

A mother of three by nineteen, Coleen Housley all but grew up with her children. Along the way, she made sacrifices to see they did not do without. "If it was clothes," said her husband, Gary, "she would make them; if it was an ice cream cone or a popsicle, she would invent a home-made version for them."

She worked until August 1993 with Gary at the Woods Credit Union.

On Labor Day weekend, 1993, Coleen and Gary married, and she gained two more children. In front of sixty relatives and friends, the couple exchanged vows as the Cherokee Queen backed out into Grand Lake. "This day was like Indian summer," recalled Gary of the two-hour cruise and reception.

Gary said he couldn't help but think of his wife as first an angel on earth, and now, of heaven. "It seemed her purpose in life was to love and help others," said Gary. "I have been left with an image of her trying to master that new set of wings, and it still makes my heart smile, because coordination was not one of her better attributes."

Observed Gary, "She was my life, my wife, my friend, my companion, and my lover." At Coleen's death, the Housleys had nine grandchildren.

GEORGE HOWARD

George M. Howard, 45, of Vallejo, CA; husband of Perla Howard; son of George L. Howard of Dallas; community planning and development representative, Office of Southern Plains Native American Programs, HUD.

Tired of skyrocketing crime and the high cost of living in the San Francisco Bay area, George Howard put in for a HUD transfer. He chose Oklahoma City because of Its proximity to Dallas, where his father, recently widowed, makes his home.

When the bombing occurred, George had been working in Oklahoma City for barely two weeks. His wife, Perla, remained in Vallejo.

Perla and George met in the Philippines in 1977; they married in Stillwater in 1987. Perla recalls her husband as a funny, energetic, spontaneous man who cofounded a motorcycle group called the Bureaucratic Bikers and once delivered twenty-six boxes of chocolate truffles to his wife after she mentioned her fondness for the candy.

A former Peace Corps member, Vietnam veteran, and public servant who worked much of his government career on behalf of Native Americans (George was one-quarter Cherokee himself), "His life was devoted to a large degree to doing things for other people," said Perla.

In Vallejo, the city has planted two redwoods in George's memory in a small park that faces the Howard home. Perla said he believed, "People should be treated like stained glass windows. We must look at them in the best light."

WANDA HOWELL

Wanda L. Howell, 34, of Spencer; wife of Melvin Howell, mother of TaShanna and Latasha, and daughter of Roger and Elmira Harris, all of Spencer; child-care attendant, America's Kids.

Growing up as the fourth of eight siblings, Wanda Howell was a peacemaker. "She was always stepping in the middle, going to the rescue, helping find solutions," said LaVonda Howell, her sister and best friend. "She always started talking to people about the Bible," added Melvin Howell, her husband of fifteen years.

Her father is a minister, and Wanda herself studied to become one. At her death, she was planning to start a youth counseling program at her father's chapel in Shawnee, where she was a member and preschool Sunday school teacher. "She always worked with children," observed LaVonda. "She wanted to have a positive influence in kids' lives."

Indeed, since she was seventeen, Wanda had worked with preschool age children. "She was crazy about kids," Melvin said.

What energy she didn't spend on her charges was expended at home on the telephone, usually with LaVonda. "She was a phone book," confided Melvin. "She loved to talk on the phone."

When Wanda and LaVonda weren't chatting on the phone, they were taking their nightly four-mile constitutional around the Star Spencer High School track, shopping, visiting the beauty shop, or enjoying holidays with their family. "We were intertwined," said LaVonda.

ROBBIN HUFF

Robbin Huff, 37, of Bethany; wife of Ronald Huff; stepmother of Corey and Matthew Huff; daughter of Richard and Barbara Buchholtz; sister of Richeal Thatcher and Rhonda Bartlebaugh, both of Oklahoma City, Renée Buchholtz of New Orleans, LA, and Richard Buchholtz of Saint Louis, MO; loan officer, Federal Employees Credit Union.

"She was ready to start her family," said husband Ronald Huff. Robbin and Ronald were expecting their first child, a girl to be named Amber Denise, in June 1995. "She always wanted kids," said Robbin's sister, Richeal Thatcher.

She had three sisters and a brother herself, and each Sunday afternoon, Robbin, Rhonda, and Richeal gathered with their families at their parents' for dinner. "We are a family that meets on Sundays," said Richeal.

Robbin and her husband bowled in a league with Richeal and her spouse, boated at Lake Thunderbird ("She was my driver while I skied," said Ronald), and country and western danced (they met at a country dance). They were married in March 1991.

Robbin spent her time at home in her flower beds tending to her morning glories and mums; she cross-stitched, decorated cakes, and liked to do crafts. A people person, she never met a stranger. "She would talk to people at the checkout stand," said Ronald. "She had a big heart, and she lived to be happy," said Richeal.

CHARLES & JEAN HURLBURT

Dr. Charles E. , 73, and Anna Jean, 67, Hurlburt, of Oklahoma City; parents of Barbie Trent of Harrah, Sherry Elliott of Temple, TX; and Dawn Barber and Betty Palmer, both of Birmingham, AL; Charles was a retired professor and director of dental radiology at OU Health Sciences Center in Oklahoma City; Jean, a semiretired RN at Deaconess Hospital; the couple was checking on retirement benefits at the Social Security Administration.

Charles and Jean Hurlburt were active members of Metropolitan Baptist Church in Oklahoma City: They both sang in the choir, Charles taught Sunday school, Jean played the hand bells, and both were on the missions board.

Jean, a nurse at Deaconess for more than twenty years, struck up friendships with everyone from aides to orderlies, patients to cleaning crew. Many a day she clocked out only to return to console a patient or talk with a coworker. "She loved her patients," Sherry Elliott and Barbie Trent echoed.

Charles and Jean met at Wheaton College in Illinois; later they spent five years as medical missionaries in Africa, then lived in Illinois and Alabama before settling down in Oklahoma City with their four daughters.

When Charles retired, Jean got him interested in cake decorating. Together, the two made countless cakes for friends, coworkers, and grandchildren. "He actually got better than her," said daughter Dawn Barber. Besides reading and studying, Charles had few hobbies, but his wife dabbled in china painting and gardening and anything else that caught her fancy. "They were people who looked for the fun," said daughter Betty Palmer.

PAUL ICE

Paul Ice, 43, of Midwest City; father of Sarah Williams of Oklahoma City and Miranda Ice of Choctaw; son of ack and Neva Ice of Midwest City; rother of Vicki Wilmott of Phoenix, AZ, Jan Barletta of Fort Myers, FL, usan Wilson of Edmond, and Kay Ice of Midwest City; senior special agent, J. S. Customs Service.

Paul Ice began his civil service areer in the early 1980s as a pecial agent with the Criminal nvestigation Division for the RS. A few years later, he moved o Customs, where he was nown as a hard-working agent vho pitched in (often without redit) when other agencies or J. S. customs offices needed his xpertise or assistance.

A former marine, Paul was nd of neatness and order, said m Robinson, assistant U.S. at-orney and a close friend since 983. Even his garden and flow-rs, said Jim, were symmetrically rranged and neat as a pin.

Paul joined the marine orps as a Second Lieuten-nt, then trained and flew as bombardier navigator in an ~6 aircraft. He later transferred o the intelligence division of e marines. He completed his me in the marine reserves and tired as a Lieutenant Colonel. retirement, he spent many of s happiest hours in his single-ngine two-seater with a friend, lative, or just the wide blue y for company.

In 1994, Paul ran in the arine Corps Marathon in ashington, D.C. In 1995, a roup of fellow runners from e Lake Runners, a group that ained on Saturdays at Lake efner, went to Washington, C., to run the same marathon his honor, and his race num-r from 1994—3072—was tired from competition. They member Paul, one said, as a pecial person, a fine person, a mendous person."

CHRISTI JENKINS

Christi Y. Jenkins, 32, of Edmond; wife of Aldo Jenkins; mother of Shimar, Shawna, Shelby, and Scott; daughter of Elcena Cummings and Acie Lee Buckner; teller, Federal Employees Credit Union.

When Christi Jenkins wasn't at work, she could usually be found taking care of her family or at church. "She loved our children," said her husband Aldo Jenkins. "Church and family were her two priorities," said Ben A. Baldridge, pastor of the New Life Tabernacle United Pentecostal Church in Edmond, where Christi taught Sunday school and was a member of the ladies' ministry. "The children were a top priority."

Christi and her husband were also involved in the evan-gelistic outreach of the church. When Christi first began going out to witness, she disliked leaving her children at home; her solution was to take them with her, said Aldo. The night before the April 19, 1995, bomb-ing, their outreach program had taken Christi and Aldo to a man's home, where they spent an hour talking to him about the church.

Said her pastor, "If you saw Christi Jenkins, it was a rare time where she wouldn't have a smile. She always had an uplifting word." She was an unofficial assistant to the pastor's wife, helping to pre-pare banquets and handling other tasks as needed. "She kept the loose ends tight," said her husband proudly.

JEAN JOHNSON

Norma Jean Johnson, 62, of Okla-homa City; wife of Carlos Johnson; mother of Edward Johnson, Vickie Cook-Lykins, Angela Richerson, and Oneta Johnson; executive secretary, Defense Investigative Service, Department of Defense.

Norma Johnson was known to work two or three jobs to help pay the bills, to be there to straighten a collar before the big performances of life, and to always have time to listen. "She was the strength of the family," said daughter Angela. "She always took care of us."

If Norma wasn't helping daughter Oneta get ready for a horse show, she was watching grandson Joshua play basketball or cheering on granddaughter Delisha in tumbling. "She was our big fan," said Oneta. "She could read your mind. She would do what needed to be done before you could ask her to do it."

Determined to earn a high school diploma, she attended night school at Southeast High School in Oklahoma City; she graduated in 1970, one year af-ter her oldest child, Edward, also graduated from Southeast.

Fond of the flowers she grew on her porch, Norma painted and made stained glass windows.

She was also an honorary member of the Fraternal Order of Police (she once worked in payroll and records for the Oklahoma City Police Depart-ment) and a one-time deputy sheriff. After a brief retirement, she joined the Department of Defense in 1989.

RAYMOND JOHNSON

Raymond L. Johnson, 59, of Oklahoma City; husband of Anne Marshall; father of Victoria Lockett of Choctaw, Andy Johnson of Wewoka, Juscindy Componation of Yukon, Deenna Johnson of Oklahoma City, Curtis Johnson of Shawnee, Josie Littrell of Durant, and Ann Deatherage of Seminole; volunteer administrative assistant, National Indian Council on Aging, Social Security Administration.

Raymond Johnson, a Seminole-Creek, worked to achieve a better life for his tribe and others. A member of the Seminole Nation, he was a former council member of the Oklahoma Indian Education Association, a member of the National Indian Education Association, and the National Congress of American Indians.

He felt strongly that Indian people should have integrity and that the U. S. government should honor its agreements with tribes. "You can live without food, but can you live without honor? You can live without electricity, but can you live without integrity?" Anne Marshall said was typical of his values.

Hired to help get a better count of Native Americans for the 1990 census, Raymond trav-eled from tribe to tribe because, said Anne, he strongly believed "people need to be counted."

Raymond attended Mary Lee Clark United Methodist Indian Church in Del City and was a member of Hilltop Indian Presbyterian Church in Wewoka. He collected arrowheads from riverbeds and enjoyed Indian art and Saturday flea markets. He had seven children, twenty-one grandchildren, and five great-grandchildren.

LARRY JONES

Larry J. Jones, 46, of Yukon; husband of Karen Jones; father of Michael, Kelly (K.J.), and Jayme; computer program specialist, Federal Highway Administration.

Larry Jones was born and raised in Pelham, Georgia; when he graduated from high school, he entered the air force. He was eighteen years old. He would spend the next twenty years of his life in the military, including service in Vietnam.

A computer specialist at the FHWA, he also taught computer science part-time at UCO. "He was a dedicated employee," said wife Karen. "He always gave 110 percent to his work. He would work all day."

Intelligent and passionate about computers and Star Trek, he was "a wonderful father," said Karen. Every night he and daughter Jayme played computer games. He coached his young son Kelly in soccer just as he had coached his older son Michael at football. "He and Kelly went to five of the World Cup games last year," said Karen.

She remembers her husband as a man people liked. "When they became friends with him, there wasn't anything for them he wouldn't do."

ALVIN JUSTES

Alvin J. Justes, 54, of Oklahoma City; brother of Violet Root of London, KY, and Billy R. Justice of Annville, KY; half-brother of Harvey Justice of East Bernstadt, KY; retired federal depository worker; customer, Federal Employees Credit Union.

Alvin Justes filled his life with books and newspapers: Most days he bought five newspapers or books; he followed both local and national news and read everything from medical tomes to history books. "He had just about any kind of hardback book," said Violet Root of her bachelor brother, on "any subject you wanted to read about ... I never saw so many books in my life except in a library."

His favorite subjects were Indians and trains. From the time he was just a tyke, he dreamed of the West and all its tribes and locomotives. When he was nineteen, Alvin packed his bags and moved to Denver (he had an uncle in Colorado); after two years he pushed on to Oklahoma City. "He believed in living," said his sister.

Though he dreamed of being a train engineer, he worked most often at factories (and later at the federal depository). He served stateside during the Vietnam War and was disabled for several years afterwards. His brother, Harvey, said the family didn't see much of Alvin (he hadn't been to the family farm in Kentucky in years due to health reasons), though several times a year they spoke on the phone and exchanged cards on holidays. His sister Violet said he often spoke about his church work. Alvin planned to finally return to his Kentucky home in the summer of 1995.

BLAKE KENNEDY

Blake R. Kennedy, 18 months; son of Steve and Laura Kennedy of Amber; grandson of Wesley and Sharan Kennedy of Amber and Loren and Betty Heavin of Verden; attended America's Kids.

Blake Kennedy had attended America's Kids since he was six weeks old (his mother, Laura, worked at Health and Human Services but received only cuts and bruises in the bombing). Blake loved green beans, Barney, and his battery-operated duck that quacked. "You couldn't have asked for a better kid," said his father Steve.

Blake's favorite words were "ball" (he was always playing with one) and "baa" (from listening to sheep on the family's small farm). At thirteen months, Blake started walking; a gregarious child, he said hi to anyone and always remembered to say thank you. He was the center of a close-knit family that included two sets of grandparents, three great-grandfathers, four great-grandmothers, two great-great grandmothers, four aunts, and two uncles—all of whom live within twenty miles of the Kennedy home.

CAROLE KHALIL

Carole Khalil, 50, of Oklahoma City; mother of Heather; sister of Jonnie Miller; daughter of Thelma O'Hern; export document clerk, U. S. Department of Agriculture.

Carole Khalil gave thirty years of service to the federal government, and her coworkers remember her as an indispensable and devoted employee with an eye for details. "She was a hard-working, intelligent person," said coworker Ada Maloney, who also recalled how supportive Carole was. "She was always telling me, 'Yeah, you can do it.' She really cared. I never remember hearing Carole complain; she would do anything for you."

At home, Carole read, sewed, and tended her rosebushes. She was a devoted mother and daughter. "Carole was the kind of person," said her sister, Jonnie Miller of Laverne, "who was always smiling and always found the good in everything."

VALERIE JO KOELSCH

Valerie Jo Koelsch, 33, of Oklahoma City; daughter of Harry and Rosemary Koelsch of Oklahoma City; sister of Gregory Koelsch of the Oklahoma City area, Terry Koelsch of Arlington, TX, and Michelle Brooks of Edmond; marketing director, Federal Employees Credit Union.

"The most striking thing about Valerie was that you felt her enthusiasm for her faith," said Anne Kirby of Saint Patrick's Catholic Church. "Her laugh and smile drew a lot of people in." A eucharistic minister at Saint Patrick's, Valerie helped launch its Young Adult Ministry, served on its parish council, and participated in its Young Adult Core Team.

Generous to strangers, she also made time for her parents, who lived nearby, as well as her three siblings and their children. When her four nieces wanted to see The Lion King, Valerie was the one to take them. "She was just a super gal," said mother Rosemary Koelsch.

An avid OSU fan, Valerie played on many coed softball teams. "Valerie was the biggest sports freak I knew. She knew anything and everything about football and basketball," said Kim Whaylen, a softball teammate and close friend (the young women met at Saint Gregory's in Shawnee and then also attended OSU in Stillwater, where Valerie graduated as a marketing major).

ANN KREYMBORG

Carolyn Ann Kreymborg, 57, of Oklahoma City; wife of Jim Kreymborg; mother of Michelle Reeder (who also died in the bombing) and Pat Kreymborg of Oklahoma City; mother-in-law of Pat Reeder of Bethany; automation clerk, HUD.

For the first time in fifteen years, both of Ann Kreymborg's children were back in Oklahoma City. "The family was finally together," said Ann's son, Pat.

Daughter Michelle, who also died in the bombing, had just returned from living overseas with her marine corps husband Pat Reeder, and Ann, an interior design graduate of OSU who had always dressed up her own house, was happily helping Michelle and Pat set up their first home.

Ann had a knack for nontraditional decorating: One year she turned tumbleweeds and white spray paint into a Christmas tree complete with white lights. A notorious contest lover, Ann once won a hundred pound pumpkin (she donated to her church).

Pat remembers a mother who juggled odd jobs, like delivering telephone books, so she could stay home with her children. "She was always there," he said. "You could count on her."

Through the years, Ann dabbled in bonds and mutual funds, took up boating and water skiing, and tended her garden. She loved the arts (especially jazz), and she was working on a second degree in computer science at night at UCO. Married thirty-five years to Jim ("They had a very beautiful marriage," said Pat), she was an active member of Saint Charles Borromeo Catholic Church in Oklahoma City.

TERESA LAUDERDALE

Teresa L. Taylor Lauderdale, 41, of Shawnee; widow of Ike Lauderdale; mother of Brian and Greg Beal; daughter of John and Gloria Taylor of Edmond; sister of Steve Taylor of Shawnee; secretary, Office of Housing, HUD.

Teresa Lauderdale "believed in service to others," said her father, John Taylor. She supported the Shawnee chapter of the Veterans of Foreign Wars, which she was introduced to by her late husband Ike, who died of a massive heart attack in October 1994. (Teresa and Ike were married only four months prior to his death.)

Sons Brian and Greg were the defining interest in Teresa's life. According to Renee Pendley, Lauderdale's best friend for two decades, "Everything she did was for those boys. She did without so they could have what they wanted or needed." Added Pendley admiringly, "I hope my kids turn out to be as well mannered."

Teresa's limited spare time was spent with her sons, making crafts with her best friend, and talking with her mother. According to her mother, Gloria Taylor, in the long days following the bombing while they waited for her body to be recovered, Teresa's oldest son quietly observed late one night: "My children will never know what a wonderful grandma they would have had."

Calling her friend "an inspiration," Pendley said Teresa emerged from a difficult personal situation years ago to become "one of the strongest people I have ever met." This Teresa, selfless but strong, is the one people will remember. "She gave so much," her headstone reads, "and expected so little."

KATHY LEINEN

Catherine M. Leinen, 47, of Oklahoma City; mother of Dawn DeArmon and William Leinen; daughter of Al and Kathleen Cagle; sister of Skip and Jimbo Cagle; grandmother of Frankie Leinen; collection officer, Federal Employees Credit Union.

Kathy Leinen was the family matriarch. "She took care of everything," said daughter Dawn DeArmon, and "she held the family together." "She was always there for everybody," agreed Kathy's mother, Kathleen Cagle.

When Dawn and her infant son, Frankie, were homeless, it was Kathy who took them in; the two lived with her for the next five years, and she became like a second mother to her grandson. When mother and son moved on, Kathy sent him cards with money inside and notes urging him to take his mother out for a Coke. "Frankie was the light of her eyes," said Cagle.

Kathy was close to her own mother, too. "My grandmother was my mother's best friend," said DeArmon. "They did everything together." Kathy loved the outdoors, crocheting blankets for her family, making crafts, hitting garage sales with her mother, and playing games. "We hung out and played dominoes," said Cagle. "She'd get just as excited playing dominoes as she would at a football game. "Her love of life sprang from a heart full of love. Said Cagle, "She was a very caring person."

CARRIE LENZ

Carrie A. Lenz, 26, of Choctaw; wife of Michael J. Lenz Jr.; mother of Michael J. Lenz III; daughter of Ken Adams and Doris Jones; step-daughter of Karen Adams and Bob Jones; sister of Chris Adams; sister-in-law of Julie Adams; granddaughter of Dorthy Musgrave and Doyle G. and the late Lola T. Adams; aunt of Kelsey Adams; stepsister of Travis and Trent Jones; Legal Technician II, Drug Enforcement Administration.

An animal lover and outdoorswoman, Carrie Lenz was uncommonly honest. "That was one of her most outstanding traits," said her mother, Doris Jones. "She had a way of saying what had to be said." And she believed in getting involved. A member of the Draper Park Christian Church, she was pursuing a paralegal degree at Rose State and anticipating the birth of her first child, a son she and husband Mike had named Michael James Lenz III. "That baby was the most important thing in her life. She couldn't have been happier," Doris said.

Mother and daughter were best friends who relished each other's company; Doris takes comfort in knowing that, according to coworkers, on the morning of April 19, Carrie was blissfully showing the office ultrasound pictures of her son taken the day before. "They told me that she was probably as happy then as she'd ever been in her life," confided Doris.

DON LEONARD

Donald R. Leonard, 50, of Edmond; husband of Diane Leonard; father of Brad, Jason, and Tim; son of the late Bratch and Esther Leonard of Edmond; U. S. Special Agent, Secret Service.

A lifetime member of the National Geographic Society, Don Leonard was amazed by the daily wonders of the world. "Sometimes at night," said his wife, Diane, "he would pull over if we were out away from the city lights and he thought the sky was unusually beautiful."

A bookworm, "He would read anything he could get his hands on," said Diane, his wife since 1974. He enjoyed fishing, golfing, sailing, and his three children. When he laughed, friends say, he "laughed all over."

Don had in recent years learned he had not only Germanic but Native American roots. He planned to retire at year's end to travel and explore his and his wife's German heritage.

A member of the National Native American Law Enforcement Association, Don was an active supporter of the Oklahoma Zoological Society, the National Cowboy Hall of Fame, Saint Jude's Childrens Hospital, and the Native American movement. A graduate of CSU (now UCO), he served both the U.S. Army with the military police and later the Oklahoma City Police Department. As an agent with the Secret Service, he protected seven presidential administrations, including Vice President Al Gore on his trip to Russia in December 1994.

Larry Kingry remembers his fellow agent as efficient and meticulous. "He would pick up a piece of paper and handle it once," said Kingry. It was no different at home, said Diane: "He always said, 'Everything has a place, and it should be in it.'"

LaKESHA LEVY

LaKesha R. Levy, 20, of Midwest City; wife of Corey Levy, mother of Corey II, daughter of Constance Favorite and Michael Richardson, all of New Orleans; Airman First Class, U. S. Air Force, Tinker Air Force Base; died while obtaining a Social Security card.

As a child, LaKesha Levy was set on becoming a doctor. Her mother encouraged her dream, buying the five year old a toy doctor's bag, complete with stethoscope and candy pills. "She religiously played with it," said Constance Favorite. Strong-willed, LaKesha (who by twenty had a husband and child) mapped out a plan to get what she wanted: joining the service so she could someday finance college and nursing school, working in the medical field in the interim, and, most recently, training at the Tinker Air Force Base hospital to be a lab technician.

Other than her career, she was light-hearted. "I'd always say, 'Girl, you are a clown,'" Favorite said. "She could make a joke about anything." LaKesha's unerring ear for voices—the born mimic could reproduce her mother's Cajun accent to a tee—was legendary in the family, said Karen Johnson, LaKesha's aunt.

DOMINIQUE LONDON

Dominique R. London, 2 years and 11 months, of Oklahoma City; son of Tonya London; grandson of Earnestine Looney; brother of Deandre Johnson, Derrick London, and Tara London, all of Oklahoma City; attended America's Kids.

On sunny days, Dominique London was outdoors—playing in the dirt, riding his Big Wheel; only on rainy days did he move inside, and then to watch his Power Rangers video. "He loved his Power Rangers," said Earnestine Looney, his grandmother and legal guardian. "He would be kicking and carrying on for days." When he turned three May 28, Dominique was to begin karate lessons, like his older brother Derrick, and move to a new daycare center at the elementary school where Derrick studies.

A pizza lover with a sweet tooth and an appreciation for McDonald's Happy Meals, Dominique was a little short fellow who stayed active most of the time, rambled on in lengthy sentences, and was into everything. "He liked to go to McDonald's," said his grandmother. "He'd go out there on that playground and you'd just have to lift him up bodily to get him out of there."

"He loved anything he wasn't supposed to mess with," she added. Dubbed "Dominoes" by his daycare buddies, he was a common sight at the side of his grandmother on Sundays at Mount Lebanon Baptist Church.

RHETA LONG

Rheta Long, 60, of Oklahoma City; mother of Valerie Tramel of Oklahoma City and John Long of San Antonio, TX; grandmother of Kenneth and Christopher Tramel, Nicholas Long of Charleston, SC, and John Long, who died in December 1994 of cancer; program clerk, Veterinary Services Division, U.S. Department of Agriculture.

At age ten, Rheta Long was hit by a drunk driver while pushing a stroller carrying her baby brother. Her brother was killed, and doctors believed it was unlikely Rheta would survive, either. But survive she did, only to be told years later that her childhood injuries precluded her from having children. She died April 19, 1995, the mother of two.

Repeatedly Rheta Long beat the odds.

The car accident left her with arthritis in her later years. Glaucoma-related complications kept her from driving, so her daughter Valerie took her most places.

Despite their closeness, Valerie knew nothing of her mother's business accomplishments—including her being named Woman of the Year by the American Business Women's Association—until she went through her mother's personal effects. Valerie knew the personal side: the grandmother who visited the Kirkpatrick Planetarium and played cards with grandsons Kenneth and Christopher, the woman who frequented the Jewel Box Theatre and Tulsa Opera and listened to books on tape.

But Rheta was also a woman of conviction who was involved with the Equal Employment Opportunity Commission's disabilities division and who often fought injustices. She attended the First Christian Church in Oklahoma City.

MICHAEL LOUDENSLAGER

Michael L. Loudenslager, 48, of Harrah; husband of Bettie Loudenslager; father of Diana and Kyle; planner-estimator, General Services Administration; rescued a coworker before he died.

The funeral procession for Michael Loudenslager included the Oklahoma City and Oklahoma County mounted patrol on horseback, acccompanied by Michael's riderless black thoroughbred.

A member of the Oklahoma Equestrian Trail Riders Association, the Oklahoma Quarter Horse Association, and the U.S. Marshal Posse, Loudenslager was a reserve deputy with the Oklahoma County sheriff's office. He was also a Mason and a Shriner. "His characteristics were like Will Rogers'," said wife Bettie. "He never met a stranger. He was always happy and outgoing, and if you ever needed help, he was always there."

The Loudenslagers had been married for twenty-seven years. They still rode to work most days together and spent their off-hours on their twenty-acre spread, where each summer they grew a garden. The couple's children, Kyle and Diana, attend college, so much of Loudenslager's time was spent with his four horses, including the black thoroughbred Bubba. Mike graduated from OSU with a degree in horticulture. After working for the University of Arkansas Extension Office, he began working in construction. The knowledge gained as a contractor helped him win the job as planner-estimator with the GSA in 1986.

Before he died April 19, 1995, Michael managed to rescue a fellow coworker.

BOBBY & DONNA LUSTER

Robert L. Jr., 45, and Aurelia Donna, 43, Luster, of Guthrie; parents of Robert Luster III, Tina, Jackie, Liz, Roy, and Carol; Bobby, a former maintenance man for Autoquip, was on disability since a 1992 heart attack; Donna was a housewife; died visiting the Social Security office.

Funds were lean enough at the Luster home to keep the family from having a telephone, but never so tight that Bobby's six children didn't on occasion get something special for Christmas or during the year. "He had a big heart," said Barbara Powers, Bob's sister. "He saved up for a long time to buy them a Nintendo."

In 1992, however, times for the Lusters went from bad to worse. Bobby suffered a heart attack, ending his lengthy career as a maintenance man. His circumstances sometimes got him down, but he remained a man who would give you his last nickel, Barbara said. Though their brood kept both the Lusters jumping (particularly Donna), Bobby managed to find time for the old western novels he so enjoyed. Said Barbara, "Bobby was a bookworm."

MICKEY MARONEY

Mickey B. Maroney, 50, of Oklahoma City; husband of Robbie Maroney; father of Alice Denison and Mickey Maroney and stepfather of Darin Fisher, all of Oklahoma City; U.S. Special Agent, Secret Service.

The youngest of eleven children, Mickey Maroney grew up in Wichita Falls, Texas, where he played defensive end for the state championship high school football team. Barry Switzer, then assistant coach at the University of Arkansas, recruited him for the Razorbacks, and Mickey played during the team's 1964 national championship season.

He went on to be a special agent who, in the course of his twenty-four-year career, protected President Lyndon Johnson and Lady Bird. His network of sources was legendary—what might take another agent two or three days, Mickey often handled with a thirty-minute phone call. Said best friend and partner Don Newsom, "There's virtually no one you could talk to in law enforcement who didn't know Mickey. He was a hell of an asset."

He was active in Special Olympics, Promise Keepers, and Sugar Smith's Make a Wish Program. "He was a big, gentle giant," said Loyd Phillips of his six foot, five inch former UA teammate. His wife Robbie remembers her husband as a family man first and foremost but also something of a jester. He was always disguising his voice on the phone, said Robbie (he once phoned his daughter and pretended to be a cement company delivering four loads of cement to her house).

Mickey was a member at Council Road Baptist Church in Bethany, where he taught Sunday school to college kids.

JAMES MARTIN

James K. Martin, 34, of Oklahoma City; son of Lorraine and Clair Martin; twin brother of Vicki Martin; brother of Lori Martin; civil engineer, Federal Highway Administration, DOT.

James was a perfectionist—said his mother, Lorraine Martin—who actually prolonged his college graduation so he could make an 'A' in every class. (The classes he fell short in, he retook the next semester.) He graduated high school from Walnut, California, and attended Mount San Antonio College before joining the marines.

When he left the service in 1985, he went to California State Polytechnic, where he received his degree in civil engineering in 1990. He hired on with the Federal Highway Administration, training in Michigan, Washington, D.C., Maryland, and San Francisco. He lived in Little Rock and Saint Paul, Minnesota, before transferring to Oklahoma City in February 1995.

James played golf and liked landscaping. "You should see our backyard," said his mother. "He'd plant all of my flowers for me."

James and his twin sister Vicki were also close (both were Star Trek fans who liked science fiction); his other love was big band music (especially Glen Miller), which he got from his parents.

GILBERTO MARTINEZ

Reverend Gilberto X. Martinez, 35, of Oklahoma City; husband of Martha Martinez; father of Michelle, Brian, Bonnie, Jillian, and Gilbert (ten days old at the time of the bombing); pastor, El Tabernacle De Fe Church in Oklahoma City; died at the Social Security office.

A pastor and father of five, the Reverend Gilberto Martinez drove his children to John Adams Elementary School every day, made sure they did their homework, and never missed a single parent-teacher conference. And John Adams principal Debbie Lobdell believes Martinez deserves credit for the school's number of Hispanic students surging from twenty (five years ago) to one hundred twenty-five.

The former teacher believed in second chances, and he befriended gang members, troubled teens, and inmates. "When they felt like talking, he was there," said Sandra Valdez, Martinez's niece. "They knew they had a friend and someone they could confide in."

Many of the young people attended his funeral.

The Martinez home was open to those who needed a place to stay. "You didn't really need to ask him for help," said Valdez. "He would just do it."

Committed to his family, his church (he belonged to the Oklahoma District Assemblies of God), and his community, Gilberto died in the process of helping one of his Spanish-speaking church members, Emilio Rangel Tapia, fill out forms at the Social Security office.

TRESIA MATHES-WORTON

Tresia J. Mathes-Worton, 28, of Oklahoma City; daughter of Vickie and J. D. Mathes; teller, Federal Employees Credit Union.

Tresia Mathes-Worton was within three days of starting a new life. The one-time Greenwood High School honor student from Midland, Texas, was moving back to Midland and planned to marry her boyfriend of three years, Travis Jobe, in July. (Her ten-year high school reunion was also set for summer.)

Born and raised in Midland, Tresia attend Midland College and earned her beautician's license from Aladdin Beauty College. She worked in business management at J. Harris clothing store and as a tanning salon manager before coming to Oklahoma in 1993. "She wanted a change," recalled her mother, Vickie Mathes; she chose Oklahoma City because her cousin lived here.

A high school cheerleader and basketball and football trainer, "Tresia was friends with everybody," said her mother. "Our house was the meeting place, and we always enjoyed the kids."

She was preceded in death by her brother in 1970.

JIM McCARTHY

James A. McCarthy, 53, of Edmond; husband of Joyce McCarthy; father of Timothy McCarthy of Durham, NC, and Todd and Kristi McCarthy of Edmond; director, Office of Housing, HUD.

The McCarthys had been in their new home in Edmond for three weeks before Jim died in the Oklahoma City bombing. (Jim took the Oklahoma City promotion in December of 1994.) Moving was second nature for the family. Joyce and Jim met at Fort Benning, Georgia (where Jim was a soldier and Joyce grew up); they married in 1961. Jim's first job was with the FDIC in Nebraska; he was subsequently transferred to Kansas City and then to Iowa; in 1991 he joined HUD and returned to Kansas City.

All the moving produced a tight-knit family. "The family attachment was so great," said Joyce. "We depended on each other." All agreed, one of the best perks of Jim's new job—after years of business trips—was the time he was able to spend at home with his wife and children.

Most days Jim walked five miles (he listened to books on tape as he strolled). He and his children fished, traveled, looked at cars, played golf, walked, and pursued other outdoor interests. Jim also attended Saint John the Baptist Church in Edmond. "He was not the kind of person who it took a lot to make happy," his wife observed. "He liked the simple things."

KENNETH McCULLOUGH

Kenneth McCullough, 36, of Edmond; husband of Sharon McCullough; father of Jessica and Patrick; special agent, Drug Enforcement Administration.

Kenneth McCullough dedicated himself to serving his nation from the day he entered college as a member of Texas A&M University's prestigious and renowned Corps of Cadets. He gave six years of service to the U.S. Army, rising to the rank of captain. He worked for the U.S. Department of Defense Investigative Service and later joined the Oklahoma City office of the Drug Enforcement Administration.

Kenneth, along with his wife, Sharon, was active in the First Baptist Church of Edmond. And his wife, also a Texas A&M graduate, said one word best describes her husband: honorable. "He was always telling our son, 'If you have no honor, you have nothing,'" she said. "Honor is the only thing that cannot be taken away from you."

BETSY McGONNELL

Betsy J. (Beebe) McGonnell, 47, of Norman; mother of Bill McGonnell of Dallas and Jamie Sly of Wichita, KS; daughter of Mary Beebe-Butts and stepdaughter of J. Crawford Butts of Oklahoma City; daughter of the late Clyde W. Beebe of Oklahoma City; niece of Carl A. and Jamie Nelson of Wichita; Charles and Wanda Woll of Belle Plaine, KS; Wayne R. Beebe of Tulsa; and Mary K. Beebe of Tulsa; clerk, Office of Housing, HUD.

Betsy McGonnell sang in the choir at Saint Michael's Episcopal Church and volunteered in its pastoral care program, tending to people hospitalized or recently bereaved.

Her singing was especially dear to her, said daughter Jamie Sly. As a student at Northwest Classen, Betsy sang in an honor choir called the Cry-Slur. More recently, she sang both with a Norman group and, along with several HUD employees, in a group called the Looney Tunes (best known for its rousing office renditions of "Happy Birthday").

Betsy spent free time with her daughter and puttering around her Norman home (she lived in Norman for more than twenty-five years). Her penchant, says her mother Mary Butts, was all things homey: home decorating magazines, The Frugal Gourmet, This Old House, Popular Mechanics, her bed of impatiens, her white poodle Maggie, and her children's two dogs. She did needlework, sewed, and knitted. She loved reading heavy, historical books, a leftover maybe from her days as an undergraduate history major at OU.

LINDA McKINNEY

Linda G. McKinney, 47, of Oklahoma City; wife of Dan McKinney; mother of Jason Smith of Oklahoma City; stepmother of Amy Stiers of Tuttle; daughter of June Griffin and the late Burl Griffin of Fittstown; sister of Eldon Griffin of Henryetta, Bobby and Randy Griffin of Fittstown, Rita Webb of Cushing, and Sherry Richardson of Latta; office manager, Secret Service.

Three years ago, Linda and Dan McKinney tied the knot western-style to the strains of "Mama He's Crazy" by the Judds and "Forever Is as Far as I'll Go" by Alabama. "She was as close to an angel as you could find on earth," said Dan of his wife.

Though she couldn't swim and was terrified of the water, Linda fished and boated with her outdoorsman husband. Said best friend Valerie Rowden, it was typical Linda: "She went fishing because he went fishing"—just as she was there to listen when Valerie needed to talk in the wee morning hours.

Friends for thirteen years, Linda and Valerie shopped together, exercised together, and dieted together (margaritas were their favorite fruit substitute). "We'd always kid each other that we had to have our fruits," said Valerie.

Linda baked for friends, family, and coworkers every Christmas, and the building's ninth floor Thanksgiving party wasn't complete without her chicken and dumplings and chocolate surprise dessert. She cooked tasty fried green tomatoes, sold Mary Kay, attended Southern Hills Baptist Church, made rag dolls, and planned to learn to quilt like her mother and grandmother.

CARTNEY McRAVEN

Cartney J. (Koch) McRaven, 19, of Midwest City; wife of Shane McRaven; daughter of Jean Morrison of Spearfish, SD, and David Koch of Rapid City, SD; Airman First Class, Tinker Air Force Base; married four days, went to Social Security office to report a name change.

They met at Tinker Air Force Base in January 1994. In the fall, he was deployed to Italy, and she, two months later, to Haiti. After e-mail, letters, and phone calls, he proposed on Valentine's Day. Two weeks before the bombing, they were reunited. They wed April 15, 1995. The marriage assured that Airman First Class Cartney McRaven and Senior Airman Shane McRaven, members of a high deployment air force unit, would be based out of the same place. The couple planned a formal wedding in December.

Their time together was spent Rollerblading, preparing gourmet meals, and serving breakfast Sunday mornings to the homeless at the Salvation Army's soup kitchen in downtown Oklahoma City. They planned to start a family in five years, if all went well. "They would thumb through the cookbooks, and then they would make these exotic meals with a seven-layered torte," recalled Cartney's mother, Jean. "Cooking became a stress reliever for them while they awaited word on whether or not they would be deployed."

Cartney dreamed of working with children and planned to pursue a degree in child psychology. She, like her husband, was a member of the Third Combat Communications Group, Thirty-second Combat Communications Squadron; she had also been named the squadron's Airman of the Year.

CLAUDE MEDEARIS

Claude Medearis, 41, of Norman; husband of Sharon Medearis of Norman; father of Catherine Alaniz and Michael Medearis; son of Olive Mullinax; twin brother of Claudette Lantz and brother of Ervin Medearis; grandfather of Andee, Taylor, and Alyssa Alaniz and Zoe Medearis; senior special agent, U.S. Customs.

Sharon Medearis remembers her husband Claude as a practical joker who once placed a tiny raccoon he was babysitting in their bed while she slept. "It scared the raccoon and didn't do me too much good, either," she said, laughing. Claude Medearis loved bad jokes and golf (though his game wasn't much better than his jokes), said Justin Jones, a former coworker and Claude's best friend. "Claude loved life; he had a passion for it. He loved his family," wrote Justin in a eulogy after his friend's death. "When Claude was around you, you just naturally felt better."

A Harley-Davidson aficionado, former Mexican customs agent, and karate black belt, Medearis' tender nature and loyalty to old friends was admired by coworkers, friends, and family. "Claude was a friend to everyone," Jones said. "He was always there if you needed him ... Claude accepted people and never judged them. In my many years of having Claude as a best friend, I never saw him angry."

Added Justin, "Many people have told me that when they would least expect it, they would look up and there Claude would be, with that patented smile of his ... Claude never was a great talker, but he smiled more than any person I have ever known."

CLAUDETTE MEEK

Claudette Meek, 43, of Oklahoma City; wife of Mike Meek; mother of Michelle and Robert; daughter of Ralph and Claudell Duke; vice president, Financial Services, Federa[l] Employees Credit Union.

Every Wednesday morning, Claudette Meek held a pep rally at work. "She would take food and have all the bells and whistles," said her daughter, Michelle. "The credit union wasn't just her job; she loved it there. She never gave less than 145 percent."

Employed at the Federal Employees Credit Union for thir[teen] years, Claudette worked her way up from teller to loan officer to vice president. "She was everyone's cheerleader," said Michelle, "and she instilled that not only in her workers bu[t] also in her family. She made us feel like we could climb mountains, even if she had to give us a little push."

She served on various committees at Southgate Baptist Church in Moore and was president of the Moore Service League (the first president ever elected to two terms). "She didn't just sign up to be a helper," said her daughter, "she signed up to be the leader of the group. Mom was busy, very active, and morally strong. She had a belief system based on right and wrong. There were n[o] a lot of gray areas. She believe[d] her children should be able to go to school and not go in deb[t]. "She was wonderful."

JERRY PARKER

Jerry L. Parker, 45, of Norman; husband of Sharon Parker; father of Sharissa, Michael, and Michelle; area engineer, Federal Highway Administration.

Born and raised in Oklahoma City, Jerry Parker graduated from Crooked Oak High School in 1967. He received his degree in civil engineering from the OU in 1973 and went to work for the FHWA a year later. His FHWA work took him to Little Rock, Los Angeles, Bismarck, Austin, and Topeka. He and his wife, Sharon, returned to Oklahoma in 1985.

A member of the Pleasant Hill Freewill Baptist Church in Norman, he served on the church's board of trustees, taught Sunday school, and participated in its men's group. He worked with computers at home and at the office, helped build and remodel his home (he and son Michael's last project was a deck), spent many a weekend antiquing (the Parkers collected stereographs, stereoscopes, and cylinder players), and enjoyed woodworking (he made daughter Michelle a rocking horse and daughter Sharissa a dinette set). "He was a quiet person with a tender heart, and he loved people," said Sharon, who he married in 1968. "Everything he did, he became engrossed in. He jumped all the way in. That's why he enjoyed his work, because he liked to jump in."

JILL RANDOLPH

Jill D. Randolph, 27, of Oklahoma City; daughter of Dale and Eva Randolph; sister of Lori Randolph Neace; certified public accountant, Federal Employees Credit Union.

Tulsa native Jill Randolph moved to Oklahoma City in 1984 with her family. A graduate of Moore High School, class of 1986, she graduated cum laude from Southern Nazarene University in 1991 with a degree in accounting. She cared deeply for her family and friends, was the owner of a fifteen-pound cat named Rascal, and centered her life around her church family.

She attended three churches in Oklahoma City: Shartel Church of God, Belle Isle Community Church, and Northwest Baptist Church, where she was active in the Single Twenties Group. "Her Bible study fellowships were almost 100 percent of her recreational activities," said her father, Dale Randolph, "whether it was playing volleyball or going to float the Illinois River."

She was said to find the humor in any situation. And, sensitive to others' feelings, she went out of her way to let people know she cared.

MICHELLE REEDER

Michelle A. Reeder, 33, of Bethany; wife of Pat Reeder; daughter of Jim and Ann Kreymborg of Oklahoma City (Ann also died in the bombing); sister of Pat Kreymborg of Oklahoma City; administrative assistant, Federal Highway Administration, DOT.

In almost fifteen years of marriage, Michelle Reeder and her husband, Pat, had worked their way around the world, living in the Philippines for three years and visiting exotic sites along the way (Singapore was their favorite).

The two met at a Putnam City football game in high school (both attended Putnam City); they married after graduation and decided their best chance to see the world was for Pat to join the marines.

See the world they did, but they also began to miss Oklahoma. In July 1994, the two returned in a two-car convoy to Oklahoma City (from Maryland, where Pat was last based), armed with walkie-talkies to chat along the way. "We were just so happy to come home," said Pat. "When we crossed the state line from Arkansas, we were both singing to each other on the walkie-talkies."

Like her mother, Ann, Michelle belonged to Saint Charles Borromeo Catholic Church in Oklahoma City, had a career in civil service, and gardened. "Whenever we had a balcony, it wasn't used for barbecues or looking at a sunset," said Pat. "It was a botanical garden."

Like Michelle's parents, they had "that kind of genuine love that comes along once a lifetime," said her brother. Agreed Pat Reeder, "Michelle wasn't just my wife, she was my best friend. She was my life."

TERRY REES

Terry S. Rees, 41, of Midwest City; wife of Bob Chumard; daughter of Doris Delman, stepdaughter of Ernest Delman, sister of Cathy McCaskell and Leslie Downey, all of Oklahoma City; sister of Steven Smith of Fair Oaks, CA; director, Program Operations Division, Office of Public Housing, HUD.

Teddy bears were Terry Rees' passion. She collected them (her personal collection numbered several hundred), attended teddy bear and craft shows, and, in many ways, resembled one herself. At her memorial service, Terry's coworkers wrote, "You can tell a great deal about a person by what they are interested in or like to do." And like her teddy bears, Terry was a source of comfort and consolation for those who needed her. "Being with Terry," her coworkers added, "brought to mind everything that results in a 'warm and fuzzy' feeling about the world."

The outpouring of support from around the world has convinced Terry's husband, Bob Chumard, and those who loved her that many more like her are among us, a realization that has brought her family comfort. Said Bob, "As a wife, friend, and confidante, Terry was truly incredible. Her sense of humor, her love of books, her love of bears, her love of shopping, her fairness, her compassion, her love of life. These qualities describe the real Terry Rees. We are blessed to have known this wonderful person, and we must celebrate her life."

MARY RENTIE

Mary L. Rentie, 39, of Bethany; wife of Ben Rentie; mother of Melissa and Melody; sister of Greg Leasure; granddaughter of "Mee Mee" Sims; public housing revitalization specialist, Office of Public Housing, HUD.

Mary Rentie worked at HUD during the day and at home at night, caring for—among others—her grandmother, "Mee Mee" Sims, and her two daughters.

Mary was a member of the First Unitarian Church, where she worked with children in the Religious Education Church School. Often she could be found carting her two daughters and their peers to church rallies and other religious activities. Fond of quilting and a fan of Red Earth (she was part Native American), she seldom slowed down and worked hard to keep everyone happy (a typical gesture was serving two kinds of potato salad at dinner to please conflicting tastes). She gardened (she especially liked pink and white azaleas), read (she had a large library), baked a great lemon cake, and took in stray cats.

At her memorial service, many friends thanked her for being a surrogate mother to their children. Sister-in-law Angela Rentie recalls Mary once actually took in a teen-aged acquaintance until a tough situation at home smoothed over. "She was just the glue that kept everything together," said Angela.

TONY REYES

Antonio C. Reyes, 55, of Edmond; husband of Dora Reyes; father of Delia Northup of Coffeyville, KS, and Michael Reyes of Bethany; grandfather of David and Leah Northup of Coffeyville, KS; equal opportunity specialist, Fair Housing and Equal Opportunity Division, HUD.

After twenty years in the navy, Tony Reyes joined the Small Business Administration in 1984 before eventually coming to HUD, where he won the 1993 Federal Employee of the Year award.

Fond of his two grandchildren, Tony made certain David and Leah spent at least one weekend a month with him and Dora, his wife of thirty-five years. Generous, outgoing, and friendly, said his wife, Tony was also an active volunteer. He belonged to the Edmond chapter of AMBUCS, the Tinker Air Force Base Hispanic Heritage Group Partners in Education program (in which he helped tutor city children), the Edmond Arts and Humanities Council (he was especially involved with the jazz and Celebration of Children festivals), and the Oklahoma Hispanic Professional Association. He served on the board of directors of the Federal Employees Credit Union and Eagle Ridge Institute, a non-profit organization that assists families and victims of substance abuse.

Four years ago, Tony also became active in the Latino Community Development Agency, where he was helping officials convert the former Riverside School into a neighborhood community center.

KATHY RIDLEY

Kathryn E. Ridley, 24, of Oklahoma City; mother of Marty and Caitlynd; daughter of Martha Ridley of Oklahoma City and Willis Ridley Jr. of Chicago; sister of James Ridley of Oklahoma City and Chris Gaddis of Chicago; student, Guthrie Job Corps (corp recruiting office was across the street from the Murrah building).

Kathy Ridley was training to become a journeyman welder but dreamed of using her vocation to become an outdoor metal sculptor. She always preferred art and poetry to school. "Her idea of high school was in the front door and out the back door and to the bowling alley," said her mother, Martha.

Yet Kathy excelled in vocal music and appreciated English and her computer classes. She blossomed in the strict Guthrie Job Corps program, rising early, attending class and work, leaving campus only rarely (and then with a pass), and earning a certificate in tack welding.

Her next step was to become a journeyman welder, but she put her studies on hold to have her second child.

Kathy is remembered by her instructor, Ernie Mack, as polite, sensitive, and kind. "She was an outstanding student," said Daniel Bates, Kathy's welding instructor. And a great friend to fellow students: "If I had a problem, I could go to her," said Debra Jones, a program colleague.

Kathy returned from maternity leave April 19, 1995; she was going to catch a ride with a recruiting officer to Guthrie. She was in the parking lot across the street from the Murrah building at Ground Zero when the bomb exploded.

TRUDY RIGNEY

Trudy J. Rigney, 31, of Midwest City; mother of Jonmichael; daughter of Lee and Haroldene Rigney of Broken Arrow; sister of Rebecca Smith and Rick Rigney; geographic information systems intern, Oklahoma Water Resources Board (located across the street from the Murrah building).

Family, friends, and coworkers remember Trudy Rigney as independent and single minded, a young woman who in recent years radiated a confidence that said, "I believe in myself." A single mother, she had seen at a local homeless shelter how tough life could be for the unskilled and uneducated, and she dedicated herself to providing something better for her own son.

With the help of Pell grants and scholarships, she entered Tulsa Junior College, where she became president of the student body for its southeast campus and maintained close to a four-point grade average. She left TJC in Tulsa to attend the University of Oklahoma in Norman, where she initially aspired to an environmental law degree (her geography studies and internship at the Oklahoma Water Resources Board had recently changed her mind, said her mother, Haroldene). She was also a youth pastor at Word of Faith Church in Norman. "Anything that had authority to it, she'd take charge of it," said her father, Lee Rigney. "She kept busy, almost too busy," added her mother in a protective voice.

Now Lee Rigney sees his daughter in his grandson. "He's a dreamer like she was," he said. "He could master just about anything."

CLAUDINE RITTER

Claudine Ritter, 48, of Oklahoma City; mother of Brian Hansen and Valerie McCoy; daughter of Lorene Ritter and the late Clyde Ritter; sister of Denita, Lane, Jeanette, and Joe; collection officer, Federal Employees Credit Union.

Claudine Ritter was tall and commanding, with large eyes that could look straight through you. "At heart she was the most sentimental person, but to watch her, you'd never know it," said her friend Gloria Holder.

After high school in Atwood, she joined the army. She was a decorated soldier, serving at the Pentagon in the Gulf War. "I don't know of a child that was ever more proud of a parent," said Brian Hansen, Claudine's son. She was in her thirtieth year of army service at the time of her death. "I told her that I swore her grass stood at attention," said Gloria.

She and son Brian were true pals. She was a strong supporter when he decided to enter the law enforcement field. In January 1995 she watched him assume the position of a communications operator for the Moore Police Department; he was eighteen.

Claudine held several degrees from different Oklahoma universities but was most proud of her teaching certificate. A single mother, she worked in banking because it allowed her to better financially support her family. "At the most trying times she could find a reason to laugh, and she could laugh at herself," said Gloria. "She knew the art of friendship and would do things that were so unselfish. She had a zest, a vigor, a zeal for life."

CHRISTY ROSAS

Christy N. Rosas, 22, of Moore; wife of Chris Rosas; mother of Shane; daughter of Bob and Debbie Pippin; sister of Michelle Floyd; receptionist, Federal Employees Credit Union.

Christy had previously been at Southwestern Bank & Trust in Oklahoma City, working her way from teller to personal banker in her five years there. On April 19, 1995, she had been at the Federal Employees Credit Union only six days.

Friends say she was extremely mature for her age and had a way of cheering people up. "You'd think, 'You know, she's right, it's not quite that bad,'" said her mother, Debbie Pippin. "That's what we've missed about her the most."

Christy spent a lot of time with her son Shane, reading and playing. Artistic, she decorated her home and designed sweatshirts. A few weeks before Easter, she planted petunias and some cannas in front of her house so it would look nice when her grandparents came to visit from Spring, Texas. "She was really proud of her little garden," said Pippin.

SONJA SANDERS

Sonja L. Sanders, 27, of Moore; wife of Mike Sanders; mother of Brooklynn and Savanna; daughter of Sheila and Ron Stroud; sister of Kristi Sanders; chief teller of operations, Federal Employees Credit Union.

Sonja Sanders raised her two daughters, tended to family needs, worked full-time, and volunteered at her church. "She was really close to her girls," said her mother, Sheila Stroud. "Sonja and Mike tried to juggle everything."

Saturdays usually began with Sonja, sister Kristi, Sheila, and daughters Brooklynn and Savanna running errands, followed by a cookout at the Strouds with their husbands. "We were blessed with a good relationship," said Sheila. "We talked two or three times a day."

Sonja was a softball player who played through high school and hoped to someday root her own children on from the bleachers as her family had. A member of Southgate Baptist Church in Moore, she volunteered with the Women's Missionary Auxiliary and attended Oklahoma City Community College, where she was working on an associate's degree in banking and business.

Light-hearted and motivated, she never backed off from a challenge. "Her assets," said Sheila, "were her personality and a big ol' smile on her face."

LANNY SCROGGINS

Lanny L. Scroggins, 46, of Yukon; husband of Cheryl Scroggins; father of Brad and Scott; staff accountant, Office of Southern Plains Native American Programs, HUD.

Lanny Scroggins served his country as both a soldier and a civil servant: receiving a Bronze Star and an Army Commendation Medal of Heroism for his 1969 to 1971 tour of duty and then working some twenty-three years for the federal government.

A Holdenville native, Lanny married Cheryl in 1978, after returning to Oklahoma. (Both Cheryl and Lanny worked for the Department of Energy at the time.) After their two sons were born, Lanny's spare time became their time. Lanny attended too many baseball, basketball, and football games to count, said Cheryl. His only hobby away from his family was fishing.

A quiet homebody who relished organized summer family vacations, Lanny's plan for the family's 1995 summer trip was to drive to the Grand Canyon, then head west to Los Angeles and Disneyland.

Lanny was someone, Cheryl said, who could always make room for one more; through the years he invited half a dozen or more nieces, nephews, and friends to live with the Scroggins family for some length of time. "He was a good partner," said Cheryl, and "a real dad."

KATHY SEIDL

Kathy L. Seidl, 39, of Bethel; wife of Glenn Seidl; mother of Clint and stepmother of Marcus; daughter of Dallas and Sharon Davis of Oklahoma City; sister of Clifford Davis of Oklahoma City, Carol Reiswig of Tuttle, and Wanda Fincher of Midwest City; investigative assistant, U.S. Secret Service.

Kathy Seidl was a dedicated employee, but family members agree, her life's aspiration was to be a wife and mother. "She wanted to get married and have four children," said her mother, Sharon Davis. Asked once by a neighbor what her hobbies were, Kathy (by then a married mother of one) answered: "being a mother and wife."

She loved the outdoors and tending her roses and azaleas. Most weekends the Seidls camped, fished, or shopped for antiques; recently Kathy had been helping her husband, Glenn, clear five acres of land near Bethel, where they planned to build their dream house.

A born hostess, Kathy never let a guest leave her home hungry, and when at someone else's home, she always lingered behind to help clean up. She collected plates and porcelain cats and had a curio cabinet filled with memorabilia—from a Lyndon Johnson ink pen to photos of her with various presidents. (Each Christmas, she ordered ornaments for Clint's teachers from the U.S. Secret Service store in Washington, D.C.) She drove a metallic lavender Honda (she loved purple), and according to Kim Rossacci, her best friend since seventh grade who now lives in Florida, "She's an angel for sure. She earned her wings here a long time ago."

LEE SELLS

Leora Lee Sells, 57, of Oklahoma City; wife of Roy Sells; sister of Dess Rousselle and Roger Lindner, both of Seward, NE, and Raymond Lindner of Grass Valley, CA; daughter of Dorthea Lindner, also of Seward; secretary, Legal Division, HUD.

When Lee Sells met her husband, Roy, in Lincoln, Nebraska, she was a die-hard Cornhusker fan who worked for the University of Nebraska's library system. And Roy said he graciously cheered her team—except when it played his beloved Sooners. When the couple moved to Oklahoma City in 1962, Lee returned the favor—save for when OU played her beloved Cornhuskers.

So it remained for six or seven seasons. Then one day in the middle of a game in which OU was trouncing Nebraska, Lee turned to Roy, announced she didn't recognize any of the Nebraska players anymore, and converted to a Sooner on the spot. Her transformation was complete: She rarely missed an OU home game (football or otherwise); she was even known to slip headphones into the choir to follow OU teams.

Lee also treasured her family and Our Savior Lutheran Church in Bethany—where she served as a Sunday school teacher, a youth counselor (for ten years), on the finance committee, and where for thirty-two years, she and her husband sang in the choir. Indeed, said Roy, family and friends always commented on how special their marriage was: "We did everything together. In thirty-seven years of marriage, we never once said a cross word to one another. We just had so much in common."

KARAN SHEPHERD

Karan D. Shepherd, 27, of Moore; wife of Jay Shepherd; mother of Brittany and Gabby; daughter of Shirley Howell; loan officer, Federal Employees Credit Union.

They called themselves the three musketeers: Karan, her oldest daughter Brittany, and her mother Shirley Howell. Indeed, the first five years of Brittany's life, the three lived together in Shirley's house; Karan was sixteen then, and the odds seemed stacked against the young single mother.

But Karan had goals. She wanted a career in banking and was determined to be a good mother. "She was really into her girls," said Shirley.

Four years ago, Karan's second daughter, Gabby, joined the tight circle of women. Karan enrolled her daughters in ballet, accompanied them to the movies and the zoo, and, with her husband, Jay, vacationed with them at her in-laws' cabin at Lake Texoma. Along the way, she reveled in the everyday moments of being a mother: The night before the bombing, Gabby was batting in a T-ball game, and Shirley recalls Karan turning to her with a smile as Gabby hit the ball and ran to first; when the little girl turned to head for second base, "Tears were running down Karan's face," said Shirley.

Karan attended Moore High School and Draughn School of Business. At the Federal Employees Credit Union, she was the youngest loan officer ever to be appointed. "I was proud to be her mother," said Shirley.

CHASE & COLTON SMITH

Chase Dalton, 3 years 10 months, and Colton Wade (far left), 2 years 2 months, Smith, of Oklahoma City; children of Tony and Edye Smith and grandchildren of Glenn Wilburn and Kathy Graham-Wilburn, all of Oklahoma City; attended America's Kids.

Chase Smith was partial to fried chicken and gravy; younger brother Colton, to food in general. Eighteen months apart, both boys weighed forty-five pounds. "Colton was a chunk," said grandmother Kathy Graham-Wilburn with a laugh. "He loved to eat."

Indeed, Colton stories are legendary in the Smith family. He was known to pop chocolate-covered kisses in his mouth (wrapper and all), suck out the chocolate kiss inside, and then spit out the tinfoil. The Christmas of 1994, he turned up missing until his mother, Edye, heard a noise coming from a closet. "She opened it," recalled Kathy, and [Colton] had taken all the children's Christmas stockings and poured them out. He was methodically] eating all their Christmas candy."

Chase was more a typical older brother: a little serious and responsible. He liked to put his baby brother to bed and

VICKEY SOHN

Master Sergeant Victoria L. Sohn of Moore, 36; wife of Sergeant First Class Greg Sohn; mother of Jessica , John, Greg Jr. , Stephen, and Vickie; master sergeant, U.S. Army Recruiting Battalion.

In 1994, the Sohn family moved into their dream house in Moore, complete with six bedrooms, three bathrooms, and a soon-to-be-installed swimming pool. Married almost two years, Vickey and Greg were also about to officially make their two families one—May 1, 1995, the couple was to sign papers adopting each other's children.

Though on active duty, Vickey was an involved and highly organized mother. She belonged to the PTA, was an assistant leader for her daughter's Brownie troop, and could be found most nights reading aloud to her and Greg's five children or caring for the youngest, John, who had asthma. "I remember lots and lots of nights of her not even going to sleep during the night," said her husband Greg, "and picking up and going to work the next day."

A perfectionist at heart, Vickey took care with everything she did, no matter how minor. "If a 't' wasn't crossed, it had to get crossed," Greg recalled. "If she was just one penny off of the

JOHN STEWART

John T. Stewart, 51, of Oklahoma City; husband of Jean Stewart; father of John Jr. and Tama of Oklahoma City and Laura McAfee of Beebe, AR; director, Program Management Division, Office of Public Housing, HUD.

John T. Stewart was likable, sensitive, and considerate, said his wife, Jean, the kind of man who helped older people cross the street and opened car doors as a rule. They married twenty-four years ago in Prague after meeting through mutual friends.

They loved horses, and at one time, they raised and raced quarter horses. After they sold their last horse, John still frequented the races to watch them run. He took up woodworking—making jewelry boxes, birdhouses, and a cedar chest for his daughter Tama—and was contemplating opening a woodworking business after he retired in December 1995.

Conscientious, he worked for the federal government for twenty-seven years, and he took his responsibility as a government worker paid by the taxpayers seriously. In cards Jean received after his death, many mentioned his fairness on the job. And even during his busiest years as a traveling auditor, he

DEE STRATTON

Dolores M. Stratton, 51, of Moore; wife of Charles Stratton; mother of Michelle and Jay Sawyer and stepdaughters Kim Fairclough and Kelly Stratton; grandmother of Jacob Sawyer, Maryann Fairclough, and Christopher Fairclough; military personnel clerk, U.S. Army Recruiting Battalion.

When childhood friends from Dolores "Dee" Stratton's days at an all-girl Catholic school in Illinois announced they would build a playground in the memory of their friend, their gesture was greeted with knowing nods of approval in Oklahoma. "It is so fitting," said Julie Lawson, a neighbor of the Strattons, "because Dee was such a kid."

She was also the ultimate movie fan. Her video collection includes more than six hundred titles. "Most of the furniture in our living room is video cabinets," observed her husband Charles. Each week Dee watched as many new videos as she could—dubbing those she couldn't squeeze in to view later. If a movie passed muster, she purchased it for her library. "She was very, very funny," recalled Julie. "She smiled all the time. Her life was so full, and she had so many friends."

EMILIO TAPIA

Emilio Tapia-Rangel, 50, of Oklahoma City; husband of the late Virginia Rangel; father of Juan and Armando Tapia of Oklahoma City and Guadalupe, Jesus, Manuel, and Jose Tapia, all of Guanajuato, Mexico; grandfather of Esther and Anita Tapia of Oklahoma City; former groundskeeper for McKinley Properties; died checking on disability benefits at the SSA.

Emilio Tapia came to the U.S. as a young man, and he worked hard to support his family both here and in his native Mexico. "He did what was needed before he was asked to do it," said Charlotte Diedrich of McKinley Properties, for whom Emilio worked as a groundskeeper before rupturing a disc in his back. Frugal, he saved enough from his paycheck to buy two houses for his family in Mexico. He loved baseball (he played outfield at company picnics) and was a member of El Tabernacle De Fe Church in Oklahoma City. "He was happy all the time," said his son Juan Tapia, whose family lived with Emilio. "He was the best dad, always there for me, always took care of me. And he told me once, someday he wanted me to take him home."

Upon his father's death, Juan honored that request, taking Emilio home to be buried in

VICTORIA TEXTER

Victoria J. Texter, 37, of Oklahoma City; wife of James R. Texter Jr.; mother of James R. Texter III; VISA program manager, Federal Employees Credit Union.

Victoria Texter was logical, down-to-earth, and helpful. "Primarily she believed in people taking responsibility for their own actions," said her husband James. "As long as people were trying to help themselves, she would go out of her way to help them." Indeed, she often assisted both friends and customers who were having trouble financially in setting up budgets they could live with.

She joined the Federal Employees Credit Union in 1981 as a teller, and, "She moved her way up through almost every position," said James. She belonged to the Sunny Lane United Methodist Church and was a member of the American Business Women's Association. At home she read and made porcelain dolls, hand-painting their faces and firing them at home. She used Rose State College in Midwest City as her personal gym—taking water aerobics and weight-training classes; across town, she took business courses at Oklahoma City Community College.

She loved the Ozarks and traveled frequently with her husband to Branson, Missouri, and Eureka Springs, Arkansas.

CHARLOTTE THOMAS

Charlotte A. Thomas, 43, of Oklahoma City; wife of John Thomas; mother of Dion, Adrion, and John John; daughter of Bettie Lewis; and daughter-in-law of Myrtle V. Thomas, all of Oklahoma City; sister of Guy Lewis of Midwest City and Cornelius Lewis III of Oklahoma City; daughter of Cornelius Lewis Jr. of Guthrie; appointment clerk, Social Security Administration.

Charlotte Thomas was a conscientious student, mother, and employee. She finished her bachelor of arts degree at Oklahoma State University in two and a half years, was "super mother" to her three children, and wrote, directed, acted, and staged her office's annual production for Black Awareness month. "She did it all," said her mother, Bettie Lewis.

Known as "Puddin" to family and childhood friends, Charlotte did the extra things that smooth the bumps of life. She was a happy-go-lucky person but quiet and tiny ("She wasn't as big as a minute," said Ylita Edd, a colleague and friend).

She avoided mingling her personal life and work. She kept a Bible at her desk and read when she had the time. She was a member of Holy Temple Baptist Church in Oklahoma City.

MIKE THOMPSON

Michael G. Thompson, 47, of Yukon; husband of Joann Thompson; father of Kimberly, Brett, Billy, and Joey; field representative, Social Security Administration.

Mike Thompson could usually be found at home with his family or tinkering out back on the green Volks-wagen beetle he bought new in 1971 and subsequently drove some 200,000 miles. "Everybody knew the bug," said his wife, Joann. "He always took the bug."

A gentle man who enjoyed working with his hands, Mike liked to build things and paint (one of Joann's favorites among his paintings is of women in a field picking wheat). At the time of his death, Mike and his children were building a storage barn from scratch in their backyard.

Mike was a Vietnam veteran. He played a little guitar and liked to visit the beach. He was a member of Trinity Baptist Church. And he worked nineteen years at the Social Security Administration.

VIRGINIA THOMPSON

Virginia M. Thompson, 56, of El Reno; mother of Phillip, Kenneth, and Shelly; grandmother of Vanessa and Desiree Thompson; employee, Federal Employees Credit Union.

Caring, giving, philanthropic, Virginia Thompson visited the elderly in rest homes, cared for the home-bound, and raised three children on her own.

Born in Okarche and raised in El Reno and Calumet, Virginia taught her children that fun can be had even when money is scarce. She and her threesome fished, rode bicycles, and played tennis—and never missed the county fair, recalled her son Ken.

An active member of Sacred Heart Catholic Church in El Reno, Virginia served on the parish council and was involved in its singles group. She spent mornings at Johnnie's Grill with a group of friends known as "The Breakfast Club" and evenings tending to her rosebushes and doing yard work (she won El Reno's first beautiful yard award).

She worked thirty-two years in the banking industry, twenty-four as manager of El Reno's Rock Island Credit Union, where she began as its only employee. "She solicited probably one-third of the members herself and enrolled them personally," said Otis Bruce, a lifelong friend and owner of Johnnie's.

An average week would see Virginia mail eight to ten thank you or get well cards. "She was the most caring person I'd ever met," said Otis. "I told her she was a nun out of season because she acted just like one. She was the best friend you'd ever had in your life."

KAYLA HADDOCK-TITSWORTH

Kayla Marie Haddock-Titsworth, 3 and a half; daughter of Chrissy and Sergeant William Titsworth of Fort Sill; sister of Katie and William Jr.; granddaughter of Bernard and Deanie Haddock, Linda and Mike Thomas, Martha Titsworth, and William Titsworth.

The Titsworth family was in the process of transferring from Fort Riley to Oklahoma City's Army Recruiting Battalion when the Oklahoma City bombing took the life of their daughter Kayla. "Just an hour before she died," said Chrissy Titsworth, "Kayla and Katie were sitting on the floor of our motel room eating Pop-Tarts. Kayla put out the finger of her right hand and said, 'If you finish all of yours, I'll give you one of mine.'

"It didn't matter who you were," added Chrissy, "Kayla would hug you. She'd talk to you. She was very loving."

The Titsworths, now stationed at Fort Sill in Lawton, remember their daughter with joy and say they will never forget Kayla's ability to empathize with others. "If you cried, she'd cry with you," said Chrissy. "Or if she didn't feel like crying, she'd come over and rub your back until you stopped. That little girl would light up any day."

RICK TOMLIN

Rick L. Tomlin, 46, of Piedmont; husband of Tina Tomlin; father of Richard and Jeremy; special agent, division program specialist, U.S. Department of Transportation.

Rick Tomlin was raised in Little River, Kansas. He studied business at Fort Hayes, served in the navy from 1969 to 1972, and went to Vietnam. He joined DOT in 1987 and came to Oklahoma City in June of 1991.

He and his wife, Tina, celebrated their twenty-fifth wedding anniversary on Valentine's Day 1995 with a trip to Las Vegas, where they visited the MGM studios and saw the Wizard of Oz set. "He loved the Wizard of Oz," said Tina. "He was totally excited. Ecstatic, like a little kid. We had to go see it two or three different times that trip, I kid you not." In fact, the Tomlins planned to return to Las Vegas for Christmas 1995 as a present to each other.

Rick snow and water skied, collected and restored old cars (he had two 1968 Plymouth Roadrunners and a 1968 Chrysler 300), and was an award-winning member of the Oklahoma Cactus and Succulent Society. "He always said that it matched his prickly personality," said Tina.

An electrician while in the navy, he was "Mr. Fix-It" to family and friends. "There was no such thing as calling the plumber or a carpenter," said Tina. At the time of his death, Rick and son Jeremy were building a garage/workshop, and all that remained to be done was the trim. "There wasn't anything he didn't know how to do," said Tina.

LUTHER & LaRUE TREANOR

Luther H., 61, and LaRue, 55, Treanor, both of Guthrie; parents of Debbie Price and Mike, Mark, and Brad Treanor, all of Guthrie; Luther was retiring after twenty-nine years delivering Townley milk; LaRue was a homemaker; the couple and granddaughter Ashley Eckles were checking on retirement benefits for Luther at the Social Security office.

Luther and LaRue Treanor lived among their children and grandchildren on 160 acres on the outskirts of Guthrie. Observed their daughter-in-law Kathleen, "They were like teenagers. You'd see them in their truck, sitting side by side." About the only argument the children ever heard was over Luther raising a herd of pigs. "Either the pigs go or I go," LaRue finally told her husband.

Luther grazed three hundred head of cattle, but he never mistook one cow for another. "He'd know which one was sick," recalled his son, Mike. "He'd say, 'You know the one with the spot under its left eye.'"

LaRue was more concerned with their circa 1899 frame farmhouse. When they bought the farm twenty-six years ago, Luther advocated tearing the house down, but LaRue resisted. Eventually, she Sheet-rocked, plastered and tore out walls and built the railing around the porch. "She breathed life back into this house," said Kathleen.

She also baked bread, canned food, made "melt-in-your-mouth cinnamon rolls," and, when her children were young, sewed their clothes. "She made everything."

The Treanors were charter members of Seward Road Baptist Church, where LaRue sang in the choir.

LARRY TURNER

Larry L. Turner, 42, of Oklahoma City; husband of Dianne Turner; father of Michael; stepfather of Demetrick; grandfather of Demeshia; U.S. special agent, Defense Investigative Service, Department of Defense.

Larry Turner was an Oklahoma highway patrolman for nine years before becoming a special agent for the U.S. Department of Defense in 1986. He majored in music at Grambling State College in Louisiana and earned a bachelor of science degree in 1980 from UCO in Edmond.

He played clarinet in the orchestra of Saint John Missionary Baptist Church in Oklahoma City, where he was also a deacon, worked with the transportation ministry, and taught an adult Sunday school class. He involved everyone in the class, said his wife, Dianne Turner. "They would tell me how they enjoyed his prayers," said Dianne.

Larry played racquetball every Saturday morning and also enjoyed tennis, softball, and golf. He loved cars and motorcycles, and he was working to become a Thirty-second degree Mason. He spent a lot of time with his wife taking walks and traveling. And he was equally fond of doing things with his granddaughter, Demeshia ("She was the apple of her papa's heart," said Dianne); grandfather and granddaughter frequented the park and children's movies.

Dianne and Larry had a close circle of friends with whom they played volleyball, picnicked, and vacationed. "He liked getting together with people. He was friendly and outgoing and could strike up a conversation with anyone," said his wife. "He was my best buddy."

JULES VALDEZ

Jules A. Valdez, 51, of Edmond; husband of Virginia Valdez; father of Marisa; program manager, Office of Southern Plains Native American Programs, HUD.

Jules Valdez was hard-working and compassionate, a man who dedicated much of his life to bettering the lives of Native Americans but always made time for his daughter, Marisa. "He was a great dad," said his wife, Virginia.

He chauffeured or accompanied Marisa to her ballet, drama, and voice lessons and rooted her on in track. He enjoyed everything about being the father of a teen-aged daughter, said Virginia.

In his spare time, Jules did pro bono legal work, fixed things around the house ("He was a self-made carpenter," said Virginia), and read.

Active in the Edmond Central Chapter of the Rotary Club (most recently as its treasurer), Jules had been honored with the Rotary's Paul Harris Fellowship Award. He belonged to the Edmond Chamber of Commerce, the Edmond Certified Cities Task Force, Leadership Edmond, and the Oklahoma Bar Association. He was a long-time member of Saint John the Baptist Catholic Church in Edmond.

In honor of his work on behalf of its people, the Ponca Tribe has named its new social service building in White Eagle the Jules Valdez Social Service Center.

JOHN VAN ESS III

John K. Van Ess III, 67, of Chickasha; husband of Dixie; father of Kevin, Dan, and Kerry Van Ess, all of Oklahoma City, and Karl Van Ess IV of Chickasha; review appraiser, Office of Housing, HUD.

John Van Ess III spent evenings sitting on his porch with his little red dachshund, Otto, chatting happily with neighbors. He relished family get-togethers and the home cooking that accompanied them. He grew up in Wewoka, where he excelled in football, basketball, and baseball; he graduated from Wewoka High in 1945. And he was a World War II-era veteran.

He is remembered as the family problem solver, rubbing his head and pacing the floor when deep in thought. He offered practical solutions in a kindly manner but was careful not to interfere. "He was just the smartest man I ever ran across," said his daughter, Kerry.

John loved to laugh and surrounded himself with others who did, too. He valued friendship, said his wife Dixie, and his friends could count on him to stay in touch and lend a hand if needed—even over the course of decades. He planned to retire in December 1995 to go into business with an old friend renovating, then selling homes.

At Easter, just four days before he died, the entire Van Ess family—grandchildren and all—sat for its first-ever clan photo.

JOHNNY WADE

Johnny A. Wade, 42, of Edmond; husband of Joannie Wade; father of Carla and Jerrel; son of Johnnie and Olivia Wade of San Augustine, TX; engineer, Federal Highway Administration.

Johnny Wade was raised in east Texas, the only child of his farmer and minister father and schoolteacher mother. He loved the outdoors and fishing. "When we lived in Arkansas, he would always go out in his boat and fish," said his wife, Joannie. "He liked going to the country. He told me that when we retired we were going back to east Texas to the country to live."

He graduated from Prairie View A & M University in Texas with a degree in civil engineering and joined FHWA in 1975. His job took him and his family all over the country; they arrived in Edmond in 1991.

Johnny liked being with his family, whether it was cooking out on the grill or playing basketball. He was a big fan of the Dallas Cowboys (even when they were losing), and he and his son, Jerrel, always kept up with the drafts.

Optimistic and something of a family motivator, Johnny had a knack for soothing his wife when she was worried or upset. Recalled Joannie, "He would say, 'Joan, just look at all the things we have to be grateful for.'"

DAVID WALKER

David J. Walker, 54, of Edmond; husband of Janet E. Walker; father of Jennifer of Edmond, LeaAnn Perry of San Diego, and Jacqueline Bowman of Tulsa; grandfather of Tyler Perry and Christian Bowman; environmental officer, Community Planning and Development Division, HUD.

David Jack Walker took to grandfathering like he had earlier taken to fathering—very well. "He was more than a man who wore a suit and tie five days a week for almost thirty-five years," said Janet, his wife of five years.

Three months away from retirement, David was planning to start his own company, Walker Environmental and Engineering, and to build a new home near Lake Tenkiller (the Walkers were in the process of buying the land).

An avid fisherman, hunter, and OSU fan (it was his alma mater), when David hugged you, Janet said in an interview with the Edmond Sun, "It didn't matter if you were a man or a woman—he hugged you until you couldn't breathe." He was a lifetime member of First Baptist Church of Nicoma Park, where he drove forty-five minutes every Sunday from his home in Edmond to attend services and served on its building committee.

For his memorial service, David's daughters, wife, and friends collaborated on a collage of his life history as a way to share their best memories of him. The end result stood four feet by five feet. Observed Janet, "My marriage was the greatest thing that ever happened to me. This man showed me a love I never knew existed. He not only was my husband, but my best friend."

ROBERT WALKER

Robert "Bob" N. Walker Jr., 52, of Oklahoma City; husband of Judy Walker; father of Robert Walker III of Prattville, AL; stepfather of Mark Lake of Oklahoma City, George Lake of Norfolk, VA, Kevin Lake of Madison, AL, and Sandra Rosenblum of New Market, AL; claims representative, Social Security Administration.

He was always one of the first to lend a hand to someone in need—be they friend or stranger. "Someone would call and say, 'My car is stuck,'" recalled his wife, Judy, "and he'd jump on his tractor and go pull them out."

An Eagle Scout and forty-six-year member of the Boy Scouts of America, Robert was assistant district commissioner for the Will Rogers District of the Boy Scouts and unit commissioner for Troop 84. In 1992, he joined the Masons—a lifelong dream. "He got his feet wet and went all the way," said Judy, becoming a member of Amity Lodge, Guthrie Scottish Rite, Fidelis-Oklahoma, Amaranth (Queen Christina Court), and India Shrine Temple. "He would always say, 'A Mason is a good man,'" recalled Judy.

He served as a microwave technician in the U.S. Army in Korea. And he combined his knack for drawing with his interest in computers to make his own Christmas cards each year. He taught Judy how to drive a tractor, hammer a nail, and use a saw—all things she once thought herself incapable of mastering. Observed Judy proudly: Robert instilled confidence in others, including his own wife.

WANDA WATKINS

Wanda Watkins, 49, of Oklahoma City; daughter of James and Mildred Watkins; sister of Junetta Watkins; aunt of Bobby Watkins, all of Rogers, AR; clerk, U.S. Army Recruiting Battalion.

When Emerson observed that winning the affection of children and the elderly was a mark of a life well lived, he might have been writing about Wanda Watkins. "Wanda had a way with children and animals," said her sister, Junetta. "When kids would be missing, I always told their parents, 'Just look for Wanda, and you'll find them.'"

Wanda became so attached to the elderly people she worked with during her five-year career as a hospital physical therapy aide, said her mother Mildred, that she finally had to change careers. "It was just too upsetting to her," said Mildred, to see them suffer.

A Leavenworth, Kansas, native and a civilian army employee, Wanda moved to Oklahoma City after her office at Fort Chaffey closed. She chose Oklahoma City so she could remain close to her family, including her sister's son, Bobby, whom she helped raise. Considerate of others, it was typical of Wanda, said Junetta, that she spent the last vacation of her life helping an aunt get settled into a new home.

MIKE WEAVER

Michael D. Weaver, 45, of Edmond; husband of Donna Weaver; father of Jeffrey and Timothy; son of Peggy Weaver of Oklahoma City; brother of Greg Weaver of Tulsa and Julie Jones of Edmond; attorney-adviser, Legal Division, HUD.

Mike and Donna Weaver met as undergraduates at the University of Oklahoma in Norman. They married twenty-two years ago, years in which Mike infused everything they did from dancing to skiing to spending time with their two sons—with fun.

He coached Jeffrey and Timothy in baseball, basketball, and soccer. But his influence extended to all his players. Wrote one basketball player after his death, "He took ten eager, misshapen and (we all thought) talented guys and made basketball players out of us. We played many teams that were bigger than us and stronger, but never did we play a team that was better coached than ours." Mike's habit of writing a personal note to each of his players at the end of the season was well known. Almost as legendary was the time his son's baseball team broke out of a bad slump after Mike showed up at the game with "magic dust," which he insisted on sprinkling on the players' mitts, bats, and hats—it may have been the first time flour was shown to have magical properties.

Devoted to family—particularly his mother and sometime golfing partner Peggy Weaver—Mike was blessed with a ready laugh and a dry sense of humor. He taught his sons, said Donna, to face the world with a smile on their face and a song in their hearts.

JULIE WELCH

Julie M. Welch, 23, of Oklahoma City; daughter of E. E. (Bud) and Lena Welch of Oklahoma City; sister of Kevin Welch of Jackson, MS; stepsister of Christopher Weeks of Oklahoma City; granddaughter of Ruby Compassi of Muskogee and Dortha Welch of Shawnee; claims representative and Spanish translator, Social Security Administration.

As a junior high student, Julie Welch once befriended a new Hispanic classmate who spoke limited English, helping the girl navigate the cafeteria line and standing up for her when others called her derogatory names. It was a life-changing encounter.

She went on to study Spanish at Bishop McGuinness High School, to spend a year in Spain as an exchange student, and to volunteer at a downtown Hispanic center. She received a Spanish scholarship to Marquette University, where she majored in Spanish (she spoke five other languages), spent six months studying in Spain, and worked with poor Hispanic children.

A member of Epiphany of the Lord Catholic Church in Oklahoma City, she planned to become a Spanish teacher and to start a program for Hispanic children in the neighborhood of Little Flower Church, where she went to mass every day after work. She also attended weekly prayer meeting at Tinker Air Force Base, where she met Lieutenant Eric Hilz, who became her best friend and boyfriend. And many an evening found her circling Lake Hefner with her mother, reciting the rosary as the two walked. Observed John Mallon, editor of Sooner Catholic, upon her death, "She must have had a real straight shot into heaven."

ROBERT WESTBERRY

Robert G. Westberry, 57, of Oklahoma City; husband of Tillie Westberry, now of Keystone Heights, FL; father of Sue Riley, Robin Brown, and Glen Westberry; grandfather of Jonathon Nelson, Frank Edwards, David Westberry, Joshua Brown, and Timothy, Stephen, and Rachel Riley; U.S. special agent in charge, Department of Defense, Defense Investigative Services.

He was a stickler for doing a job right, but Robert Westberry also believed in taking care of the people who did the work. He encouraged employees to stay home and care for sick children, said his wife, Tillie, assuring them that their job would always be there. "In turn," said Tillie, "they would be better employees. He always bent over backwards for them."

A former Daytona Beach police officer and Florida state trooper, Robert joined navy intelligence in 1969; his work with the civilian navy security branch took him to Vietnam from 1970 to 1971. In 1972, he joined the Department of Defense. The family moved to Oklahoma City in November of 1992 to be closer to Tillie's mother.

In recent years, Tillie and Robert had begun traveling, often in the process visiting their three children and seven grandchildren ("They loved their papa," said Tillie of the grandkids). He was preceded in death by their daughter Mathilda Ann Lansing in April of 1988.

Dependable, considerate, and kind-hearted, Robert was the kind of person who joked and chatted with anyone who crossed his path in the course of a normal day, providing for those he encountered—both strangers and friends—a welcome friendly face.

ALAN WHICHER

Alan G. Whicher, 40, of Edmond; husband of Pam Whicher, now of Rockville, MD; father of Meredith, Melinda, and Ryan; son of Bette and the late Victor Whicher; assistant special agent, U.S. Secret Service, Oklahoma City field office.

Twenty minutes before the explosion on April 19, 1995, Alan Whicher phoned his wife, Pam, at home to give her a pep talk and wish her good luck before she gave a speech that day at a women's Bible study at Oklahoma City University.

Accustomed to excelling in his own endeavors, he encouraged others to do the same. "He was so type A," said Pam, "that when he started something, he saw it through."

Health-conscious and industrious, Alan religiously chose salads over burgers, was up by seven on Saturday mornings ready to tackle his weekend chores ("I finally talked him out of mowing the lawn at eight," said Pam), and pumped iron four times a week ("He had muscles upon muscles," said Larry Kingry, a friend and fellow agent). "As a kid," said his mother, Bette, "he used to wax his car so much, he'd wax the color right off it."

A member of Saint John the Baptist Catholic Church in Edmond, Alan gave up drinking alcohol every Lent, and it didn't matter what party he attended, he wouldn't drink. "He was never swayed by a crowd," said Pam.

He protected presidents and princes, and he told his staff upon his arrival in Oklahoma City, "People say that I'm hard but fair." Observed Kingry, "He was fair, but he wasn't hard."

JO ANN WHITTENBERG

Jo Ann Whittenberg, 35, of Oklahoma City; daughter of Lee Ann Whitten-berg; twin sister of Mary Ann Whittenberg; niece of Otto Caldwell; program support assistant, Office of Public Housing, HUD.

Jo Ann Whittenberg and her mother, Lee Ann, and sister, Mary Ann, were unusually close. In fact, until six months prior to the bombing, Jo Ann lived at home, and she called home every morning. "She was such a good daughter," said Lee Ann. "I always tell people, 'I didn't get my gray hair from my children, I got it from my dog.'"

Born at Saint Anthony Hospital and a graduate of John Marshall, "Jo Ann was always smiling, always friendly to everyone," said Lee Ann. After her death, her mother received notes from many of the small businesses which Jo Ann patronized, telling her how much the merchants appreciated Jo Ann's ready smile and genuine friendliness.

Situated in her own apartment, Jo Ann gardened, baked gourmet desserts (her Italian cream cakes and 7-Up pound cakes were in constant demand at work), and fancied herself a do-it-yourself mechanic who proudly fixed her own flats and did other repair work on her car. Since her daughter's death, Lee Ann said she has been touched by how wonderful everyone at HUD has been. "They were truly a family," she said of the HUD crew.

FRAN WILLIAMS

Frances Williams, 48, of Oklahoma City; daughter of Mozelle Bibb and mother of Dawn Mahan and Matt Story, all of Oklahoma City; grandmother of Matthew and Michael Mahan and MiCayla Story; secretary, Community Planning and Development Division, HUD.

Fran Williams was known to loan money to people when they needed it, to give a lift to anyone who needed a ride (wherever they needed to go), and to visit her eighty-eight-year-old mother sometimes as many as three times a day. "She would do anything to help other people," said her daughter, Dawn. "She was a very, very giving person." Indeed, Fran was known to have once taken a homeless woman into her home for a month until the woman could get back on her feet.

She entertained her grandchildren most weekends, taking them to the movies and McDonald's or baking cookies with them at her home (Fran had a notorious sweet tooth and often ate cake for breakfast, to her daughter's chagrin). Fran and her eldest grandson, Matthew, said Dawn, were best friends.

At HUD, Fran was a popular employee. Repeatedly, coworkers and families of HUD employees mentioned her friendly demeanor and warm voice over the telephone. "She was just a special person," her daughter said, "and I really miss her. But I know where she is, and I know she's watching over us."

SCOTT WILLIAMS

Scott D. Williams, 24, of Tuttle; husband of Nicole Williams; father of Kylie Nicole Scott Williams; son of Bob and Connie Williams of Tuttle; brother of Craig Williams of Tuttle; salesman, William E. Davis and Sons Food Inc. of Oklahoma City; was making a delivery to the Murrah building when the bomb exploded.

Whenever Scott Williams got excited—whether from pre-game jitters or good news—he would get red, "little pork chop cheeks," said his mother, Connie Williams. And sure enough, when Scott learned he was to be a father for the first time, his cheeks responded accordingly.

He and wife Nikki chose the name Kylie for their daughter, and exactly three months from the date Scott died, Kylie Nicole Scott Williams was born.

A business education gradu-ate of UCO, Scott had become a salesman with William E. Davis. He hoped to someday coach, but he liked being a salesman.

Scott was a fan of Ryne Sandberg of the Chicago Cubs, played second base and shortstop, and was a member of Tuttle High School's 1988 championship baseball team (the first state championship in a team sport in Tuttle's history). "All he really wanted to do was play baseball," said Paul Lekawski, Scott's uncle. "He was a competitor," added Connie.

Scott went on to become a UCO graduate assistant baseball coach during the Bronchos' record-setting 1994 season that saw the team make the NCAA Division II playoffs.

Two years ago, Scott, a member of Beverly Hills Baptist Church in Oklahoma City, was baptized with his mother. "He was one of the good guys of life," she said.

STEVE WILLIAMS

William S. Williams, 42, of Cashion; husband of Barbara Williams; father of Sara, Allysone, and Meryl; op-erations supervisor, Social Security Administration.

Steve Williams knew "a little bit about a lot of things" and "a lot about most things," said Bar-bara Williams. At times, his wife and three daughters teased that their resident MENSA member had to be a relative of Cliff Clavern from the television show Cheers.

He owned four hours of self-narrated, taped tours of Civil War battlegrounds and was a math whiz, but he also practiced his golf swing in the wheat field behind the family's house and serenaded family and friends on his Fender guitar. Once in a great while, said Barbara, he would "fire up the amplifier and drag out his Fender Stratocaster and get together with old friends for a big jam session." Steve had twenty years with the SSA and planned to retire young and build a recording studio.

He enjoyed discussing the topics of This Week with David Brinkley, climbing Mount Princeton, and riding the Shockwave at Six Flags five times in a row—all, of course, with his family. "He had a laugh," confided Barbara, "that made others laugh."

CLARENCE WILSON

Clarence E. Wilson Sr. , 49, of Oklahoma City; husband of Gloria Cole Wilson; father of Clarence Jr. of the Washington, D.C. area and the late Mark Wilson; former father-in-law of Beth Wilson of New York City; brother of Thomas Wilson of Oklahoma City, Bernice McGee of Lawton, and George F. Wilson and Patsy Jones, both of Savannah, GA; area counsel, Legal Division, HUD.

In high school in Lawton, Clarence Wilson Sr. was student council president. As an undergraduate at OU, he was a member of the President's Leadership Class, a cofounder of the African-American Student Union, and an officer of Omega Psi Phi Fraternity. In 1968, he graduated with honors from OU, the fourth African-American in the school's history to earn a bachelor's degree in pharmacy. In 1971, he earned a juris doc-torate from OU.

Universally wise and "always right," Clarence Sr. was known to patiently explain his position over and over again until, invari-ably, the other person would have to concede. "[It] was a little hard to live with," admitted his son Clarence Jr., a doctoral student in pharmacology at Howard University.

Clarence Sr. liked throwing elaborate, catered parties for his friends but also enjoyed manning his big outdoor grill and wrestling up barbecue. He tinkered at home on his white 1965 and turquoise 1985 Jaguars. At his death, he served as legal counsel and a member of the Board of Representatives for his fraternity; he was also a member of Saint John Mission-ary Baptist Church. Observed one family friend, "Clarence Wilson, Sr. must have been one of the most well liked people in the world."

RONOTA WOODBRIDGE

Ronota A. Woodbridge, 31, of Edmond; wife of Gary Woodbridge; daughter of Ron and Beth Newberry; pavement materials engineer, Fed-eral Highway Administration.

Not long before the Okla-homa City bombing, Ronota Woodbridge—unbeknownst to her family—took the Profes-sional Engineering Exam. Only after her death did they learn she had passed the test that would have made her eligible to go into private practice. "She studied hard for that one," said her husband, Gary. "They only have a thirty to forty percent pass rate."

Ronota earned a bachelor's degree in engineering physics from Abilene Christian Univer-sity and bachelor's and master's degrees in civil engineering from the University of Arkansas. She joined the FHWA in 1990.

Described by family as a wonderful Christian wife and daughter, Ronota was known for trying to make others feel good and for offering encouragement when someone else was having a bad day. A member of the Edmond Church of Christ and the Federal Eagles Toastmaster Club, she liked to sew and col-lect rocks.

Married eight years, Ronota and Gary often hunted, fished, and skied at Lake Arbuckle, which reminded them of Ar-kansas; the couple had recently canoed the north fork of the White River in southern Missouri. "We had just gotten into tandem bicycling and really enjoyed it," said Gary. On nice evenings, the couple could be seen riding their tandem bicycle around Lake Arcadia and back to their Edmond home.

JOHN YOUNGBLOOD

John A. "Buddy" Youngblood, 52, of Yukon; husband of Kathy Youngblood; father of Tammy, Becky, Robin, John (Bud) Jr. , and Ann Walker; special agent, Office of Motor Carriers, Federal Highway Administration.

"He devoted his whole life to the public," said Kathy of her husband, John. "His whole goal was to try to make the world a better place through law and order."

John "Buddy" Youngblood joined the New Mexico State Police Department in 1972. A criminal justice major in college, he began his career with the U.S. Department of Transporta-tion Federal Highway Adminis-tration in 1980—duty stations included Little Rock, Lubbock, Oklahoma City, and Austin, final-ly returning to Oklahoma City with the Transportation Safety Institute in 1989. Then in March 1995, he was transferred back to FHWA, just six weeks before the bombing. Prior to his death, he was a volunteer policeman in Lubbock as well as El Reno. At the time of his death, he was a member of the Yukon Police Reserve.

John liked camping, fish-ing, deer hunting, and being outdoors. He was an assistant coach for John Jr.'s baseball team, and he enjoyed attend-ing his football practices and games. "He was very gentle, had a very good sense of humor, and was good hearted—too good hearted," said Kathy. "He'd give you the shirt off his back. John wasn't just your friend; he was your best friend, and he'd do anything for you."

THE CHILDREN

I am the voice of the children—
simple and honest and clear.
Forever the light in the darkest of night.
I have not gone away, I am here.

I am the eyes of the children—
with vision beyond my years.
I focus my sight, unblinking and bright,
unclouded, except for my tears.

I am the soul of the children—
innocent, blameless, and pure.
My spirit, undaunted, through violence flaunted,
will conquer and ever endure.

Remember the trust of the children.
Darkness will not have its day;
take hold of my hand, and we'll both understand
that the children will show you the way.

*—This original poem by Susan Hill Custer was recited
by Kristen Bramble at the Statewide Prayer Service,
April 23, 1995.*

BRINGING IT DOWN

'The survivors need to grieve for those who died. Bringing the

building down can begin the whole process of healing.'

IT STOOD FOR WEEKS like a gaping wound open to the sun and elements. Opinions on whether it should stay or go—whether it was monument or brutal reminder—were as compelling as the thousands who came to see it in the weeks following the bombing.

Governor Frank Keating pushed for the Alfred P. Murrah building to be bulldozed and a memorial to be built on its site. President Clinton vowed to provide funds to rebuild, replace, or relocate the federal building, depending on what the people of Oklahoma ultimately wanted. And Mayor Ron Norick weighed in on the side of demolition, after consulting with victims' families, including two whose loved ones were known to be entombed inside.

Though building designer Ron Loftis of Oklahoma City believed no technical obstacles prevented the circa 1977 building from being repaired, all conceded psychological barriers might well exist.

In the end, the General Services Administration pronounced the building structurally unsound and, in the name of expediency, declared explosives should be used to demolish it: implosion would take a matter of seconds; a wrecking ball, some three weeks at best. It went without being said that the sooner the building was leveled, the sooner the bodies of the last victims could be recovered and returned to their families.

On the eve of the implosion, the largest crowd of spectators yet descended on the site to take one last look at what terrorism had wrought.

May 23, 1995, dawned clear and windy. At 7:01:09 a.m., a hundred and fifty pounds of dynamite, packed strategically in the nine-story building, was detonated. The building crumpled into a thirty-foot heap of concrete and twisted metal. And the Alfred P. Murrah building was laid to rest. Some two thousand people were on hand to witness the building's demise. There was no applause or cheers. Instead, quiet groups of people, some with tears in their eyes, simply turned their backs and walked away.

About 150 pounds of explosives were distributed at some 300 spots in the Alfred P. Murrah Federal Building; it collapsed in 7 3/4 seconds.

Controlled Demolition Inc. of Phoenix, Maryland, shrouded parts of the Murrah building in fireproof cloth to prevent debris from flying.

Governor Frank Keating, Mayor Ron Norick, Deputy Fire Chief Jon Hansen, and the families of Christy Rosas and Virginia Thompson watched the implosion from the fifteenth floor of the Regency Tower apartments.

An estimated two thousand people watched the Murrah building implode; afterwards, police barricades—in place since the blast—were removed, allowing people to walk within a half-block of the bombing site.

It took almost two rainy months for Midwest Wrecking of Midwest City to clear the building site (work was slowed to allow the last three victims to be recovered and so evidence could be gathered); the debris was placed in a special plot at a southwest Oklahoma City landfill owned by BFI Waste Systems.

TEACH YOUR CHILDREN WELL

By Thom Hunter

THE TEACHER WALKED CALMLY into the room, clutching a twisted tissue in her right hand, running her left hand through her hair. She hesitated, looking sadly at the children who trusted her to teach them history, to read them riddles, to drill them on multiplication tables, to referee four-square and to pull them from the bottom of the pile when the playground bullies got too big. Her bottom lip trembled as she wished this task could fall to someone else. She knew that for the rest of their lives, if they remembered nothing more about her, they would remember the morning Miss Adams told them... "Something terrible has happened," she said. And then she sighed and began to try to explain a tragedy she herself could not comprehend.

It was November 22, 1963. I was in that elementary school classroom, and President John F. Kennedy had been killed in Dallas. I went home and for days sat transfixed in front of a black and white TV as another little boy saluted his fallen father and a nation bowed in fear, sorrow, and disbelief. I remember.

I remember May 4, 1970. I was in high school, civil riots had erupted around the nation, and anti-war fever raged out of control at Kent State in Ohio. It appeared we Americans would drown in discontent and destroy each other in anger. I remember.

I remember January 28, 1986. I was a young father, and the space shuttle *Challenger*, a symbol of our nation's pride and progress, disintegrated in air off the coast of Florida, taking with it some of our brightest adventurers. I watched with four young sons, bright-eyed and excited about spaceships and adventure. Suddenly, their eyes turned to me for an explanation. When I close my eyes, I remember.

But democracy continued, and new leaders emerged, and those who rioted forgave, and most found ways to work within the system, and we journeyed on into space and found new frontiers. While we didn't forget, a strong nation moved on, tempered by pain, eyes opened, resolve stronger, more powerful than any man-made tragedy. Repeatedly, this nation of very diverse individuals has come together to take the twisted remains of tragedy and re-mold them into a monument of our collective strength. We children who heard the chilling news from Miss Adams that morning in 1963 are in our forties now. And she was right, we never forgot the news she delivered. Millions more memories have crowded in on that morning, yet it remains alone. It is a part of each of us. Tragic though it was, however, it did not alone define who we became. Fear faded in the face of baseball and Barbie dolls, summer vacations, and Christmas trees. Time passed. And we were, for all practical purposes, fine.

Then came April 19, 1995.

"I heard there'd been an explosion in downtown Oklahoma City," said Patrick, eleven. "I heard them say it was the federal building, and I thought 'Cool, an explosion.' I didn't even know what a federal building was. I found out later that the explosion was bad and the building was big and people were killed and I got mad. But I wasn't sure who to be mad at."

Anger. To whom should they direct it?

"The teacher told me to go to the office, where the principal handed me a green slip of paper that said 'Your Dad is okay. He wasn't in his office,' " remembers Donovan, thirteen. "They asked me not to say much in class because they didn't want kids to get upset. But I couldn't help talking about it. It was scary."

Fear. But of what?

"I sat beside Mom and watched television after school until we got hungry," remembers Lauren, nine. "Then we ate and watched some more. When I went to sleep, I saw it all again, as if I was there. There were children crying, and I couldn't help. It was a nightmare."

Frustration. What can relieve it?

"You hear a lot about grownups killing each other, and I always wonder why," said Russell, fourteen. "When I saw it on television, at first it was like watching a movie. But when I saw the children, I had to go outside and play basketball. It was too real. It was too sad."

Sorrow. How can they overcome it?

"I wanted to get in my car and drive to Oklahoma City and find the bomber," said Zachary, seventeen. "It's not fair that he could do something that terrible and then just go on about life. I wanted to make him watch as people were taken out of the building and make him listen as people found out their family members were killed. It isn't fair."

Fairness. Every kid craves it.

Given the choice, there is not a mother or a father in Oklahoma who would not have protected every son and daughter from exposure to the horror of April 19. The choice wasn't given. The news coverage was pervasive, the tragedy entered every conversation, and the building itself stood for weeks like an open wound. As we drove along the roads to school or to a baseball game or to church, every yellow moving van reminded my children of the tragedy. Indeed, a drive in the country brought it all back in a way only a child would create: "See those cows," said Patrick. "They make fertilizer from their manure, and fertilizer was used to blow up the federal building." Suddenly, it seemed cows were dangerous. Unless, of course, someone helps make some sense of it all.

And that's what we parents are for. Someone else rescued the survivors. Someone else cleared the debris. Someone else memorialized the lost loved ones. Someone will counsel the victims. Someone is distributing funds to rebuild. Someone will prosecute the crime. Someone will see that punishment is carried out. And the parents of the children of Oklahoma will help to make some sense of it all. "People are good overall, aren't they?" asked Lauren, watching long lines of people donating blood, dropping off donations. " I guess it takes a really bad guy to blow up a building."

"Yes, Lauren," I said. "Overall, people are good."

Four days after the bombing, a seven-year-old boy had a dream that someone parked a truck in front of his house and blew it up. He woke up, screaming for Daddy, and Daddy came. They looked out the window. There was no truck. They talked. They prayed. They slept. And in the morning, the little boy went out front and played in his yard in the bright morning light. No fear.

Parents listen to many dreams. Some are bright and beautiful; some are dark and troubling. And, in my own family the dreams of seventeen-year-old Zach and nine-year-old Lauren differ greatly. Indeed, the only thing not different is the listening part. In fact, perhaps this tragedy has instilled in us a new resolve to make it clear what family means in Oklahoma. Perhaps we hold our children a little closer now than we used to, keep a little better eye on them; spend a little more time explaining things; check on them a little more through the night. In the midst of all that anger, fear, frustration, and sorrow, perhaps we found something with which to cope. Love.

The bombing left family of those who died aching with a need to do something. The answer for some was a June 5, 1995, press conference on the Capitol grounds in support of habeas corpus reform (it would speed up the death penalty appeals process and expand wiretapping powers, among other things). President Clinton endorsed the bill, the Senate passed it (98-1) June 7, and the House Judiciary Committee supported a version, but at year's end opponents still had strong moral problems with the bill, and the House had not called a vote. Above, Glenn Seidl (obscured), Clint Seidl, Bob Denison, Dan McKinney, Jason Smith, Mike Reyes at podium, Gary Bland, Earl Adams, Kay Ice, Suzanne Britten, and Senator Don Nickles

CELEBRATION OF THE SPIRIT

On October 19-22, 1995, the Oklahoma Arts Institute brought family members of bombing victims, survivors, and professional artists together at Quartz Mountain for a first-of-its-kind arts workshop entitled "Celebration of the Spirit." Together, attendees explored the healing properties of art.

THIRTY-FIVE OF Caren Cook's HUD coworkers died in the Oklahoma City bombing: "On April 19, 1995," Caren wrote, "our world exploded." On the six-month anniversary of the bombing, Caren joined 127 other survivors and family members at Quartz Mountain hoping to find some solace in art. In the shadow of one of Oklahoma's oldest mountains, men, women, and children made memory boxes and delicate mobiles of gold thread, wove baskets, explored dance movements and group song, and scrawled journal entries. Working side by side, they also shared stories—of those they lost, of lives led.

Selected works from the workshop—from a memory quilt made by the children (they sewed private personal messages into its hem) to selected pieces of poetry, basketry, and sculpture—comprise an exhibit that creators hope will someday tour the United States (it debuted at the state capitol in the Governor's Gallery in December). At the very least it may prove—as one participant found—that, "Art does lift our spirits and free our souls."

See the people dying, hear the babies crying,
and I mourn.
Want to wake up so I pinch myself,
and sadly enough, it is far worse than a dream.

And I can't help but feel hate to the
cowards that did this.
I know that the Lord above will turn
this tragedy into love.

Some thought they heard thunder
but how could they have guessed
it was a bomb?

Physical and emotional pain throughout the world.
169 gone.

Patrick McCullough, Edmond, Age 10
from "Celebration of the Spirit"

Note: At the time this poem was written, rescuers
widely believed there were 169 victims.

An Explosion of Grace, *by Caren Cook contains mementos of her coworkers. Wrote Cook, "Many lives of precious people were sacrificed to show the world that grace and love overcome evil."*

Various memorabilia hangs on the chainlink fence surrounding the bombing site.

THE FOLLOWING PAGES PRESENT A SELECTION OF
OFFICIAL DOCUMENTS, PUBLIC STATEMENTS, PRIVATE
MESSAGES, AND OTHER RECORDS DEALING WITH THE
BOMBING OF DOWNTOWN OKLAHOMA CITY.

© 1995 DAILY OKLAHOMAN

THE DAILY OKLAHOMAN

The State Newspaper Since 1907

OKLAHOMA CITY, OK   THURSDAY, APRIL 20, 1995   60 PAGES   50¢

MORNING OF TERROR
City Struggles With Shock of Deadly Bombing

An Oklahoma City firefighter runs through rubble near the Alfred P. Murrah Federal Building after an explosion caved in the front of the building Wednesday. The blast damaged other buildings within several blocks.

Small Children Victims In Day-Care Center

By Diana Baldwin
Staff Writer

Five small children, badly injured and bloodied, and a toy doll were among the first to be removed from the Murrah Building's second floor day-care center.

"You couldn't even tell they had been little boys or little girls," said Lydia Winfrey, a licensed practical nurse, who assisted with the children wrapped in blankets and lying on the brick patio of the federal building.

One child was decapitated and others had severe head injuries.

Winfrey said. A hole in one child's head was filled with plaster pieces. The medical examiner photographed the young, innocent victims.

The toy doll, which was found near one victim, was brought out of the rubble in hopes it would help identify that victim, Winfrey said.

Dr. Kathy DeHart, a local dentist who volunteered at the southside triage center, said it appeared the blast hit the children in the face, blowing them backward.

"It was just totally devastating in the explosion in downtown Oklahoma City on Wednesday.

A firefighter carries a child injured in the explosion in downtown Oklahoma City on Wednesday.

Scores Killed In Bomb Blast; State Stunned

By Steve Lackmeyer
and David Zizzo
Staff Writers

A thunderous bomb blast rocked Oklahoma City on Wednesday, ripping a huge slice from a federal building and killing at least 150 to 200 people, many of them children.

The bombing, felt throughout central sections of Oklahoma, shattered the downtown district and left a grieving state wondering why.

The explosion, shortly after 9 a.m. demolished about a third of the Alfred P. Murrah Federal Building, causing all nine stories, including a day-care center on the second floor, to "pancake" into a pile of rubble.

Workers in their offices tumbled out of the nine-story building to the street below. One man fell into the 30-foot-wide bomb crater.

Victims fled the building, their clothes ripped off by the blast. Others wandered in a daze. Some victims with gashes on their arms and legs, or with head injuries, blood streaming down their faces, sat on curbs, quiet and shocked.

Shortly after 10 p.m., rescuers pulled a 15-year-old girl from the rubble of the building parking lot, the first survivor found in hours.

The girl was listed in critical condition late Wednesday.

See BLAST, Page 3

Inside

Weatherline ®
Call 478-3377 for local reports, forecasts.
Mostly cloudy skies are expected in the metropolitan area today, with a high temperature of 89 and a low of 47.
— Page 28

Tinker Air Force Base boosters speak in support of the Air Force's recommendations to shift work there.
— Page 6

One of two candidates withdraws his name in the search for a new Oklahoma City schools superintendent.
— Page 11

Features
Ann Landers 10	Prime Time 10
Billy Graham 10	Public Records 28
Bridge 48	Sports 29-36
Business 21-26	TV Log. 27
Classified 36-47	
Comics 48	**4 Sections**
Crossword 48	
Dear Abby 10	Delivery Service 478-7171
Editorial 8	Want Ads 475-3000
Entertainment 12	Other Calls 475-3311
Horoscope 10	
Markets 21, 23-26	Entire contents copyright 1995. The Oklahoma Publishing Co. Box 25125, Oklahoma City 73125, Vol. 104, No. 75.
Obituaries 28, 38	
Oil 22	

Prayer for Today

WHEN life gets weary, Lord, remind us to count our many blessings you give us every day. Thank you for helping to ease our fears or heartaches. Amen.

Terror in the Heartland

Coverage of the bomb blast and its aftermath is on Pages 4, 5, 7-9, 11-14, 21-22 and in a Special Section on Pages 15-20.

Fresh Day in City Turns Into New-Found Horror

By Penny Owen
Staff Writer

Oklahoma City will never be the same.

This is a place, after all, where terrorists don't venture. The heartland, people kept saying. Car bombs don't kill children here.

Wednesday changed everything. In an explosion felt at least 15 miles away,

the fresh, innocent morning turned to horror. In five seconds, witnesses said, floors at the Alfred P. Murrah Federal Building "cascaded on top of each other."

Those there drew all kinds of initial conclusions. A plane crashed. An earthquake hit. Armageddon.

Once the smoke cleared,
See QUESTIONS, Page 2

By 1995's end, the Daily Oklahoman *had run some 3,000 stories and 1,000 photographs related to the Oklahoma City bombing. The newspaper employs 140 full-time editorial staffers, and according to Managing Editor Ed Kelley, "Every single one of them got a piece of this story." Sports copy editors wrote headlines for news stories, and columnists pitched in to write profiles of those who died. "We decided from day one," said Kelley, "that our readers would judge us on how we treated the people who died, the people who were injured, and the families who were related to those who died." According to Kelley, from the outset the* Daily Oklahoman *tried to stake out the high ground, helping to establish a road map for how the tragedy should be covered as media from around the world flocked to the site.*

STATEMENTS BY THE PRESIDENT

On April 19, 1995, at 5:30 p.m. EDT, President Bill Clinton delivered the following statement to the capitol press corps in the White House briefing room.

The bombing in Oklahoma City was an attack on innocent children and defenseless citizens. It was an act of cowardice, and it was evil. The United States will not tolerate it. And I will not allow the people of this country to be intimidated by evil cowards.

I have met with our team, which we assembled to deal with this bombing. And I have determined to take the following steps to assure the strongest response to this situation:

First, I have deployed a crisis management team under the leadership of the FBI, working with the Department of Justice, the Bureau of Alcohol, Tobacco and Firearms, military and local authorities. We are sending the world's finest investigators to solve these murders.

Second, I have declared an emergency in Oklahoma City. And at my direction, James Lee Witt, the director of the Federal Emergency Management Agency, is now on his way there to make sure we do everything we can to help the people of Oklahoma deal with the tragedy.

Third, we are taking every precaution to reassure and to protect people who work in or live near other federal facilities.

Let there be no room for doubt—we will find the people who did this. When we do, justice will be swift, certain, and severe. These people are killers, and they must be treated like killers.

Finally, let me say that I ask all Americans tonight to pray—to pray for the people who have lost their lives, to pray for the families and the friends of the dead and the wounded, to pray for the people of Oklahoma City.

May God's grace be with them.

Meanwhile, we will be about our work. Thank you.

On April 21, 1995, at 4:05 p.m. EDT, President Bill Clinton addressed the capitol press corps in the White House briefing room before taking questions.

Good afternoon. First let me say how very proud I am of the swift and decisive and determined work of law enforcement officials on this case throughout the country. I know every American is proud of them, too. Their continued vigilance makes me sure that we will solve this crime in its entirety and that justice will prevail.

Today I want to say a special word of thanks to the Justice Department, under the able leadership of the attorney general, to Director Freeh and all the hundreds of people in the FBI who have worked on this case, to the men and women of the Bureau of Alcohol, Tobacco, and Firearms, to all the federal authorities, and to all the state and local enforcement officials, especially those in Oklahoma who have been working on this case. And, of course, I'd like to say a personal thanks, as I know all Americans would, to the Oklahoma lawman whose vigilance led to the initial arrest of the suspect.

As I said on Wednesday, justice for these killers will be certain, swift, and severe. We will find them. We will convict them. And we will seek the death penalty for them.

Finally, I know I speak for all Americans when once again I extend our deepest thanks to the brave men and women who are still involved in the rescue teams. Let us not forget them. There is a lot of work for them still to do. It is difficult and it is often heartbreaking now.

Our thoughts and prayers continue to be with the people in Oklahoma City. And let me say again: You will overcome this moment of grief and horror. You will rebuild. And we will be there to work with you until the work is done.

THE BOMB SITE

The impact of the explosion blew plate-glass windows out all along Northwest 23rd Street—some twenty blocks north of Ground Zero. Of the 168 victims, 163 were in the Alfred P. Murrah Federal Building, two at the Water Resources Board, one in the Athenian Building, one streetside, and one on-site after the bombing. The blast itself rocked buildings as far away as Guthrie, some thirty miles north.

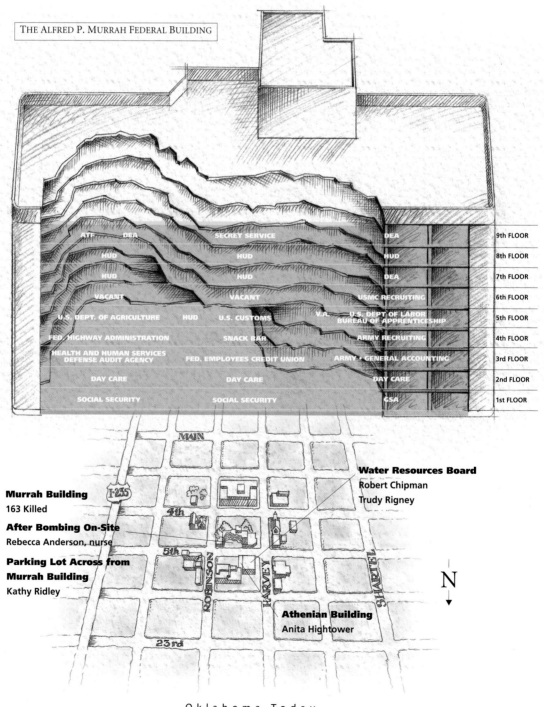

THE ALFRED P. MURRAH FEDERAL BUILDING

ATF	DEA	SECRET SERVICE	DEA	9th FLOOR
HUD		HUD	HUD	8th FLOOR
HUD		HUD	DEA	7th FLOOR
VACANT		VACANT	USMC RECRUITING	6th FLOOR
U.S. DEPT. OF AGRICULTURE	HUD	U.S. CUSTOMS	V.A.	U.S. DEPT OF LABOR BUREAU OF APPRENTICESHIP	5th FLOOR
FED. HIGHWAY ADMINISTRATION		SNACK BAR	ARMY RECRUITING	4th FLOOR
HEALTH AND HUMAN SERVICES DEFENSE AUDIT AGENCY		FED. EMPLOYEES CREDIT UNION	ARMY · GENERAL ACCOUNTING	3rd FLOOR
DAY CARE		DAY CARE	DAY CARE	2nd FLOOR
SOCIAL SECURITY		SOCIAL SECURITY	GSA	1st FLOOR

MAIN

Water Resources Board
Robert Chipman
Trudy Rigney

Murrah Building
163 Killed

After Bombing On-Site
Rebecca Anderson, nurse

Parking Lot Across from Murrah Building
Kathy Ridley

Athenian Building
Anita Hightower

N

PRESIDENTIAL PROCLAMATIONS

On April 20, 1995, President Bill Clinton signed the following presidential proclamation ordering that American flags be flown at half-mast; twenty-four hours later, he proclaimed Sunday, April 23, 1995, a national day of mourning in memory of those who died in the Oklahoma City bombing. On May 3, 1995, the president submitted to Congress the "Anti-terrorism Amendments Act of 1995," in which he asked for more legal tools and resources for law enforcement officials to fight terrorism.

LOWERING U.S. FLAGS
A Presidential Proclamation

On April 19, 1995, the Alfred P. Murrah Federal Building in Oklahoma City was brutally bombed in an appalling act of cowardice. As a mark of respect for those killed in the bombing, I hereby order, by the authority vested in me as President of the United States of America by section 175 of title 36 of the United States Code, that the flag of the United States shall be flown at half-staff at the White House and upon all public buildings and grounds, at all military posts and naval stations, and on all naval vessels of the Federal Government in the District of Columbia and throughout the United States and its Territories and possessions through Monday, April 24, 1995. I also direct that the flag shall be flown at half-staff for the same length of time at all United States embassies, legations, consular offices, and other facilities abroad, including all military facilities and naval vessels and stations.

IN WITNESS WHEREOF, I have hereunto set my hand this twentieth day of April, in the year of our Lord nineteen hundred and ninety-five, and of the Independence of the United States of America the two hundred and nineteenth.

A DAY OF MOURNING
A Presidential Proclamation

As we seek justice for the evil done in Oklahoma City on April 19, 1995, good and decent people everywhere mourn the loss of innocents. Our sons and daughters, parents and friends were stolen from us. Their families can never replace the gift of their laughter. Our nation can never replace the spirit of their character. But even as we grieve, we resolve today in solemn promise that those on earth shall never be bowed by murderous cowards. This sin against humanity shall not go unpunished.

It has been said that, "In every child who is born, the potentiality of the whole human race is born again." We lost unimaginable potential this past week. And we will miss our loved ones dearly. But the children who died in this violence may yet lift up humanity. We do them no greater honor than by taking from their deaths the memory of their hopes, by carrying with us always their dreams, their kind and trusting ways. We redeem the value of their lives no further than by heeding the voices of children everywhere, who ask simply and invariably for peace and love.

We take comfort in knowing that all who perished are in God's hands.

NOW, THEREFORE, I, WILLIAM J. CLINTON, President of the United States of America, by virtue of the authority vested in me by the Constitution and laws of the United States, do hereby appoint Sunday, April 23, 1995, as a National Day of Mourning throughout the United States. I ask the American people assembled on that day in their homes and places of worship to pay homage to the memory of those lost in the Oklahoma City tragedy and to pray for them and their community. I invite all those around the world who share our grief to join us in this solemn observance.

IN WITNESS WHEREOF, I have hereunto set my hand this twenty-first day of April, in the year of our Lord nineteen hundred and ninety-five, and of the Independence of the United States of America the two hundred and nineteenth.

A RESOLUTION FROM THE U.S. SENATE
104th Congress   *Senate Resolution 110*

WHEREAS, on Wednesday, April 19, 1995, a car bomb exploded outside the Alfred P. Murrah Federal Building in Oklahoma City, Oklahoma, collapsing the north face of this nine-story concrete building, killing and injuring innocent and defenseless children and adults;

WHEREAS, authorities are calling this the deadliest terrorist attack ever on United States soil;

WHEREAS, Federal law authorizes the imposition of the death penalty for terrorist murder; and

WHEREAS, additional anti-terrorism measures are now pending for consideration in the United States Senate: Now, therefore, be it

RESOLVED, That the Senate of the United States—

(1) condemns, in the strongest possible terms, the heinous bombing attack against innocent children and adults at the Alfred P. Murrah Federal Building in Oklahoma City;

(2) sends its heartfelt condolences to the families, friends, and loved ones of those whose lives were taken away by this abhorrent and cowardly act; and expresses its hopes for the rapid and complete recovery of those wounded in the bombing;

(3) applauds all those courageous rescue and volunteer workers who are giving unselfishly of themselves and commends all law enforcement officials who are working determinedly to bring the perpetrators to justice;

(4) supports the President's and the United States Attorney General's position that Federal prosecutors will seek the maximum penalty allowed by law, including the death penalty, for those responsible;

(5) commends the rapid actions taken by the President to provide assistance to the victims of the explosion and for promptly beginning an investigation to find the perpetrators of this crime, and it urges the President to use all necessary means to continue this effort until the perpetrators and their accomplices are found and appropriately punished; and

(6) will expeditiously approve legislation to strengthen the authority and resources of all Federal agencies involved in combating such acts of terrorism.

RESOLUTION OF THE OKLAHOMA LEGISLATURE

The following resolution was adopted by the Oklahoma House of Representatives on April 24, 1995; Three days later, it was adopted by the Oklahoma Senate. The resolution joined eight other resolutions and seven acts passed by the Oklahoma legislature dealing with the aftermath of the bombing—from victim compensation funds, to commendations for civil servants who participated in rescue and recovery efforts, to a concurrent resolution urging members of Oklahoma's congressional delegation to obtain any and all federal support possible to rebuild downtown Oklahoma City, to an act creating the Oklahoma Alfred P. Murrah Service Medal.

WHEREAS, on Wednesday, April 19, 1995, at 9:02 a.m., the Alfred P. Murrah Federal Building in Oklahoma City, Oklahoma, was the target of a cowardly terrorist bomb attack that virtually destroyed the building, damaged dozens of buildings in the downtown area, and killed or wounded hundreds of persons; and

WHEREAS, this attack on the very fabric of our national community is the worst bomb attack in the nation's history on American soil and has shocked, frightened, angered, bewildered, and saddened the citizens of Oklahoma and the United States; and

WHEREAS, despite our fear and emotions, hundreds of individuals almost instantly descended on the Murrah building to begin the urgent and arduous task of helping those who were injured and have continued their search efforts in the face of unspeakable horror and danger; and

WHEREAS, these heroes, which included law enforcement officers, state and federal military personnel, firefighters, search and rescue professionals, doctors, nurses, emergency medical technicians, medicolegal officials, office workers, and volunteers from throughout the country as diverse as our shared heritage; and

WHEREAS, the rescue effort continues as our entire nation continues its prayers that more of the victims of this blast will be found alive in the rubble and that the healing process for us all can begin; and

WHEREAS, as the magnitude of this attack has become clear, countless other everyday citizens continue to give of themselves, ensuring this cowardly, evil attack does not achieve its goal of planting dissension and fear in the United States; and

WHEREAS, people are donating their time, food, clothing, and money to relief organizations, donating blood to ensure the injured have a chance to recover, donating vital equipment to the search and rescue teams still combing the remains of the building for survivors and victims; and

WHEREAS, the list of individuals, organizations, churches, and businesses who have come together in one of the largest relief efforts in American history is virtually endless, encompassing the entire mosaic of people that is the United States; and

WHEREAS, the people of this state and nation have responded to unspeakable violence and cowardice with unsurpassed courage and compassion.

NOW, THEREFORE BE IT RESOLVED BY THE HOUSE OF REPRESENTATIVES OF THE FIRST SESSION OF THE FORTY-FIFTH OKLAHOMA LEGISLATURE, THE SENATE CONCURRING THEREIN:

That the Oklahoma Legislature hereby praises and commends the countless men, women, children, businesses, and organizations who have participated in the search, rescue, recovery, and relief efforts in the wake of the cowardly terrorist bomb attack on the Alfred P. Murrah building in Oklahoma City.

That the Oklahoma Legislature expresses its boundless admiration and deep gratitude, on behalf of all Oklahomans, to the countless men, women, children, businesses, and organizations who are coming together to provide comfort and compassion to the victims of this attack and their families.

That the Oklahoma Legislature hereby expresses its strong intent that this state will not be torn asunder by this cowardly, evil attack on the Alfred P. Murrah Federal Building.

That the Oklahoma Legislature expresses its deep sorrow for all those who have been harmed by the unconscionable act of these terrorists.

The Dade County, Florida, search and rescue team showed its continued support in many ways.

COMMENTS IN THE WORLD PRESS

The most chilling fact about the Oklahoma City bombing was that it struck children eating breakfast and playing in a day-care center one floor above the street. And the only way to respond to the ache the incident created is to clasp all surviving children tightly—even those thousands of miles from harm's way—and pour out a fearful love.

—Harrison Rainie
U.S. News & World Report

Pearl Harbor comes to mind. A sneak attack strikes like a cobra during a tranquil morning...This time the target is a federal building in Oklahoma City. Then there was an immediate declaration of war on a well-defined enemy, and Americans marched off to battle in droves. This time there is no clearly defined enemy, but Americans are once again in a mood to march to battle—this time against terrorists, whoever they may be.

—Norman A. Lockman
The (Wilmington, Del.) *News Journal*

They call it the Heartland, a cliche that claimed its truth at 9:02 one warm Wednesday morning when a nine-story concrete and marble government office building in a quiet midwestern city was ripped apart by a powerful explosion. To the millions of Americans who watched body after body borne from the wreckage—some of them so small that weeping firefighters couldn't bear to look down at what they so gently cradled—it seemed as if the heart of the nation itself had been sundered.

—George Howe Colt
Life Magazine

How much practice did it take to plan a human sacrifice? How many mornings had the killers sat outside that federal building, making judgments about where and when to park their bomb, which recipe to use, how to make sure that the full force of the blast hit the building square in the belly? And when the day finally came, the truck loaded and the time set, did they wait and watch the children go in, hand in hand with their parents, before they drove away?

—Nancy Gibbs
Time Magazine

The shattered building, its innards exposed to the camera; the black smoke; the confused people hastening, they hoped, away from danger; the bloodied bodies on the street; the crying babies; the agitated local reporters...Like the anchors, the Oklahoma officials who showed up periodically with more adjectives than news ("brutal, callous, vicious," said Governor Frank Keating) were reassuring presences. So, of course, was the President, who spoke to the country in the afternoon in the company of Attorney General Janet Reno. It was confirmation that matters were in hand and that all Americans were in this together.

—Walter Goodman
New York Times

Those inspired by the human drama of caring people working in the midst of the Oklahoma bombing should take comfort that society isn't defined by its maniacs but by its saviors.

—Barbara Reynolds
USA Today

"ALL I KNOW *IS* WHAT
I READ IN THE PAPERS"
—WILL ROGERS

One visiting tabloid reporter donned a priest's vestments to try to sneak into the church where distraught relatives of bombing victims were struggling with their losses. Another posed as a firefighter in an attempt to shoot video inside the ruined federal building as workers pulled bodies out from the rubble...Meanwhile, local Oklahoma City TV news reporters read homespun poems to calm their anxious viewers and skipped reading sports scores because they suddenly seemed frivolous. The local newspaper opened a hot line so readers would have some place to vent their sorrow. Something like a journalistic holy war was waged in Oklahoma City, pitting the nation's purveyors of sensationalist tabloid journalism against local TV and print reporters who staked out a higher moral ground.

—Howard Witt and Hugh Dellios
Chicago Tribune

IF IT CAN HAPPEN HERE...

OKLAHOMA CITY

MIKE SMITH
Las Vegas Sun, 1995
NORTH AMER SYND.

The homemade bomb that blew open the federal office building in Oklahoma City left hundreds dead or missing—and a nation feeling vulnerable. As rescue workers searched for signs of life, the FBI closed in on a suspect and several "material witnesses," leaving the rest of the country to ask how Americans could do such a thing.

—*Newsweek*

Those who perpetrate such unspeakable horror are sadly mistaken. They misread the human spirit and misinterpret the American psyche. We enjoy great comforts, especially in the heartland, but we are not so soft as to accept this sitting down. We have sharp, sometimes irreconcilable differences with each other, aired for all the world to see, but we are not so divided that we won't unite and defend each other to the death.

—*The Topeka* (Kan.) *Capital-Journal*

"We will not be cowed."

—*Los Angeles Times*

They came from the Valley of the Sun to climb a mountain of rubble, work in the shadow of death, and look for hope in the ashes. They came as strangers in our midst, but they leave as lifelong friends.

They came from California's capital city to Oklahoma's, toting dogs eager to sniff for warmth in our cold rains. They came from earthquake zones and hurricane country, some with memories of death and destruction still fresh. Others came as veterans of another downtown bombing, the one which telegraphed to America that terrorism had reached our shores.

From sea to shining sea, the rescuers came in waves—from Phoenix, Sacramento, south Florida, and New York; from Washington state, Southern California and the Bay Area; from Maryland and Virginia.

Hundreds more came on their own instead of in teams—firefighters from surrounding states and beyond. Lest we forget, many of the rescuers culling debris and bringing out the dead came from across town. For them, the dead could be a friend or a neighbor, a member of their church or softball team.

The rescuers were away from home just when their own families needed them most, when their kids sought hugs and reassurances. These men and women saw unspeakable horror here and found so few signs of life. But they became heroes in a city that suddenly discovered it is full of heroes.

As we rise from tragedy, these heroes are the wind beneath our wings.

Soon, the world's attention will shift from this place—but not entirely. Many will want to come see for themselves this icon of grief and recovery. But Americans from coast to coast won't have to travel far to touch someone who was here when we needed help.

As they return home, these heroes take our gratitude for their sacrifice. They moved a mountain for us. They wept with us. They experienced Oklahoma at its darkest, and yet its finest, hour.

We invite them all to return one day to experience our normalcy, to see our sights, to walk our streets, eat our food—and receive a hero's welcome.

—*The Daily Oklahoman*
April 26, 1995

WASSERMAN
©'95 BOSTON GLOBE
DIST. BY L.A. TIMES SYNDICATE

AND THE LETTERS CAME FROM AROUND THE WORLD

WE WENT TO Oklahoma City to assist with a horrible situation that centered on death and destruction, but we went home with a lesson in life and how a community should react to adversity.

Phoenix Fire Department
Urban Search & Rescue Team

I HAVE FOUND a new family—the citizens of Oklahoma City. I find myself constantly watching television for any news from Oklahoma City. I sit and cry, knowing my new family is dealing with such pain and anger. I did not want to leave Oklahoma and neither did any of the other members of the task force.

My thoughts and prayers will be with you always.

Jimbo Meagher
Virginia Task Force 2

AS A MOTHER, I think someone should enlarge all your photos of those beautiful and innocent children and paste them to the walls of the prison cells of the people responsible for this senseless and ignorant tragedy.

Janet Lukaswitz
Port Chester, New York

GOD BLESS YOU all. You are America at its best.

Jimmy and Marilyn Whitehead,
Wilmington, Delaware

I CAN'T TELL you how many tears I have shed. My heart goes out to all the victims' families. To those who did the bombing, may you burn in hell.

JoAnn Nelson
Longview, Washington

I CAN'T TELL you how much of a shock the April 19, 1995, bombing was to me here in Hawaii—because it targeted my fellow federal employees in my home state. I pray for God's mercies upon the survivors and the families of those who died in the explosion.

David Ware
Hawaii

NOT UNTIL I had my own child did I realize the magnitude of what it might be like to lose my most precious possession—an innocent child. I share the profound sadness of loss of all the mothers who can no longer hug their babies every day, and offer my condolences to every one of you.

Nancy Friedman-Margolin
New York City

THE BOMBING OF the federal building will be followed by calls for legislation. We should stand vigil against these. For while a crisis of this magnitude provides the enemies of liberty with opportunity, it also provides us with the opportunity to demonstrate that we are neither a rabble nor a mob, but a people.

David Rogers
Oklahoma City

WE ARRIVED IN the aftermath of the bombing equipped with camera crews, reporters, and many good intentions. Time and time again, we were overwhelmed by your hospitality, spirit, and invincible strength.

We are indebted to you for allowing us to intrude on your grief and for allowing us to share it...We will not forget you. You have set an example to the rest of America: That people can come together to overcome the worst of tragedies.

John Walsh
America's Most Wanted

A day after the bombing, this Bureau of Alcohol, Tobacco, & Firearms truck sits near the site.

WORDS TO REMEMBER

"This isn't American; this can't be America."
　　　　　　—Sam Gwynne, Austin bureau chief, *Time*

"There are places we have to crawl over bodies to get to other people. People are crying out to us. There are areas where we can reach through and try to touch their hands. There are some areas we can't get to at all."
　　　　　　—Jon Hansen, Oklahoma City
Fire Department
April 20, 1995
New York Times

"We believe in miracles. Pray for us, will you? Please."
　　　　　　—Oklahoman Kay Chisum
to *U.S. News & World Report*

"The most-asked question on April 19 was 'Why?' And all I could say was that I didn't know."
　　　　　　—an Oklahoma City chaplain
to *Life* Magazine

"The first thing I did was grab the phone and call her work number. And of course, there was no work number."
　　　　　　—Charles Stratton, on trying to contact his wife,
Dolores, a clerk in the federal building's army recruiting
office (she died in the blast)

"I've done this in Beirut, Somalia, Bosnia. The last thing you expect to do is come here."
　　　　　　—Tom Brokaw
NBC anchor

"We're having a real hard time getting them to take a break."
　　　　　　—A rescue team leader, speaking of rescue workers who had been on twelve hour shifts

"It's not Jerusalem. It's not Baghdad. It's not Bolivia. It's Oklahoma."
　　　　　　—Bombing survivor V.Z. Lawton

"They trusted the people walking around to leave things alone and they did. No one was picking up anything."
　　　　　　—Sundra Wiley-Everly, R.N.,
on bomb site security
Muskogee Daily Phoenix

"I've never been more emotionally distraught in my life. I keep finding more people who have done things to help or who have lost friends and loved ones."
　　　　　　—Ben Robinson, state senator
Muskogee Daily Phoenix

"...The terrorists, by choosing a heartland target, have made a strategic error. The pursuit will be relentless, the appetite for retribution overwhelming."
　　　　　　—Norman Lockman, syndicated columnist

"I saw things in there I wish I had never seen."
　　　　　　—Robert Buckner, Oklahoma City resident,
on the inside of the Murrah building

"The people don't have to stare at it anymore and see the heartache. Now it's only in the people's faces."
　　　　　　—Paula Lombard after the Murrah building
was demolished
May 24, 1995
The Daily Oklahoman

"We need to show the bomber that we're starting over, and we're going to be better."
　　　　　　—Rich Barnard after the Murrah building
was demolished
May 24, 1995
The Daily Oklahoman

"I think I'll go home and have a good cry."
　　　　　　—Dennis Garland after the Murrah building
was demolished
May 24, 1995
The Daily Oklahoman

"The loss you feel must not paralyze your own lives."
　　　　　　—Victoria Cummock whose husband died
on Pan Am 103
In Their Name

"When the explosion did come, it was no respecter of persons. The young and the old, the innocent and the guilty, the black and the white—all trapped in the rubble of life. And for a brief moment, you brought us together as a family. The lions and the lambs are lying together, and none are afraid as we seek peace in the valley."
　　　　　　—The Reverend Jesse Jackson
May 27, 1995
The Daily Oklahoman

"Through it all, make us better and not bitter. Let us learn something about ourselves and each other."
　　　　　　—The Reverend Jesse Jackson
April 27, 1995
The Daily Oklahoman

"You put it back together...You redo those people."
　　　　　　—5-year-old Peder Davis of Oklahoma City

Weary firefighters take a break from sifting through the rubble of the Alfred P. Murrah Federal Building.

EULOGIES AT THE MEMORIAL SERVICE

From the April 23, 1995, prayer service at the Oklahoma State Fair Arena in Oklahoma City.

By President Bill Clinton

Today our nation joins with you in grief. We mourn with you. We share your hope against hope that some may still survive. We thank all those who have worked so heroically to save lives and to solve this crime—those here in Oklahoma and those who are all across this great land and many who left their own lives to come here to work hand in hand with you.

We pledge to do all we can to help you heal the injured, to rebuild this city, and to bring to justice those who did this evil.

This terrible sin took the lives of our American family, innocent children in that building, only because their parents were trying to be good parents as well as good workers; citizens in the building going about their daily business; and many there who served the rest of us—who worked to help the elderly and the disabled, who worked to support our farmers and our veterans, who worked to enforce our laws and to protect us. Let us say clearly, they served us well, and we are grateful.

But for so many of you they were also neighbors and friends. You saw them at church or the PTA meetings, at the civic clubs, at the ballpark. You know them in ways that all the rest of America could not. And to all the members of the families here present who have suffered loss, though we share your grief, your pain is unimaginable, and we know that. We cannot undo it. That is God's work.

Our words seem small beside the loss you have endured. But I found a few I wanted to share today. I've received a lot of letters in these last terrible days. One stood out because it came from a young widow and a mother of three whose own husband was murdered with over 200 other Americans when Pan Am 103 was shot down. Here is what that woman said I should say to you today: "The anger you feel is valid, but you must not allow yourselves to be consumed by it. The hurt you feel must not be allowed to turn into hate, but instead into the search for justice. The loss you feel must not paralyze your own lives. Instead, you must try to pay tribute to your loved ones by continuing to do all the things they left undone, thus ensuring they did not die in vain."

Wise words from one who also knows. You have lost too much, but you have not lost everything. And you have certainly not lost America, for we will stand with you for as many tomorrows as it takes. If ever we needed evidence of that, I could only recall the words of Governor and Mrs. Keating: "If anybody thinks that Americans are mostly mean and selfish, they ought to come to Oklahoma." If anybody thinks Americans have lost the capacity for love and caring and courage, they ought to come to Oklahoma.

To all my fellow Americans beyond this hall, I say, one thing we owe those who have sacrificed is the duty to purge ourselves of the dark forces which gave rise to this evil. They are forces that threaten our common peace, our freedom, our way of life. Let us teach our children that the God of comfort is also the God of righteousness. Those who trouble their own house will inherit the wind. Justice will prevail. Let us let our own children know that we will stand against the forces of fear. When there is talk of hatred, let us stand up and talk against it. When there is talk of violence, let us stand up and talk against it. In the face of death, let us honor life. As St. Paul admonished us, let us not be overcome by evil, but overcome evil with good. Yesterday Hillary and I had the privilege of speaking with some children of other federal employees—children like those who were lost here. And one little girl said something we will never forget. She said we should all plant a tree in memory of the children. So this morning before we got on the plane to come here, at the White House we planted a tree in honor of the children of Oklahoma. It was a dogwood with its wonderful spring flower and its deep, enduring roots. It embodies the lesson of the Psalms—that the life of a good person is like a tree whose leaf does not wither.

My fellow Americans, a tree takes a long time to grow, and wounds take a long time to heal. But we must begin. Those who are lost now belong to God. Someday we will be with them. But until that happens, their legacy must be our lives. Thank you all, and God bless you.

By Governor Frank Keating

This arena holds at most a few thousand people, but today it contains the heart of a nation. We have come here in shared sorrow to grieve the loss of beloved neighbors, to honor brave comrades, to join our souls in close communion with God.

The tragedy of April 19th shocked America. Its unspeakable evil sickened the world. Never in the history of our country have Americans witnessed such senseless barbarism. It has been suggested that those who committed this act of mass murder chose us as their victims because we were supposedly immune—the heartland of America.

Well, we are the heartland of America. Today we stand before the world, and before our God, together—our hearts and hands linked in a solidarity these criminals can never understand. We stand together in love.

We have seen the terrifying images and read the heart-touching stories. Some of us have lived them: The firefighter clutching the body of a sweet, innocent child. The policeman reaching through rubble to grasp an outstretched hand. The volunteer stretcher bearers—some black, some white, some brown, all linked in courage and compassion—rushing aid to the wounded. The healers embracing life...the mourners lamenting death. The endless lines of donors and helpers and givers—giving their labor, their hopes, their treasure, their very blood.

Through all of this—through the tears, the righteous anger, the soul-rending sorrow of immeasurable loss—we have sometimes felt alone. But we are never truly alone. We have God, and we have each other.

Today we have our neighbors—some three million Oklahomans, and never have we drawn so close. There is something special about Oklahoma. We have always known that; now, so does America, and the world.

Today, we have our fellow Americans—from the power of our federal relief and investigative agencies to the prayers of millions. They will bring us justice as they have already brought us hope, and we will be forever grateful for this wonderful outpouring of love and support. Today we have our families—so

many of them torn by sorrow and hurt, but families still, strong through the generations, stronger yet through this terrible ordeal. Today we have our heroes and heroines—saints in gray and blue and white and khaki—the rescuers and the healers. They have labored long and nobly. And they have cried for us. Today we have our leaders: Mister President, Reverend Graham, we are moved by your presence. The warmth of our welcome may be dimmed by tears, but it is one of deep gratitude. Thank you for coming to touch our lives. Today we have our children—Oklahoma is still a young state, and our young people are very special to us. We have been brutally reminded of how precious they are by the events of the last few days. For them we reserve our warmest hugs and gentlest touch. Today we have our God. He is not a God of your religion or mine, but of all people, in all times. He is a God of love, but He is also a God of justice. Today He assures us once again that good is stronger than evil, that love is greater than hate, that each of us is His special child, embraced by the Father's love.

Our pain is vast. Our loss is beyond measure. We cannot fathom this act, but we can reach beyond its horrible consequences. The thousands of us gathered here today are multiplied by God's love, anointed by his gentle mercy. Today we are one with Him and with one another. It is right for us to grieve. We have all been touched by an immense tragedy, and our sorrow is part of the healing process. For some of us stricken with intense personal losses, it will be a long and tortured path. For all of us it is a journey through darkness. But darkness ends in morning light. That is God's promise, and it is our hope.

There is a lovely parable of a man who looked back on his life and saw it as an endless series of footprints in the sand. At times there were two sets of footprints, side by side, and he remembered these times as happy. At others there was but one set of prints—the times of sadness and pain.

He confronted God and asked why He had ceased to walk beside him when he most needed that support. Why, he wondered, had God abandoned him?

And God answered: But my son, those were the times I was carrying you. He carries us today, cupped gently in his loving hands.

Two mourners pay their respects during a memorial service on April 23, 1995, at All Sports Stadium in Oklahoma City.

Reverend Billy Graham at the Oklahoma State Fair Arena on April 23, 1995

THE PRAYER AT THE MEMORIAL SERVICE

Given by the Reverend Billy Graham on Sunday afternoon, April 23, 1995, at the state-wide prayer service at the Oklahoma State Fair Arena, Oklahoma City, Oklahoma.

No matter how hard we try, words simply cannot express the horror and the shock and the revulsion we all feel over what took place in this city last Wednesday morning. That terrible and senseless tragedy runs against the grain of every standard, every belief, every custom we hold as a civilized society, and the images of the devastation and human suffering we have seen here will be indelibly imprinted on each one of our minds and hearts as long as we live.

That blast was like a violent explosion ripping at the heart of America, and long after the rubble is cleared and the rebuilding begins, the scars of this senseless and evil outrage will remain.

But we come together here today to say to those who masterminded this cruel plot, and to those who carried it out, that the spirit of this city and this nation will not be defeated by their twisted and diabolical schemes. Someday the wounds will heal, and someday those who thought they could sow chaos and discord will be brought to justice as President Clinton has so forcefully and eloquently said. The wounds of this tragedy are deep, but the courage and faith and determination of the people of Oklahoma City are even deeper.

The Bible says in Psalm 147:3, "He heals the brokenhearted and binds up their wounds." And so with this service today we stand together to say: Let the healing begin!

But how do we understand something like this? How can things like this happen? Why does God allow this to take place?

Over three thousand years ago a man named Job struggled with the same questions. He was a good man, and yet disaster struck him suddenly and swiftly. He lost his seven sons and three daughters. He lost all his possessions. He even lost his health, his body covered with sores so unsightly that others could hardly recognize him. Even his wife and his friends turned against him.

In the midst of his suffering he asked, "Why?" "Why did I not perish at birth?" he cried out in his agony (Job 3:11). Perhaps that is the way you feel, and I want to assure you that God understands those feelings.

The Bible says in Isaiah 43:2, "When you pass through the waters, I will be with you...When you walk through the fire, you will not be burned: the flames will not set you ablaze." And yet Job found there were lessons to be learned from his suffering—even if he did not fully understand it. And that is true for us as well. What are some lessons we can learn from this tragedy? How do we understand it?

First, that it is a mystery. I have been asked on hundreds of occasions why God allows tragedy and suffering. I have to confess that I can never fully answer to satisfy even myself. I have to accept, by faith, that God is a God of love and mercy and compassion even in the midst of suffering.

I can remember many years ago lying on the dirt floor in a field hospital in Korea and looking up into the face of a soldier suspended in a frame who was horribly wounded, and asking myself, "Why?" I can recall standing at the bedside of children who were dying and asking, "Why?" I can recall walking through the devastation left by hurricanes in Florida and South Carolina and typhoons in India and earthquakes in Guatemala and California and asking myself, "Why?"

The Bible says God is not the author of evil, and it speaks of evil as a "mystery" (2 Thessalonians 2:7). There is something about evil we will never fully understand this side of eternity. But the Bible says two other things that we sometimes are tempted to forget. It tells us that Satan is real, and that "He was a murderer from the beginning" (John 8:44). And it also tells us that evil is real and that the human heart is capable of almost limitless evil when it is cut off from God and His moral law. The prophet Jeremiah said, "The heart is deceitful above all things and beyond cure. Who can understand it?" (Jeremiah 17:9).

That is one reason we each need God in our lives, for only He can change our hearts and give us the desire and the power to do what is right and keep us from wrong. Times like this will do one of two things: They will either make us hard and bitter and angry at God, or they will make us tender and open and help us reach out in trust and faith. I pray that you will not let bitterness poison your soul, but that you would turn in faith and trust to God, even if we cannot understand. It is far better to face something like this with God's strength than to face it alone and without Him.

But the lesson of this event has not only been about mystery, but a lesson of a community coming together. What an example Oklahoma City and the state of Oklahoma have been to the world these past few days! And the cooperation between officials of every level no matter what religious group we belong to or what our political views may be. None of us will ever forget the picture of a weary fireman tenderly cradling the body of a bloodstained infant or the picture of hundreds of people standing patiently in line to donate blood. The work of the Red Cross, the Salvation Army, and a host of other humanitarian organizations, as well as the emergency workers and the doctors and nurses, have inspired us and humbled us.

A tragedy like this could have torn this city apart, but instead it has united this city, and you have become a family. We have seen people coming together in a way we never could have imagined, and that is an example to us all. Hundreds if not thousands of prayer groups across the nation have arisen to pray for Oklahoma City. The forces of hate and violence must not be allowed to gain their victory, not just in our society, but in our hearts. Nor must we respond to hate with more hate. This is a time of coming together, and we have seen that and been inspired by it.

This tragedy also gives us a lesson in comfort and compassion.

The Search Goes On

We have seen an outpouring of sympathy and help not only in Oklahoma City but from all over the nation and the world. We have been reminded that a cruel event like this, which so vividly demonstrates the depths of human evil, also brings out the best in us of human compassion and sympathy and sacrifice.

But this can also teach us about God's comfort and compassion.

Some of you today are going through heartache and grief so intense that you wonder if it can ever go away. But I want to tell you that God cares, and the Bible says that He is "the God of all comfort, who comforts us in all our troubles" (2 Corinthians 1:3-4). Jesus said, "Blessed are those who mourn, for they will be comforted" (Matthew 5:4). I pray that every one of you will experience God's comfort during these days as you turn to Him, for God loves you, and He shares in your suffering.

Finally—difficult as it may be for us to see right now—this event gives us a message of hope for the present, and hope for the future. Yes, there is hope. There is hope for the present because I believe the stage has already been set for restoration and renewal in this city. I am not just talking about buildings that will be repaired and rebuilt. I am talking about a new sense of community and service to each other that will endure long after the memory of this event begins to fade.

Today let every American rededicate ourselves to a new spirit of brotherhood and compassion, working together to solve the problems and barriers that would tear us apart. But there also is hope for the future because of God's promises. As a Christian I have hope not just for this life, but for the life to come. Someday there will be a glorious reunion with those who have died and gone to Heaven before us. I believe that includes those innocent children whose lives were taken from us. I pray that you will have this hope in your heart.

This event also reminds us of the brevity and uncertainty of life. It reminds us that we never know when we too will be called into eternity. I doubt if even one of those people who walked into the federal building last Wednesday morning thought that it would be their last day on earth. That is why we each need to face our own spiritual need and commit ourselves to God and

His will now. It is ironic that this terrible event took place just three days after the churches in this city were filled with people celebrating Easter—just one week ago.

For the Christian, the cross tells us that God understands our suffering, for He took it upon Himself in the person of Jesus Christ. From the cross, God declares, "I love you, and I know the heartaches and the sorrows and the pain you feel." But the story does not end with the cross, for Easter points us beyond the tragedy of the cross to the hope of the empty tomb. It tells us that there is hope for eternal life, for Christ has conquered death. And it also tells us that God has triumphed over evil and death and hell. This is our hope, and it can be your hope as well.

I was deeply moved Friday night when watching Larry King talking to Edye Smith, who lost her two little boys in the explosion. Her brother, a twenty-eight-year-old police officer, was dispatched to the crime scene to help, and in searching the rubble found one of his nephews. The boys' grandfather is a Christian evangelist who said that conducting their funeral is the hardest thing he has ever faced but that his faith has been crucial in helping him through the tragedy. He quoted Romans 8:28, "And we know that in all things God works for the good of those who love him" and said that if that were the only verse we had in the Bible, we could work through all our problems in life if we believed it.

President and Mrs. Clinton will remember at the National Prayer Breakfast in Washington earlier this year, Andrew Young (who had just gone through the tragic death of his wife) closed his talk with a quote from the old hymn "How Firm a Foundation." The fourth verse says:

The soul that on Jesus hath leaned for repose
I will not. I will not desert to its foes;
That soul, though all hell should endeavor to shake,
I'll never, no, never, no, never forsake!

My prayer for you today is that you will feel the loving arms of God wrapped around you and will know in your heart that He will never forsake you as you trust Him.

A view to the north from the rubble-free Alfred P. Murrah building site

GOVERNOR'S SPEECH AT FLAG RAISING CEREMONY

On July 4, 1995, at 8:30 a.m., Governor Frank Keating, standing on the south steps of the state capitol in Oklahoma City, gave the order for flags across Oklahoma to be raised.

For the past seventy-six days, since the morning of April 20, 1995, flags have flown half-staff across Oklahoma in memory of those who died in the Murrah federal building bombing.

Today we restore our flags to their rightful place—proudly, as free men and women who will never bow to tyranny or terror.

Today we honor the brave and the caring—our rescue workers and our volunteers.

Today we remember those we lost—the innocent victims of this terrible act.

Today, as on every July 4 for 219 years, we celebrate American Independence. Independence Day has a special meaning for us this year. And so does our flag. In the days after April 19, that flag was once again a symbol of power and significance to so many Oklahomans. It flew from the damaged building. It shone proudly from the uniforms of firefighters and police officers. It draped the caskets of our victims. It adorned our homes, our places of work, and our hearts.

We have said so many heartfelt thank yous in recent weeks.

We have thanked the rescuers and the volunteers, as we will again today. We have voiced our love and gratitude to those from distant cities who came to our aid—and many of them have returned to be with us this morning. We have thanked our neighbors. There is a spirit and a closeness in our state and our community. Some say it emerged from tragedy. I say it was always there, and will always be there, because we are Oklahomans. We responded in the only way we knew how—with love and compassion and strength and dignity.

That is Oklahoma.

Much has been said of the way we responded to this terrible act. Those who came to us from across the nation marveled at our strength and our solidarity. They spoke of a new standard—the Oklahoma Standard.

We were not surprised. Oklahomans have always been capable of greatness. We showed our true nature to the world, and let the world take note: the days of pessimism and despair about Oklahoma are over. The spirit of April 19 was not an accident. It will carry us into the next century and make of Oklahoma what we always knew was possible. Good enough is no longer acceptable...we know we are capable of the very best.

Our Independence Day is a time for joy and celebration. This year, our joy is tempered by sorrow and our celebration is muted by the magnitude of our losses. But we do have cause for joy. We do have something to celebrate.

Our flag flies untarnished.

With us today are those who saved lives—and those whose lives were saved. And our system of justice—established by free people to assure their freedom—will bring to account those responsible for the bombing.

On a cold and rainy night in April, I had the honor of accepting, on behalf of the people of Oklahoma, the first American flag recovered from the ruins of the Murrah building. It was stained and it was torn—and it was beautiful. The rescuers who brought it out had tears in their eyes—but they also had pride. They knew what that flag symbolized. It stood for those who died in its service, for those who refused to bow to terror, for all that is good in our state and our nation.

In a few moments you will hear the songs of our nation. Listen to the words.

You will see the valiant rescuers. Thank them with your cheers.

You will see our flag. Honor it with your deepest gestures of respect.

Those songs, those valiant rescuers, that flag—they are one today as we remember 219 years of freedom—as we pledge once again, on this our day of Independence, that the beacon of liberty shall never, ever die.

The Oklahoma City National Memorial was dedicated on April 19, 2000, five years after the bombing.

Two visitors to the Oklahoma City National Memorial look at a remaining portion of the Alfred P. Murrah Federal Building. Remnants of the building were incorporated into the memorial's design.

HEALING HEARTS

As a new millenium dawns, the Oklahoma City

bombing becomes a distant but palpable memory.

J.D. MERRYWEATHER

G RIEF, CHILLING IN its emptiness, is among the most profound of our passages: necessary for transcendence but hol-
low in its manifestation. In the darkest hours, sorrow seems as if
it will exist forever. And perhaps, in many ways, it does.

In the aftermath of hell on earth, as 200 Northwest Fifth Street
instantly became on April 19, 1995, grief fully and unapolo-geti-
cally inserted itself into the national landscape. The physical and
emotional pain it caused was immeasurably deep and seemingly
impossible to overcome. We lost loved ones, and we lost innocence.
A black shroud hung heavy over the soul of a people, a city, and
a nation.

In time, for some, but not all, blackened hearts have yielded to
new warmth. Days upon days have brought bits of laughter and
a lighter gait. The choice to live fully has eventually overruled the
paralyzing inertia of anger and fear.

In a year already distinguished by the historic dedication of the
Oklahoma City National Memorial, *Oklahoma Today* chose to
revisit the aftermath of the bombing. In telling the rest of the
story—if there can ever be a final chapter—we examine the continuing lives of those most affected, the courtroom drama and
ensuing legal twists, and the memorial itself, a beautiful monument
to serenity, recovery, and hope. A public place for private, lingering
sorrow, the memorial stands as a powerful acknowledgement of
our collective grief.

In accepting the monstrous fate and insurmountable pain of
the Oklahoma City bombing, Oklahomans may now walk tall,
victorious and resilient, connected to the mystery and the wonder
of the world's ways. Survivors we are.

Louisa McClure

HUMBLE HEROES

THE MEN AND WOMEN OF
THE OKLAHOMA CITY FIRE DEPARTMENT

By Maura McDermott

Editor's Note: Oklahoma Today *named the Oklahoma City Fire Department its 1995 Oklahoman of the Year for courageous rescue and recovery efforts in the aftermath of the Murrah bombing.*

WE ARE NOT HEROES." The Oklahoma City firefighters tried to tell us this during the sixteen days they rescued the survivors and recovered the victims of the bombing of the Alfred P. Murrah Federal Building in downtown Oklahoma City. Firefighters tried to point out who they considered the real heroes of the tragedy. The innocent dead. The families of the victims. The survivors. The unnamed, untrained folks who ran into the building minutes after it fell to pull the shocked and bleeding out of the dust. The Red Cross and other volunteers. The police, emergency medical workers, doctors, nurses, soldiers.

As for why practically everyone but they were heroes, the explanation was simple: "We were doing our job." They were right. If the bombing was the biggest event in the history of the Oklahoma City Fire Department, it was also simply a more intense version of what firefighters deal with every day: scenes of destruction where some people are saved, others lost. It was one of about forty thousand calls or rides Oklahoma City firefighters take each year—to fires, to car wrecks, to heart attacks, to chlorine spills, to hot air balloons fallen out of the sky. "Anytime the light kicks on, we are expected to take care of it," says Corporal Rick Harris of Fire Station 1, located just five blocks from the site of the Murrah building. So, on the morning of April 19, 1995, Harris and others on the red shift at Station 1 took a ride to the worst terrorist attack ever on American soil.

Because of the magnitude of the attack, the world, however, insisted on thinking of the rescuers, especially the firefighters, as heroes. Figures in smudged helmets and baggy brown coats and pants, OKLA CITY in big block letters on their backs, appeared daily on our television screens and on the front pages of our newspapers. Mostly nameless, often faceless, they did tasks no one should ever have to do. From time to time one of these figures would take off his helmet and tell us a story—of carrying a lifeless infant into the light, of clutching a living hand sticking out of the rubble like a battered flower, of finding a toy fire truck among the fallen walls—and then go back to his work. They downplayed the dangers to their bodies and minds, but we knew better.

No matter how much they denied it, they were our heroes, symbols of sanity amid a landscape of madness. And of course we were right, too, if you define a hero as someone noted for feats of courage or nobility, as the dictionary does. Agreeing with the public, in September 1995, the International Association of Fire Chiefs awarded the Oklahoma City Fire Department the International Benjamin Franklin Fire Service Award for Valor. Usually given to an individual, the medal is the highest honor the fire service bestows. "I couldn't be prouder," says fire chief Gary Marrs of his firefighters. In a letter of commendation each firefighter received in June 1995, Marrs wrote, "You have shown this community and this country the best part of human nature: the willingness to help others in time of great need...You have proved that this is the best fire department in the nation."

THE WORKING LIFE

DINNER WAS READY. The firefighters working the red shift at Station 1 were about to load their plates with chicken fried steak, mashed potatoes, baby carrots, and black-eyed peas, when suddenly the overhead lights flashed brighter for an instant and a signal sounded. Instantly, firefighters jumped to attention. As the dispatcher ran through the address and the reported problem, four firefighters abandoned their plates and, just like in the movies, slid down poles to their truck. In the space of a minute, the rescue squad was making a ride—siren on, red lights flashing—down the quiet dinnertime streets to Pathways, a nearby residence for the mentally disabled. Over their heads, a Christmas tree shone in green lights on top of a downtown office building.

Carrying orange boxes of medical gear, the four bounded out of the truck and into the building and a room painted with a bright tropical scene of palm trees and pounding surf. A thin, gray-haired man sat alone at the end of the room, and though he was surrounded by palm trees, he was shaking as if frozen to the marrow. Drops of blood dotted the linoleum floor. The squad was all calm efficiency: pulling on gloves, taking the man's blood pressure and pulse rate, getting his medical records, questioning the staffer who had called 911. The sick man would not speak and could not stop shaking; before long, Rick Harris, the lead emergency medical technician on the call, gently strapped an oxygen mask across his face. A minute passed, and the man laid his head back and began to wail like a heartbroken dog on the end of a chain. Frightened, an onlooker began to cry. "These people know what they're doing," the staffer reassured her. "They're A number 1!"

Before long, EMSA arrived to take the man to the hospital, and the squad was able to leave this small scene of misery and return to dinner. Citywide, seventy percent of fire department calls involve medical emergencies. The squad stays busy, called out on the average about seven to nine times per twenty-four hour shift. In contrast, there were two fire calls that day. Be-

Oklahoma City firefighters work at the Murrah building site.

cause of better building codes, heating systems, and public education efforts by the fire department, the number of fires has gone down in the last twenty or so years, says Dick Miller, assistant fire marshal. Fire deaths, too, are way down, because of increased use of smoke alarms.

Consequently, firefighters these days have to do more than "put the wet stuff on the red stuff," or in laymen's parlance, put out fires. All firefighters know basic emergency medical techniques, and many have advanced skills. A special team at Station 5 handles the hazardous materials (there were four hundred HAZMAT calls last year), and a special team at Station 8 specializes in underwater rescue. Some firefighters have also trained in the techniques of confined space rescue and high angle rescue (using ropes)—both critically in need in the Murrah building rescue. Firefighters with specialized training are scattered among the city's thirty-five fire stations. "We've tried to evolve into a full-service organization," says assistant

fire chief Kenneth Bunch. His firefighters have to be prepared for everything, because, as Bunch explains, "In the majority of incidents, we roll up and don't know what it is."

Today there are one thousand firefighters in Oklahoma City, up by about two hundred in the last five years. They ought to borrow "the few, the proud" slogan from the marines, because competition for a spot in the fire academy is fierce—for each class of twenty, twenty-five hundred have applied. After written and physical exams and an interview, the chosen go through sixteen weeks of training and then a year of probation.

This is a far cry from thirty years ago, when Dick Miller became a water squirter. After a rudimentary screening process, he was on the job a month before acquiring any formal training. His first day was memorable: Just as the station officer was about to sound a test alarm so Miller would know what to expect, a real alarm went off. The officer said, "That's it—jump on," and Miller did, one arm stuffed in his coat sleeve, the

In most instances, firefighters arrive on the scene with no clue as to what they will find there.

other holding onto the rescue squad truck for dear life. Upon arrival at the fire scene, "I had no idea what to do," he recalls. He learned by watching the old hands. Those were the days of the mighty smoke eaters, firefighters with leather lungs who regularly entered burning buildings without air masks and usually came out—tops of ears sizzling, tips of the fireman's trademark mustache singed—to tell the tale. The long-term results, however, were not so inspiring: high rates of lung and heart disease caused by smoke exposure.

The days of naked heroics are over. Firefighters still enter burning buildings, but they must wear a breathing apparatus similar to what scuba divers use. They are clothed in bunker gear made of space-age fabrics that protect at temperatures of more than 800 degrees, whereas the smoke eater made do with cotton or polyester. Hazardous materials teams wear even more specialized protective gear nicknamed "moon suits." The safety upgrades extend to the fire trucks: Firefighters ride inside now, and there are doors on the cabs. These days chain saws have replaced axes, and even computers have infiltrated the stations.

Despite the modern accouterments, a day at the fire station is still a mix of routine and excitement, as it always has been. Shifts are twenty-four hours long and start at 7 a.m. First thing, firefighters check all their equipment and apparatus, clean the station, and do stretching exercises together. They eat breakfast together, too—firefighters at Station 1 take turns fixing meals and draw for cleanup chores. Each day brings a mandatory two hours of school in fire or rescue techniques at the fire station, or alternatively, practice sessions of fire or rescue tactics, sometimes with other companies. Fire companies also make safety inspections and draw up prefire plans of businesses in their districts as well as test each of the city's ten thousand fire hydrants each year.

These activities are in addition to calls. Despite busy schedules, the camaraderie remains strong. Twenty-four-hour shifts make the firehouse more like a second home than a place of employment. The atmosphere inside is jovial, and practical jokes abound; firefighters at Station 1 liken it to summer camp or a slumber party. The enthusiasm for the job gets passed down; firefighters often follow in their father's or uncle's or cousin's footsteps. Chief Marrs himself is a third-generation firefighter.

The allure of the shiny red fire engine, it seems, is hard to resist. And while the modern firefighter may be a renaissance man (or woman), expected to know how to both comfort the hurt and clean up toxic chemical spills, down deep what really gets his or her heart pumping is a good, working fire. Despite the risks, or perhaps because of them, fighting fires is a thrill. Lieutenant Tommy Phillips of Station 1 compares fighting a fire to taking a roller coaster ride. "When you kick in the front door, it's scary," he says. Inside a burning building, it is usually pitch-black with smoke-filled air, and it can be difficult to locate the fire. Fires are also unpredictable—at one moment

On-duty firefighters respond to more calls for Emergency Medical Services situations than fire-related scenes.

apparently tamed, the next, springing on you like a wildcat. But after the fire is out and everyone is safe, he explains, euphoria follows: "You're jumping up and down, hooting and hollering, 'Let's do it again!'" Such moments, he says, make firefighting "the best job in the world."

The flip side to the adrenaline rush, however, is how hard it can be to turn it off—especially for rookies. A case in point: Fire alarms used to be accompanied by a distinctive click, which sounded just like the click of an electric light switch, says eighteen-year veteran Oliver Moore of Station 1. This made an afternoon nap on days off nearly impossible; with the flip of a switch in the next room, a firefighter was up and running (the solution was installing silent switches). The longer a firefighter, on the other hand, the harder it is to get the adrenaline flowing—especially in the dead of night, when the firefighter has to go from "gumbyland" to "full-tilt boogie," as one firefighter put it, ready to rush into a burning building or aid a heart attack victim. One older firefighter confesses to having awakened at the wheel halfway to a call.

Psychological strain adds to the pressure. On Captain Nathan Shipman's first day on the job, he was faced with a mother who had just strangled her child. Firefighters see things that make it hard to come back and eat dinner, no matter how good the firehouse cook. The stress takes its toll: Firefighters reportedly have higher than average rates of divorce and suicide. While once they tried to cope by holding emotions in, during the last few years, the macho approach shows signs of going the way of leather helmets. Even old-timers like twenty-eight-year veteran David Bowman have embraced talking it out. The new attitude, Bowman hopes, will keep young firefighters from quitting and others from taking early retirement, maybe even keep marriages intact as well.

While talking is a good strategy for coping with the horrors of the job, it cannot beat the boost that comes from actually saving someone's life. And rescuers often forge strong emotional bonds

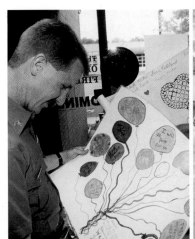

Above, from left to right, Firefighter Brian Arnold smiles at a child's card; John Williams, Carl Glover, Bob Edwards, Tim Farmer, and Ed Koch at work; police sergeant John Avera, Baylee Almon, and Chris Fields on April 19, 1995. Opposite page, Major Homer Jones has been with the fire department since 1987.

with those they rescue. Oliver Moore and other firefighters from Station 1 went to the hospital to visit bombing survivors they helped rescue on April 19, 1995, including a seriously injured man Moore found in an alley pinned under pieces of the Journal Record Building roof. "I needed to see that he made it," Moore explains. "It helped me out a lot." Echoes Harris, "If you can help somebody, that's about as good as it gets."

MAKING A DIFFERENCE

NINETEEN EIGHTY-NINE WAS A pivotal year for the Oklahoma City Fire Department. In retrospect, one can see that the events of that year prepared the department for what was to be its greatest challenge thus far, the rescue and recovery at the Oklahoma City bombing.

Nineteen eighty-nine was also the department's centennial. In 1889, the department began as a volunteer bucket brigade. Its first piece of apparatus was an old beer wagon equipped only with ladders and buckets, pulled by hand to fires. By 1891, finances had improved to the point that two horses, Babe and Jumbo, were purchased to do the pulling. Firemen were justly proud of their horses, who reportedly could distinguish the ring of the fire phone from the local phone and were always in place before the firemen had time to slide down their poles.

The horses did some heavy work—including hauling a 1907 water tower, a platform that extended sixty-five feet into the air. But by 1910 the department had its first piece of motorized equipment—a dazzling white chemical and hose truck with fancy gold lettering, complete with a perfect silver bell in front (now on display at the Oklahoma Firefighters Museum in Oklahoma City, a toy dalmatian in the driver's seat). Over the years, the citizens of Oklahoma City consistently passed bond issues and sales taxes to modernize and expand the fire department. By 1951 the department counted twenty-two stations and five hundred gallon per minute engines; by 1971, the

number of stations had reached thirty, and the engines were pumping a thousand gallons per minute.

Along with equipment changes came social changes. The first black firemen were hired in 1951, and their station, Number 6, subsequently earned the most efficient station award three years in a row. Firemen became firefighters in the mid 1980s with the hiring of the first women (today there are about twenty-five in Oklahoma City). By its centennial in 1989, the OCFD was a thoroughly modern department with a good safety record. Though eleven firefighters had been killed responding to or battling fires since 1911, the last had been Dan McQueen, who died in 1950 while battling a lumberyard blaze.

The department's fortunes, however, were about to change at a modest one-story frame house in southwest Oklahoma City. On March 8, 1989, a four year old playing with a stick in an open flame heater started a fire. Before it was extinguished, three firefighters—Jefferey Lindsay, Bennie Zellner, and Jimmy Ayers—were killed in a flashover, a fireball created when flammable gases become superheated and explode into flame. The fire, which reached temperatures approaching 1000 degrees, was so intense it burned away the men's protective clothing and breathing apparatus.

The death of the three was a shock to the whole department. The trauma prompted the later formation of the peer counseling groups called Critical Incident Stress Debriefing (CISD) teams, which proved to be so helpful during the long Murrah rescue. Firefighters on the teams provide a sympathetic ear and advice on how to recognize symptoms of posttraumatic stress disorder and what to do about it. The CISD teams enabled firefighters to hold on to their humanity during the sixteen-day Murrah ordeal, writes assistant fire chief Jon Hansen in his 1995 book *Oklahoma Rescue*. Bowman suspects the mandatory sessions might be why OCFD firefighters are coping better than some predicted.

While the department was recovering emotionally after the fatal house fire, community leaders stepped forward. They began a petition drive to put a new sales tax referendum for the department on the ballot. Two months before the fatal fire, a similar tax proposal had been defeated by 105 votes. The petition drive was successful, as was the vote, and the subsequent increase of three-fourths of a cent was split between the police and fire departments.

Hansen is still emotional about the deaths of the three firefighters; he was on the scene and comforted Jefferey Lindsay's brother, Mike, who was fighting the fire when his brother died. "Those three guys gave their lives for the community," he says, "and the community repaid them by passing the tax." Firefighters would later credit the sales tax as a crucial variable in the department's successful handling of the Murrah rescue. The sales tax revenue bought new equipment, engines, and other vehicles, including a 135-foot ladder truck, the only ladder long enough to reach survivors in some parts of the Murrah building. Perhaps most importantly, the tax bought new firefighters, making possible the dual manning of fire stations and the bombing recovery effort. "Those three guys were with us in that building," says Hansen. "They made a difference."

THE OKLAHOMA STANDARD

THE OKLAHOMA CITY FIRE Department began as a bucket brigade in 1889, so perhaps it is fitting that in the department's finest hour, it again embraced the lowly bucket—this time not as a vessel for water, but for rubble. This is not the kind of work that earns you a cover photo on *People* magazine, but it was essential: Hundreds of firefighters, working in teams, removed by hand some 450 tons of the shattered Murrah building, while what remained of the building shifted and swayed in the wind. While the process was tedious, firefighters derived satisfaction from watching the rubble pile slowly shrink. "We felt like we accomplished a feat that hasn't been done anywhere else in the U.S.," recalls Bowman.

The rubble was removed in order to recover the dead, a labor of love and duty that the Oklahoma City Fire Department took upon itself. By May 4, 1995, all but three of the 168 victims of the bomb—those buried near a dangerously unstable support column of the Murrah building—had been recovered, and the recovery effort ended. The rescue had begun sixteen days earlier when squads, engines, and trucks from a number of stations dispatched themselves to the bomb site; before long, Chief Marrs ordered a general alarm—calling in all on-duty units and the off-duty shifts—the first in the history of the city. By the end of the first day, all of the survivors trapped in the building had been rescued, with the Oklahoma City Fire Department having a hand in nearly all of the rescues.

In an initial report analyzing the rescue operation, investigators from the International Fire Protection Association gave the department high marks for speedy recovery of survivors (most were rescued in the first hour and a half). They praised firefighters for making decisions that "were almost universally correct and were instrumental in saving lives—which reflects well on the level of training and preparedness of the companies and command officers." They also praised the department for its safety precautions. Save for Rebecca Anderson, a nurse who died of head injuries after hurrying to the site to help, the firefighters were able to prevent other serious injuries among the hundreds of rescuers despite extremely dangerous conditions. And as help from around the state and country poured in to downtown Oklahoma City, it fell to the Oklahoma City Fire Department to coordinate the extensive rescue and subsequent recovery operation. "It was a learning experience for all of us," says Hansen, who points out that the effort was marked by exceptional cooperation between a large number of local, state, and federal agencies. This high level of cooperation has since been dubbed "the Oklahoma standard" by Federal Emergency Management Agency (FEMA) officials.

The department's successful management of the rescue effort earned it new respect. In 1996, Marrs and assistant fire chief Bunch gave a presentation at a conference in Virginia attended by fire officials from such terrorism hot spots as Tokyo, Israel, and France. Bunch confesses that prior to April 19, 1995, they probably would have never attended such a conference. Still, these days Marrs finds himself fielding calls from other chiefs impressed by the way his department handled the bombing and curious about how they run other programs. One telling observation: They are never content. Despite accolades that would make a sailor blush, Marrs and the department continue to look for even better ways to be prepared for the worst that might hit their city, whether the disaster be natural or manmade. Plans call for the department to add specialized search and rescue teams, modeled after the urban search and rescue teams that flew in to help at the Murrah building.

Marrs has also made community involvement a high priority. Soon firefighters may be attending neighborhood meetings, teaching CPR classes in the station, and working with businesses and community groups to prevent arson fires. The public education staff has already been beefed up. Two large-scale public education programs target children, who are responsible for fifty percent of reported arson fires and a million dollars worth of damage each year. These same children are often victims of the fires they set.

Many kids who set fires do so simply because they are curious, says Major Sheila Hays, who is part of a particularly innovative program called Operation FireSAFE. Matches and lighters (which Hays compares to loaded handguns) are left out, and children experiment. But about forty percent of child arsonists are children in crisis. Hays' job is to interview children who set fires, conduct a fire safety program with them, and if need be, refer them to a mental health professional who decides if they need further help.

Hays was the second woman in the department to perform firefighting duties, and during the five years she worked on the rigs, she went through some tough times proving that she could

Assistant fire chief Jon Hansen became a common sight after the bombing; later in 1995 he penned a book, Oklahoma Rescue, *chronicling the fire department's rescue efforts at the Murrah building.*

do the job. But listening to the stories some children tell, she says, is every bit as hard on her emotionally.

Some of the children she interviews have been abused physically or sexually. One little girl used fire as a way to stop family violence. Knowing someone would call the fire department, the six year old set fires whenever her father began beating her mother. Hays contends that troubled children who play with fire don't stop until an intervention, and she is proud that her program has achieved a low recidivism rate of fifteen percent. "As a fire department we want to stop that fire-setting behavior, but we also want to help the child as a whole," she says. "We're talking about a better community, a better society."

THE REAL HEROES

SHORTLY BEFORE CHRISTMAS, Amy Petty kept a promise she made on April 19, 1995, to four firefighters from Oklahoma City's Station 8. The men formed the core of a group who worked for five hours to dig her out of a black hole of mangled office furniture, concrete, electrical wire, and rebar, while a refrigerator dangled in the air over their heads and cantaloupe-sized chunks of concrete fell around them. Petty couldn't see the four (Allen Hill, Christopher Thompson, Mike Roberts, and Vernon Simpson) who would eventually free her, but she could talk to them and listen to them discuss the problems to be overcome. "I could tell it wasn't an easy thing," she recalls.

It wasn't. At 9:02 a.m., Petty had "taken a slide," in rescue parlance; that is, she fell from the Federal Employees Credit Union on the third floor to what had been the ground floor of the building. After that split-second descent into what must have seemed like hell, Petty at times was terrified. She would say, "I'm going to die, aren't I?" recalls Hill, and he would promise her, "No, Amy, you're not going to die." At other times throughout the ordeal, everyone did his best to keep the conversation light; in one such attempt, Petty said, "Well, I guess when I get out of here, I'll owe you guys a cup of coffee," to which she got the reply: "Well, I sure do like chocolate chip cookies," and then after a pause, another voice cracked, "I like chocolate chip cookies and

beer." Petty recalls laughing and saying she could probably handle the cookies.

But it was awhile before she felt she could handle seeing the firefighters and talking about what had happened to her on April 19. Finally, two kinds of chocolate chip cookies in hand and husband in tow, she walked into Station 8. "It was so wonderful to meet and talk to them," says Petty. "She looked a lot different," jokes Hill. Looking at pictures of where she had landed, Petty was filled with gratitude. "Tons of people," she says, helped to free her, but she feels especially grateful for these four—they risked staying with her during the second bomb scare (she was left alone during the first), and they made the right decisions, she says, hard choices about what to cut and what to move that eventually freed her. "I really do owe my life to them," she says. "I will always support that fire station."

"The citizens of this community have been behind us for a long time," comments Hansen, but even he was surprised by the outpouring of support in the days following the bombing. Ten thousand volunteers had arrived by Friday, he says with amazement—and there would have been more had radio and television stations not urged folks to stay away. "I couldn't go anywhere without being offered a drink or a meal," he says. Donations of food also flooded fire stations. In fact, he believes many firefighters actually gained weight during the rescue. At a final meeting for volunteers, Chief Marrs summed up the department's attitude: "From the men and women of the Oklahoma City Fire Department, we love you and thank you very much."

The feeling was mutual. Messages poured in from around the world: almost two hundred thousand pictures, posters, banners, signs, wreaths, paper chains, and, of course, letters, many of them illustrated with hearts and rainbows and flowers. Most were from children. "Dear heroes," many of them began. "I love you," many of them ended. The children who wrote seemed to be able to bore right to the heart of the experience. One child from Waco, Texas, wrote: "I think y'all are the bravest people on earth. It must take lots of courage to go into a building that had just been bombed." Another letter, neatly typed on a computer from a sixth grader in Wisconsin, addressed the firefighters of Station 1: "I can't even imagine how sad it was to see all those hurt people. I hope you can get over this terrible incident. When I grow up I would like to be a firefighter just like all of you."

Little did the children realize that their hope and faith was fuel desperately needed by the men and women in yellow, as it became ever more clear that what had started out as a rescue effort was fast becoming an effort to retrieve the dead. "The kids were the ones," says Hansen, "who helped us keep our faith in a situation that could have sent us into the depths of despair." The missives greeted rescuers as they ate and rested and were

Clockwise from top, Firefighters and other rescuers removed by hand some 450 tons of shattered building; Amy Petty brings cookies to rescuers Vernon Simpson, Allen Hill, Christopher Thompson, and Mike Roberts.

distributed around to the fire stations. At Station 1, firefighters plastered the usually spartan station walls with the colorful letters. At Station 31, Lieutenant Gary Thurman found that he couldn't get enough of the letters. Thurman, though off duty, had arrived at the Murrah building early on. The scene was surreal—at one point he found himself sitting down waiting for help to remove four victims when hundred dollar bills began raining down around him; not long after, he noticed "the baby doll with blood all over it, the teddy bear, a little tricycle," and it dawned on him he was near the daycare area.

After the rescue was over, Thurman says he had a nagging feeling that there was something left for him to do. He also worried that firefighters, anxious to get back to normal, would set aside the letters and might eventually throw them away. He shared this concern with Monte Baxter, who had entered the Murrah building within a few minutes of the explosion. Baxter had already retrieved some of the mail from a station dumpster. The mail had historical significance, Thurman believed, and should perhaps become part of the planned bombing memorial.

So Thurman took it upon himself to load everything up. It took three trips in his van to gather items at the Myriad Convention Center, where rescuers had been fed and housed and cheered by the letters; then he made a sweep of the fire stations. In the end he filled up a two-car garage and a spare bedroom in his house. "It was overwhelming," confesses Thurman. He and retired firefighter Harold Colbert nevertheless dug in, laughing and crying over the precious messages. "It's letters from kids that make you appreciate your job," Thurman says. "I wasn't throwing nothing away."

He noticed that many of the cards asked firefighters to write back, and he was eager to do it. But how? Help came from the Oklahoma Historical Society. Archives director Bill Welge rounded up volunteers to sort the items by state and compile a list of names and addresses. On December 1, 1995, the fire department's public education office unveiled its "Answering the Call" campaign. A line drawing of a firefighter holding a teddy bear (taken from a photo of Thurman) illustrates the reply cards and envelopes sent out to fire stations along with the first thousand of about fifty thousand names OHS was able to compile. The program is voluntary, but Thurman, who has written almost two hundred letters thus far, is optimistic his fellow firefighters will take time to write some thank yous. "We will be the first fire department to write back the world," he predicts. For Thurman, a soft-spoken nineteen-year veteran, the letters have already worked their magic, leading him away from the horror of the Murrah building. "The letters woke me up and made me feel good about life again," he says. "There is more good out there than people realize."

Maura McDermott of Checotah is a contributing editor for Oklahoma Today.

AFTER TWO FEDERAL TRIALS,
JUSTICE PREVAILS.

By Julie DelCour

AP/WIDE WORLD PHOTOS/MICHAEL CAULFIELD

IT BECAME A ritual. A few minutes before 9 a.m. each day, Roy Sells arrived in the Denver courtroom, always taking the same seat next to the wall at the end of a particular row. Pressed against a wooden bench that never got softer on his back, Sells listened to evidence that never got easier on his heart, as first one trial and then another unfolded for two men whose crimes had left him a widower.

Sells never missed a day of testimony in the 1997-98 proceedings for Timothy McVeigh and Terry Nichols, which, at various points, were covered by 130 news organizations numbering 2,500 employees from six continents.

Sells was there when McVeigh's trial began on March 31, 1997. Security was tight, with concrete barriers snaking around a federal complex that covered an entire city block. Bomb-sniffing dogs, armed city police, federal marshals, security officers, and mounted patrols were a constant presence. Only a limited number of spectators were allowed in the courtroom.

The trial lasted ten weeks, with the prosecution calling 162 witnesses and the defense calling 52. Almost five hundred exhibits were introduced, including everything from the controversial *Turner Diaries: A Novel*, which prosecutors said was the blueprint for the bombing, to a ten-foot Ryder truck axle and a miniature model of the six-block crime scene.

Opposite page, Stephen Jones, center, defense attorney for Timothy McVeigh, is surrounded by members of the media outside the federal courthouse in Denver on May 29, 1997, prior to closing arguments in the McVeigh trial. Above, La-Donna Battle, right, and Cindy Flenniken, left, embrace Jannie Coverdale as they leave the federal courthouse after hearing the guilty on all counts verdict in the trial of Timothy McVeigh.

On June 2, 1997, jurors returned with a guilty verdict on eleven first-degree murder, conspiracy, and weapons charges. In anticipation of the verdict, the streets and sidewalks near the courthouse were lined with citizens standing shoulder to shoulder to hear the outcome. The punishment stage of the trial ended eleven days later, on a Friday the thirteenth, with a death verdict.

Sells sat through the fifteen-week Nichols trial, which began that fall. Jurors delivered a verdict two days before Christmas that victims found both confusing and heartbreaking. Jurors had found Nichols guilty of the bombing conspiracy but acquitted him of blame for the actual attack. He also was convicted on eight counts of involuntary manslaughter in the deaths of eight law enforcement agents but was cleared of first and second-degree murder charges. In the punishment phase, United States District Judge Richard P. Matsch took the case away from jurors at the beginning of a third day of deliberations because they could not agree on Nichols' sentencing. With the case out of the jurors' hands, Nichols could no longer receive a death sentence. It would be up to Matsch to decide on a sentence of life imprisonment or less.

Almost six months later, on June 4, 1998—the day that Matsch gave Nichols a life sentence, the harshest punishment allowable for the earlier verdict—Sells arose from his seat and left the courtroom forever, having attended all of what were called "the trials of the century."

Outside on the courthouse plaza, his voice firm against a mountain wind, Sells emphasized that he had not spent all that time in the courtroom for vengeance. "I was in there for justice, and I think justice was served."

Now Sells, along with so many other Oklahoma City bombing victims, waits and wishes for justice again. In this newly minted millennium, they prepare for yet another "trial of the century."

This trial will deal with unfinished business. Oklahoma County District Attorney Bob Macy hopes that an Oklahoma jury will do what one Colorado federal jury did with confidence against McVeigh but what a second jury could not do against Nichols—impose the death penalty.

That case began March 29, 1999, only days after McVeigh's death sentence had been upheld by the U.S. Supreme Court. With Nichols' federal appeals still pending, Macy filed 160 counts of first-degree murder and three lesser charges against him.

"I promised a lot of people that I would see to it that whoever committed this crime would be held accountable," Macy said in March 1999. "I'm trying to keep my word."

Macy's decision to seek a state trial for Nichols, forty-five, unleashed a torrent of criticism, with polls suggesting that most Oklahomans were against it. Legislators, complaining about the exorbitant cost, threatened to withhold funds. Victims appeared divided. Some, insecure over the outcome of Nichols' federal appeals, agreed that a state trial was needed. Others, such as Bud Welch, a vocal death penalty opponent, argued that the trial would be an emotional drain and a financial waste.

"There are so many of us who are trying to go forward," Welch, who lost his daughter, Julie, in the blast, told the *Daily Oklahoman* in March 1999. "We're trying to build a memorial. We've got the dirt turning down there. We're getting ready to pour the foundations for the gates. We're making progress. We're trying to go forward. And this damn state trial is not going to do anything but set all of us back."

Undaunted, Macy pressed ahead, personally ironing out security concerns with U.S. Attorney General Janet Reno over Nichols' return to Oklahoma from a maximum-security prison in Florence, Colorado.

Finally, on a cold winter night, federal marshals flew Nichols to Oklahoma City, arriving at 1:10 a.m. on January 31, 2000. He was escorted by a caravan of seven patrol cars to the Oklahoma County jail, where he remains, checked every fifteen minutes by deputies and isolated in a 108-foot-square cinder block cell with a video camera on the door.

Meanwhile, McVeigh, thirty-two, is held on federal death row in Terre Haute, Indiana. His second appeal, which claimed juror misconduct and ineffective assistance of counsel, despite an estimated $15 million defense, was rejected by Judge Matsch on October 12, 2000. Pending further review, an execution date will be set. (The last federal execution, a hanging, took place in 1963.) His appeals have moved rapidly because of a 1996 law, pushed by bombing victims, that shortens the appeals process for federal inmates.

A third figure in the bombing case, government star witness Michael Fortier, thirty-two, continues to battle a twelve-year sentence originally imposed in May 1998 and later set aside by the Tenth Circuit U.S. Court of Appeals. Fortier was resentenced

in October 1999. He appealed, claiming a judge was vindictive, had used an improper sentencing guideline, and had abused his discretion in reimposing the same sentence.

Fortier, an army buddy of McVeigh's, pleaded guilty to failing to warn authorities of plans to bomb the Alfred P. Murrah Federal Building, lying to FBI agents in the aftermath of the bombing, and helping McVeigh move and sell stolen weapons, whose proceeds, prosecutors claimed, later were used to finance the bombing. At issue is whether Fortier knew the proceeds would be used in a crime resulting in deaths. Last September, one judge in a three-member federal appeals court panel hearing oral arguments said that Fortier may have been resentenced incorrectly and too severely. The panel has not yet ruled on his latest appeal.

The Oklahoma City bombing case has had other developments. In 1997, then-state representative Charles Key spearheaded an initiative petition to empanel an Oklahoma County grand jury to probe whether the federal government had prior knowledge of the bombing and whether others than those convicted were involved.

In December 1998, the eighteen-month, $525,434 investigation ended. The panel had interviewed 117 witnesses. In their report, grand jurors said they could "state with assurance that we do not believe that the federal government had prior knowledge that this horrible terrorist attack was going to happen. We also do not believe that this was a sting operation that went too far or that this was a terrorist attack financed or conceived by individuals outside this country. This was an act perpetrated by Americans on Americans."

Jurors said that while they could not "affirmatively state that absolutely no one else was involved in the bombing," they did not receive information "sufficient to indict any additional conspirators."

While the $82.5 million federal bombing probe—the costliest criminal investigation in American history—has largely wound down, FBI agents say they will continue to pursue leads should new evidence emerge.

In October 1999, the U.S. Supreme Court upheld Nichols' federal convictions. He is pursuing another federal appeal, claiming the FBI withheld information about the possibility of other suspects.

In his state case, Nichols awaits a preliminary hearing, which has been delayed twice and assigned to two different judges. If he is bound over on charges, yet another judge would conduct the trial. As of October 2000, nearly a million dollars from the Oklahoma County court fund had been allotted for his defense.

In October, district judge Ray Dean Linder of Alva disqualified Macy and his staff, saying that published comments made about the case by Macy violated a court-imposed gag order.

"I have never seen such a blatant open violation of the rules of professional conduct. There is no doubt in my mind that Mr. Macy is too closely involved," said Linder, who was acting on a defense motion to remove Macy.

Clockwise from top left, News crews set up outside the federal courthouse, left, and federal office building in Denver on February 20, 1996 after an announcement that the Timothy McVeigh and Terry Nichols trials would be held there; U.S. District Judge Richard Matsch at the federal courthouse in Denver on April 24, 1996. Matsch was the presiding judge in both the McVeigh and Nichols trials; defense attorney Stephen Jones outside the U.S. Courthouse in Denver after the jury sentenced McVeigh to death; in this illustration, defense attorneys Stephen Jones, left, Michael Tigar, McVeigh, and Nichols are shown in federal court on October 4, 1996; victims' family members cheer lead prosecutor, Joseph Hartzler, after hearing the verdict in the McVeigh trial.

Macy may appeal. If the appeal is denied, it would be up to Oklahoma Attorney General Drew Edmondson to appoint another district attorney, who could choose to drop the case.

Bud Welch has not changed his mind about opposing the trial. But other victims, such as Jannie Coverdale, who lost two young grandsons, Aaron, five, and Elijah, two, in the bombing, support the prosecution. Even Coverdale, though, is troubled by the length of the process.

"It will hurt to go through this again, but I want the trial to start. I want somebody to pay for killing my grandsons. I will be here for however long it takes," she says.

Coverdale has rebuilt her life, taking a new job and befriending a small boy named Adrian. "His mother shares him with me. He reminds me of Elijah, and he takes away some of the loneliness. Adrian went with me to the dedication of the Oklahoma City memorial."

A few weeks ago, Adrian was visiting when a report on the bombing came on the TV. With almost sixth-sense empathy, Adrian, seven, touched Coverdale's arm. "Granny, does that make you sad?" he asked.

Coverdale said that it did.

"Don't be sad," Adrian replied. "You have me now."

. . . .

Julie DelCour covered the Oklahoma City bombing case, including the federal trials and appeals of Timothy McVeigh and Terry Nichols, for the Tulsa World, *where she has worked for twenty-three years.*

WE COME HERE TO REMEMBER

*Five years after the bombing, the Oklahoma City National
Memorial becomes a healing and symbolic reality.*

By Mike Brake

*One hundred and sixty-eight lighted chairs sit on the south
lawn of the Oklahoma City National Memorial. Each
inscribed with a name, the chairs represent the lives that were
lost April 19, 1995.*

TWO DAYS BEFORE the April 19 dedication of the
Oklahoma City National Memorial, Brandon Denny and
Trey Florence told the world that this year, things would be
different.

Brandon was in the Alfred P. Murrah Building daycare center
on April 19, 1995. He was found after the blast, barely alive, a
chunk of concrete embedded in his brain. He still walks with
a limp and has limited use of one hand, but according to his
mother, Claudia, he is "all boy."

Trey was a long-awaited blessing to David and Linda Florence.
His mother worked for the Department of Housing and Urban
Development in the Murrah building. On the Friday before the
bombing, Linda walked downstairs to snap photos at the daycare
center Easter party. Five days later, she died. When her husband
processed the film, he insisted that the daycare families receive
copies of the last pictures taken in life of their children.

Brandon Denny and Trey Florence were toddlers in 1995.
They have attended somber anniversary ceremonies and heard
countless tales of the small yet dramatic roles they played in
a city's history. They are beginning to understand that one of
the many funds established to help bombing victims will one
day send them to college. At a reception for the scholarship
families two days before the memorial dedication, they were
playing, seated side by side at a table and giggling like the two
happy small boys they are. Life, they seemed to be saying, has
been renewed.

It is impossible to overstate the impact the bombing had on
this city. One survey suggested that almost half of the residents
of central Oklahoma—more than 400,000 people—had a direct
connection to the event. They knew someone who died. They
volunteered to give blood or serve food. They loaded bottled
water and work gloves and lined up for hours at one of the

Clockwise from top left, The "Jesus Wept" statue depicts a mourning Christ, standing with his back to the bombing site; the memorial at night with the Regency Tower in the distance; Hans and Torrey Butzer, the memorial architects, at the dedication on April 19, 2000; a scene from dedication day, including the honor guard.

The inscription on the Gates of Time reads, "We come here to remember those who were killed, those who survived and those changed forever. May all who leave here know the impact of violence. May this memorial offer comfort, strength, peace, hope and serenity." The memorial site covers three and a half acres and sits on the north side of downtown Oklahoma City.

dozens of collection points. They prayed and they cried, and in the end they took an immense and justified pride in how their city responded to the most horrendous domestic terrorist massacre in American history.

The residents of Oklahoma City were changed, and so was their city. At first, it seemed that no city could sustain such a staggering physical and emotional blow and emerge intact—and we didn't. We became a better place, and if there is a symbol of that renaissance, it is made of bronze, stone, glass, and water, the newly dedicated Oklahoma City National Memorial.

Before the bomb, Northwest Fifth between Robinson and Harvey was an ordinary street flanked by some unremarkable buildings and an old elm tree. After the bomb, it became a holy shrine, and five years later, a president and the national media and Oklahomans by the tens of thousands came to stand in awe.

On dedication day, a man who had steered one of the rescue dogs through the mangled wreckage stood beside the memorial reflecting pool with his young son.

"Being here and being part of all this made me a better man and a better father," he says quietly. "It changed me in a fundamental way. We will come here often, my family and me. It is...sacred ground."

A S THE FINAL truckloads of rubble left Northwest Fifth in 1995 and as the wrecking ball advanced to demolish a half-dozen crippled structures around the perimeter, Mayor Ron Norick

appointed a 350-member task force to investigate how Oklahoma City would memorialize this spot and the events that took place here. The task force included bombing survivors, rescuers, relatives of the slain, and civic leaders. Local attorney Bob Johnson agreed to serve as chairman. He later recalled that emotions were still raw among many who had been through the fire. All that emerged from that early task force was a mission statement that proposed some sort of memorial. A statue, perhaps.

Then the people of Oklahoma City took over. They turned a simple chainlink fence that had been erected to keep people off the site into an ever-growing memorial of their own. They hung pictures on the fence and key chains and little poems wrapped in plastic. Visitors from out of state pried the license tags from their cars and wired them to the fence. There were banners from Alaska, children's drawings from Georgia, flowers pulled from nearby gardens. Every few weeks, archivists came to remove the items, cataloguing them with fine care. Within days the fence was covered again.

On the first anniversary of the bombing, following a private memorial service for families and survivors, thousands still lined the fence at midnight, gazing at new grass where the old building had stood, looking up into the dark and gaping windows of the Journal Record Building across the street, its walls still spray-painted with arrows and instructions to the April 19 search parties. Four years before the real memorial was dedicated, the fence had become a shrine.

N DEDICATION DAY, Jane Thomas sat on a stone ledge halfway down from the Survivor Tree and watched thousands as they walked between the empty chairs or pointed to names on the Survivor Wall. As archivist for the Memorial Foundation, Thomas has lived with the artifacts of the bombing from the earliest days. She spends her working hours among stained police and fire uniforms, shoes filled with glass, a calendar taken from a desk still open to April 19, 1995, a warped door from the Journal Record Building, and hundreds of thousands of documents.

"I wondered how it would feel to see people here," she says. "For so long we've felt like it was ours alone, the memorial staff and the committees." A family passed by, snapping photos of the Rescuer's Wall that guards the Survivor Tree. Thomas watched them and smiled. "It feels just fine. I like it."

In the fall of 1996, the original Memorial Task Force became the Oklahoma City National Memorial Foundation. The foundation announced an international design competition, and within months, its offices were flooded with 624 suggested designs. A screening committee narrowed that field to five finalists, and a jury made up of eight family members and survivors, three community leaders, and four design professionals chose a concept submitted from Berlin, Germany, by Hans-Ekkehard Butzer, his wife Torrey Butzer (a native of Nowata, Oklahoma), and Sven Berg.

The outdoor portion of the memorial would have seven central components. Twin "Gates of Time" at each end of the site would symbolize 9:01 and 9:03 a.m., the minutes flanking the bomb's explosion at 9:02. A sweeping reflecting pool would connect the gates. Where the Murrah building stood, 168 lighted, empty chairs would bear the names of the dead. On the surviving east wall of the building, carved in granite salvaged from the rubble, would be the names of those who survived. Across the street, a promontory would surround the Survivor Tree, an American elm that dates at least to the 1920s. To the west, a Children's Area would remember the many messages of support from young people. Between the tree and the Children's Area, an orchard would honor the rescuers and volunteers.

The foundation later added a section of the beloved chainlink fence, where visitors could continue to leave messages and keepsakes.

AYING FOR THE memorial was no small challenge. From the beginning, the foundation was determined to raise most of the nearly $30 million it would take, largely from private sources. Most sites of national remembrance are entirely federally funded. But as it had in the first hours of April 19, 1995, Oklahoma City would take the lead.

There were big checks from corporations, "in memory of" checks from thousands of individuals, and bags of pennies from schoolchildren nationwide.

On October 25, 1998, ground was broken for the memorial. The next day, hundreds of family members, survivors, and rescuers hoisted the fence above their heads and moved it to the west end of the site. The Butzers were on hand, too. They had moved to Oklahoma City, not just to oversee the birth of their design but to call it home. Like the hundreds of rescuers and volunteers who came to Oklahoma City in 1995, they have a permanent connection to a city and its people.

This page, More than two hundred honor guard members represented the rescue and recovery agencies from the 1995 bombing at the private ceremony on April 19, 2000, prior to the public opening of the memorial. Guards escorted families in, one at a time, to the chair representing a lost loved one.

Close to seven thousand family members, survivors, and rescuers attended a private ceremony on dedication morning, five years to the moment from an explosion that changed a city. They read the names of the dead and observed 168 seconds of silence—it seems endless, that 168 seconds which has marked every anniversary since 1995—and then they filed into the memorial to place wreaths and to stand quietly in front of the chairs, the wall, and the pool. And then something happened. It was like a door closing...the memorial was finished. What began with unutterable agony and continued through five long years as a dull, abiding pain seemed to be easing for so many of those who had feared an endless night. They looked at the sun on the gates and on the pool, and there was a palpable sense of completion.

The crowd at the afternoon ceremony was even larger, and people continued to come well into the night. They looked and they touched, always quiet and subdued, like people visiting a cathedral. Many of them simply sat on the terrace ledges beneath the Survivor Tree. Hundreds tossed coins into the pool. They seemed determined to make this memorial endure, or perhaps to leave a bit of themselves behind. They—we—were once again family.

WHEN FRAN FERRARI walked to the Survivor Wall, she looked at her name. Her office window on the third floor of the Journal Record Building had overlooked the old elm tree in the parking lot—"my tree"—in a direct line to the spot where the bomb truck was parked. Ferrari was on the phone that morning.

The blast imploded the window frame, fracturing her skull. She was peppered and blinded by glass. When the rescuers brought her out for the ride to the hospital, they had to carry her in an office chair. Ferrari has vision, hearing, and balance problems. Her right hand refuses to grip things as it once did, and she calls her scars "my souvenirs."

Ferrari turned from her name on the Survivor Wall and said, "I am part of it now." She walked slowly past the pool and the chairs to the west gate.

"Nine-oh-three," she said softly. "I'm going to walk through it." She did, then entered the Children's Area, where kids are invited to chalk sentiments on the sidewalk. Ferrari selected peach- colored chalk and carefully drew a chair, like the one that had taken her from chaos to rescue five years before, her grip now sure despite the bumps which she thinks may be still-embedded fragments of the bomb truck itself.

And then she wrote: "This chair isn't empty—I lived."

Mike Brake is the chief writer for Governor Frank Keating. He was the principal oral history editor for In Their Name (Random House).

On dedication day, Michael Butzer, 3, and Maddie Butzer, 5, nephew and niece of memorial architect Hans Butzer, splash a rose in the reflecting pool.

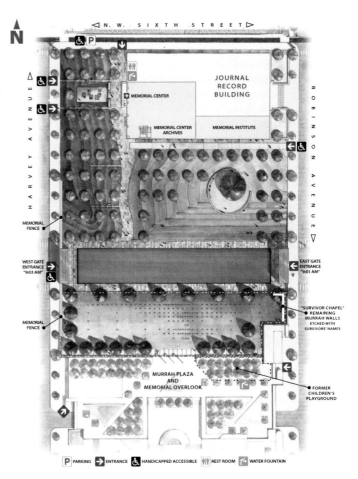

A TRIPLE-FACETED MEMORIAL

The Oklahoma City National Memorial is comprised of three components: the outdoor memorial, a museum, and a terrorism institute.

The indoor component of the Oklahoma City National Memorial, the Memorial Center, will occupy the three lower floors at the west end of the Journal Record Building. Its permanent exhibit will display artifacts from the huge memorial archives, from equipment used by the rescuers to items salvaged from the bombed buildings.

While admission to the outdoor portion of the memorial is free, a small admission will be charged for the Memorial Center to support the memorial's ongoing operations and upkeep.

The Institute for the Prevention of Terrorism is the third component of the Oklahoma City National Memorial, and it represents the city's effort to give something back to a world that helped so much in 1995.

Headed by General Dennis Reimer, former chief of staff of the U.S. Army and a native of Medford, Oklahoma, the institute has two central goals—to act as a worldwide clearinghouse for information that can help prevent terrorist acts and to speed rescue efforts when such attacks do occur. One of its primary efforts will focus on training public safety agencies in how to respond to terrorism in the first crucial hours.

LIFE GOES ON

For three Oklahomans touched by the bombing, the first five years bring pain, loss, challenge, change—and new joys.

By Mike Brake

Eight-year-old singer Mikaila Enriquez hugs Patti Hall after a Fourth of July tribute to survivors in 1995.

IF YOU WERE at the center of the vortex like Patti Hall, standing in the Alfred P. Murrah Federal Building's third-floor credit union, there was no sound—only sudden shock and terrifying darkness.

For John Avera, a half-mile away, the blast was a thunderclap. Fragments of ceiling tile rained down on him, and he watched, amazed, as a rigid glass window bowed in a full six inches, then snapped back without shattering.

There was not even a distant rumble in Tulsa, where Diane Leonard kept her morning business appointment. Later, a ringing phone brought accounts of the bombing and the unbelievable news that her husband was among the missing.

For Patti Hall, for John Avera, for Diane Leonard, and for thousands who were directly touched by the bombing, that moment at 9:02 a.m. on April 19, 1995, was life shifting. In the words of Civil War veterans who tried to tell their grandchildren about combat, all had "seen the elephant."

Those who have worked closely with bombing survivors—defined as people who lost family members, people injured or directly shaken by the blast, rescuers, volunteers, everyone who was there—believe most have achieved a "new normal," that in many ways the so-called "victims" are stronger than before the bomb so dramatically disrupted their lives. There have been a handful of tragic suicides, some increased drug and alcohol abuse, and a number of divorces and other personal catastrophe among the several thousand Oklahomans most affected by the bombing, but for the most part, the fifth anniversary and the dedication of the Oklahoma City National Memorial signified another milestone in what can hopefully be termed a steady process of recovery.

Gwen Allen directs Project Heartland, a free community mental health and counseling program created in 1995 to serve bombing survivors. "I think we have done better than many people expected," Allen says, "but one reason is that we had the safety net in place early on. From Project Heartland to many private mental health and church resources, people have had a place to turn." That was true as early as the first hours after the bombing, when a family information and support center opened at Oklahoma City's First Christian Church. By that first

Diane Leonard, right, hugs a victims' advocate after a memorial service for Oklahoma City bombing victims in Denver on January 7, 1998, the day jurors in the trial of Terry Nichols deadlocked in the penalty phase.

A group of people sing "God Bless America" next to the fence of the Murrah bombing site after the announcement that Timothy McVeigh received the death penalty. Among those holding the flag is survivor Patti Hall, in the wide-brimmed hat.

Oklahoma Today

weekend after the bombing, hundreds of volunteer pastors and counselors were on duty around the clock to support the grieving process.

By mid-2000, Project Heartland had delivered counseling services to more than nine thousand Oklahomans. The center still sees an average of twenty-five new clients each month, Allen says. Significantly, many are police and fire personnel, who routinely experience stresses and traumas that bring back memories of the bombing. Allen also confirms an impression shared by many bombing survivors—that those who were stable and healthy before 1995 have come through the first five years, in many cases, stronger than before. "You bring your own personal history to something like this," she says, noting that people who have solid emotional and spiritual reserves call on them in times of crisis.

STEPPING FORWARD

IT TOOK PATTI HALL several years to find the positive. A nine-year employee of the credit union, she was at work on the third floor of the Murrah building that morning. At 9:01 she grabbed a can of air freshener and stepped into the hallway outside the teller windows to douse a bad odor. "I pushed the lever on top of the can at the exact second the bomb went off," Hall says. "I thought I had done something to cause it!" Hall felt herself lifted and blown backward. "It was like fainting and being levitated at the same time." She lost consciousness and awoke some time later under part of the massive rubble slide that the Murrah building had become. One of the first rescuers to rush to the site was standing on her face.

"I stuck my hand up," she says. "When they finally dug me out, one of the rescuers was a General Services Administration employee I knew well from the building, but he said he didn't even recognize me." At Southwest Medical Center, doctors called Hall's relatives with word to rush. "They said I was dying." Hall had a fractured shoulder and collarbone, broken ribs, a punctured lung, a shattered pelvis, and crushed legs and feet. Her body's oxygen level, which ought to be near 100 percent, registered less than one percent. "They placed me in what they call a medically induced coma," she says. "Because of all the injuries, they said I could not have survived any other way." For five weeks, through multiple surgeries, attached to a respirator, and strapped to a rotating bed, Patti Hall's comatose body fought the odds. She finally awakened to the news that she might never walk again.

"I said, 'Really?' and they said, 'You will if you want to,'" she recalls. "I wanted to." By the early spring of 1996, as the first anniversary of the bombing approached, Hall stepped successfully out of her wheelchair, graduated to a walker, and soon began moving about and even driving on her own. But she was alone, with her aged mother her only local relative. She depended on regular home nursing care. She avoided her fortieth Central High School reunion in Oklahoma City and became more and more of a recluse. Soon she was medicating herself with alcohol.

"Finally, my therapist told me I needed to go to rehab," she says. "I was reluctant. But I went and I learned. And I recovered." Her mother was now living in a retirement center, half of her credit union family had died in the bombing, but Patti Hall had a new family—Alcoholics Anonymous.

By the fourth anniversary of the bombing, and after enduring four years without a job, she was forced to face a second reality. "The doctors told me I could never return to work. I had always worked and supported myself, but my body is just not dependable. Some days I simply can't get up and around well, and the injuries to my lungs caused asthma. Well, that news did a number on me. It was like I had lost everything."

Hall attended that year's anniversary ceremonies at the Murrah building site, the last such event before construction began on the permanent memorial. She was placing flowers on the building footprint along with other surviving credit union employees, when, she says, "I just fell to pieces. I broke down. I was alone." She looked up to see a familiar face—the First Lady of Oklahoma, Cathy Keating. They talked about Hall's situation, and one day soon her phone rang.

"I was despondent and thought, why bother to answer it? But I did. It was Cathy Keating asking me to come help manage the gift shop at the capitol."

Five years after the bombing, Patti Hall was volunteering at the gift shop and for the Salvation Army, attending AA meetings—and planning to enroll in a public speaking class.

"When God pulls you out like this, you know you have a job to do," she says. "I am more determined than ever to keep going. When they need me, if I can, I go. Of course I still have a few down days. But I get up and get going. I'd like to be known for more than just the bombing. I am not going to wallow in it."

The new Patti Hall sees herself as "stronger, yes, more independent than I ever realized. This has given me insights into strengths I never knew I had."

A MAN IN FULL

JOHN AVERA HAD seen most of the death, misery, crime, and blood associated with a long career as an Oklahoma City police officer, but his journey into the depths of the shattered Murrah building on April 19, 1995, changed him, too.

Avera was at work in a building across the street from police headquarters, moving some crime lab equipment, when the blast rocked his office. He ran outside and began sprinting in the direction of the rising smoke column. At the building, a man grabbed him and shouted that there was a daycare center on the second floor. Avera climbed over the rubble pile and found himself in hell.

After helping a barefoot and bleeding woman out of the chaos, Avera and a fellow policeman, Don Helmuth, ventured back inside.

"I heard a baby crying," Avera says. He and Helmuth began digging, and almost simultaneously, each uncovered a small form. Helmuth had found P. J. Allen, who would survive. Avera cradled year-old Baylee Almon, who would not.

Outside, he handed the still form of Baylee Almon to a firefighter, Chris Fields. Neither man knew that two other men with cameras were independently recording the handoff—a series of photos that would win the Pulitzer Prize and appear on the front pages of virtually every newspaper around the world.

On April 20, 1995, John Avera awoke to find himself a symbol. It seemed the media could not get enough of the policeman who went into hell to rescue Baylee Almon, the firefighter who carried her to the ambulance, Baylee's mother, Aren—and the dead child herself. Even schoolchildren sending "get well" cards to Oklahoma City in the days after the bombing etched their own crude versions of the scene. Baylee Almon and her rescuers were icons.

"I have to say it was not pleasant," Avera says five years later. "During the first year, up through the first anniversary of the bombing, the interview requests were almost constant. I couldn't go anywhere without being recognized." Avera became close with Fields, Almon, and Chuck Porter, the young banker whose photos won the Pulitzer Prize. They formed a mutual support system at the center of a media whirlpool. But there was a cost.

"I just had no time to think," Avera says. "There was no release. In police work, you see a lot of bad things, but there are release mechanisms—jokes and black humor that civilians would not understand. You did not joke about the bombing."

Avera had nightmares. When he saw young children—especially groups of small children performing in school programs or at church—he suffered breathlessness and anxiety attacks. He twice went to a Massachusetts mental health facility that specializes in sup-

porting public safety employees traumatized by work experiences. He retired from the Oklahoma City Police Department in February 1997 with twenty-seven years of service, opened an Edmond computer store, and in 1999 went to work for the City of Edmond as a computer specialist.

"I have learned to live with these emotions," he says. "For a long time, I was really grumpy at home." Avera had married his wife, Benita, at the police station in the 1970s, when they were both young dispatchers there. Their pictures were in the paper, a happy "cop couple." They had three children and a marriage that seemed immune to the rocky times that plague so many in law enforcement. Thanks to Benita's work as a fingerprint technician, she understood the work and the stresses better than most law enforcement wives, and their partnership has endured.

But the nightmares have not ended for John Avera. In those shadowy dreams, he is in a dark, dusty, and confining place with screams all around him, yet he is powerless to help. He wakes up sweating and drained. And there are daytime flashbacks as well. The nineteenth of April remains a ponderous presence.

"Just this week they were asking for volunteers at church to teach Sunday school," he says. "The kids were there. They showed pictures of all the church volunteers, and it was like those quick pictures of all the dead from the bombing. It's still inside me. When I feel it, when something triggers it, I have learned to get up and leave, go outside."

Avera says he has accepted the fact that experiences and his unwanted celebrity have left him indelibly marked. "I'm doing good otherwise," he says. "I'm enjoying myself in many ways. The new job is fun."

There was always a twinkle in John Avera's eyes, an irrepressible impishness that made him a much-loved character at police headquarters. It's still there, but when he talks about that day, he gazes into the distance and sighs.

"You do not forget," he says.

Opposite page, Senator Don Nickles looks on as Diane Leonard pauses during a Capitol Hill news conference on April 15, 1996, to discuss antiterrorism legislation. Above left, Diane Leonard holds back tears as she talks about victims' rights at a press conference in Oklahoma City in November 1996. Above right, Oklahoma City police sergeant John Avera, left, and firefighter captain Chris Fields at the funeral of one-year-old Baylee Almon on April 24, 1995.

A WOMAN OF SUBSTANCE

ON THE DAY of Don Leonard's funeral, his widow, Diane, stood and told the crowd, "Don would want us all to take time to stop and smell the roses." It would be almost five years before she followed her own advice.

Leonard was a Secret Service agent less than a year away from retirement on April 19, 1995.

"We had all these plans," Diane Leonard says, "and they were literally blown to pieces." She was in Tulsa on a sales call for a greeting card company when news of the bombing came. Through two sleepless nights she waited—and on Friday, April 21, word came that her husband's body had been recovered from the building rubble. There was grief, sorrow, despair—and a deep anger at terrorism and those who practice it.

"The kind of work I had been doing had no meaning any longer," she says. "I had to do something to help, to fix what had been broken."

Diane Leonard is a natural leader, and within weeks she emerged as a powerful and persuasive spokesperson for bombing families. She met with Oklahoma Attorney General Drew Edmondson and became an instant activist on behalf of the growing victims' rights movement, embodied in federal legislation to reform and speed the criminal appellate process. By June 1995, Leonard was leading delegations to Washington, where the bombing families and survivors were a potent force in the ultimate passage of criminal justice reforms and a new antiterrorism bill. In the photos and news clippings from that period, Diane Leonard is ever present—lobbying senators and congressmen, standing behind the president at a White House bill signing, making her case on the evening news.

Back home, she soon joined Edmondson's staff as a crime victims' advocate. She went to court and to executions with relatives of the murdered. She served on committees to create the Oklahoma City National Memorial and was chosen for a select survivors' committee that coordinated travel to Denver for Oklahomans attending the trials of Timothy McVeigh and Terry Nichols. When the judge in the McVeigh trial imposed an unpopular order that banned family members who planned to testify in the trials from attending any of the proceedings, Leonard was enraged.

"I went to Washington with language that would change federal law to permit family members to testify in impact statements and attend the trial as well," she says. Several weeks later, within forty-eight hours, the legislation passed in both the House and Senate and was signed into law. Another Diane Leonard mission accomplished.

Later, she helped organize the December 1999 burial of the unidentified fragments of human remains which had never been matched with specific victims after the bombing. "That was very important to me and to many of the families, because we knew, some of us, that our loved ones had been terribly damaged on that day, that those remains very probably included some of our own."

During the Nichols trial, Leonard worked with Oklahoma City police chaplain Jack Poe to secure a federal grant creating an organization to provide counseling and support services for rescue workers from across the nation who had come to Oklahoma City after the bombing. Soon she was serving as administrator of the program, planning and participating in workshops on both coasts. Leonard was a frequent speaker at professional meetings on the impact of traumatic rescue service on fire and police personnel.

"McVeigh and Nichols won enough on April nineteenth," she says bluntly. "They were not going to win anything else, to steal any more lives." When an Oklahoma City policeman who had participated in the rescue killed himself in 1996, Leonard redoubled her efforts on behalf of the rescuers.

She was out to save the world. And she was not taking time to smell the roses. In the spring of 1999, after four years of struggle, she touched bottom.

"I was driving home late one night from a meeting in Stillwater and I thought, 'There is nothing but ugliness in this world.' I would sit there day after day and hear the stories of these rescuers. I had a broken heart every day. And that night I wanted to just drive off a bridge."

Leonard's mother had committed suicide in 1986. "I promised myself then that I would never do that to the people around me. So I drove home that night."

Soon she relinquished her rescuer workshop duties. "I needed some light in my life, against all that darkness," she says. By late 1999,

she was redecorating her home, doing much of the work herself, and in 2000 she began crafting stained glass, which soon became a small home business. Days that had been frantically filled with advocacy and meetings with members of Congress soon gave way to quiet times in her home workshop, surrounded by the bright blues and reds and yellows of her elegant glass creations.

"What happened on April 19, 1995, changed who I was," Leonard says. She fought some stirring battles and won some important victories, but the personal cost was high. As one friend told her, "You cannot save the world."

"Now, five years later, I can see beauty in a sunset again." Leonard remains a member of the board which provides support to rescuers, and she often visits the memorial, where one of 168 chairs bears her husband's name. She has no plans to withdraw entirely from the various activities that still involve victims and families and rescuers, but the compulsion she once had to drive the bus has waned.

The thorns of Diane Leonard's life—and of Patti Hall's and John Avera's and so many others—once again have blooming roses.

Above, left to right: Patti Hall, John Avera, and Diane Leonard at the Oklahoma City National Memorial, more than five years after the bombing; Patti Hall works at the gift shop in the capitol building on Tuesdays and Thursdays; John Avera with his wife, Benita, and their two children, at Lake Hefner in Oklahoma City; and Diane Leonard in her home art studio, where she creates stained glass. (All portraits were taken in October 2000.)

REMARKS BY THE PRESIDENT AT THE OKLAHOMA CITY NATIONAL MEMORIAL DEDICATION

On April 19, 2000, at 6:05 p.m., President Bill Clinton addressed the Oklahoma City public and the nation as the keynote speaker for the Oklahoma City National Memorial dedication. At his side were cabinet members representing each arm of the federal government which lost employees in the bombing.

THANK YOU VERY much, Governor Keating. I wanted to be here today, and I was grateful to be asked. I wanted to thank you and Cathy for all you have done. Thank you, Senator Nickles and members of the congressional delegation. Thank you, Mayor Humphreys, and I thank your predecessor, Mayor Norick. Thank you, Chairman Johnson; thank you, Karen Luke.

I thank all of the federal leaders who are here today who lost their employees and worked so hard—Attorney General Reno and our Secretaries of Health and Human Services, Housing and Urban Development, and Transportation; the leaders of the Office of Personnel Management; the Customs, the ATF, and the Secret Service and many others. I thank Bob Stanton and the Park Service for making sure this place would be well cared for, forever.

I thank the unknown number of people who contributed to the building of this magnificent monument and to the scholarship fund. I thank General Ferrell and all those who are working and will work here from now on to combat terrorism. I congratulate the young couple who designed this magnificent memorial, and I think we should give them a round of applause.

I thank the
Oklahoma City Philharmonic Brass and the Memorial Community Choir and Shawntel Smith for their ringing and wonderful music today.

Most of all, I thank the families who lost your loved ones, the survivors and your families, the rescue workers, and the family of Oklahoma for setting an example for America. I can add little now to the words and music, even less to the silence and amazing grace of this memorial. Its empty chairs recall the mercy seat of Old Testament scripture—a place for the children of God to come for renewal and dedication.

So this is a day both for remembrance and for renewal. Hillary and I will never forget being with you at that first memorial service while the rescue teams were still searching. I know the last five years have not been easy. I hope you can take some comfort in knowing that, just as I said five years ago, America is still with you, and that with this memorial you can know America will never forget.

As the governor said in alluding to Gettysburg, there are places in our national landscape so scarred by freedom's sacrifice that they shape forever the soul of America—Valley Forge, Gettysburg, Selma. This place is such sacred ground.

I think you should all know that it was on this exact day 225 years ago that the American Revolution began. What a 225 years it has been. The brave Americans we lost here 220 years later were not fighting a war, but they were patriots in service to their fellow citizens, just as much as the police and fire and other public servants are here among us today. And they were children whose promise keeps our old democracy forever young.

Five years ago, the cowards who killed them made a choice—a choice to attack this building and the people in it, because they wanted to strike a blow at America's heartland, at the core of our nation's being. This was an attack on all America and every American.

Five years later, we are here because you made a choice, a choice to choose hope and love over despair and hatred. It is easy for us to say today, and even, perhaps, easy for you to clap today—but I know that this wise choice was also a very hard one, especially for the families of the victims. I know there are still days when the old anger wells up inside you, still days when tears fill your eyes, when you think your heart will surely break. On those days in the future, I hope you can come here and find solace in the memory of your loved ones, in the honor of your fellow citizens.

I hope you can find the strength to live a full and loving life, free of hatred, which only cripples. I believe your loved ones would want you to have that life. And though you have given too much, you still have so much to give.

The great writer, Ralph Ellison, who was a native of this city, once said, "America is woven of many strands...our fate is to become one, and yet many." On April 19, 1995, our many strands became one—one in love and support for you and in our determined opposition to terrorism. You taught us again how much stronger we are when we all stand together in our common humanity to protect life, liberty, and the rule of law for all.

We may never have all the answers for what happened here. But as we continue our journey toward understanding, one truth is clear: What was meant to break has made you stronger.

As I left the White House today, I looked, as I often do, at your tree—the beautiful dogwood Hillary and I planted on the south lawn five years ago for those who were lost here. Five years later, that tree stands a little taller, its spring flowers are a little fuller, its roots have dug in a little deeper. But it's still a young tree.

Five years isn't a very long time for trees to grow or for wounds to heal and hearts to mend. But today, like your beautiful dogwood tree on the White House lawn, Oklahoma City clearly is blooming again. For that, all your fellow Americans—and, indeed, decent, good people all over the world—are grateful to you. And grateful to God for the grace that led you on.

In Romans it is said, "The night is far spent, the day is at hand. Let us cast off the works of darkness, and let us put on the armor of light."

May you keep on your armor of light, may you keep your light shining on this place of hope, where memories of the lost and the meaning of America will live forever.

May God bless you, and God bless America.

Remarks by Governor Frank Keating at the Oklahoma City National Memorial Dedication

ONE HUNDRED THIRTY-SIX years ago, Abraham Lincoln spoke at the dedication of another American shrine, the battlefield at Gettysburg, Pennsylvania. He said, "The world will little note, nor long remember, what we say here, but it can never forget what they did here."

We have come full circle, to another American shrine, another patch of hallowed ground, another place of memories. We, too, will never forget what they did here—our friends and neighbors and so many of those wonderful helpers who have come back to be with us today.

They showed great courage.

They exhibited boundless compassion.

They suffered and triumphed—and 168 of them gave their lives.

Make no mistake, the names inscribed on those chairs on a smooth grassy slope where a building once stood are the names of heroes and heroines all. So are the names on the wall that records the survivors. And so are all of you, members of a vast and loving family that has been through so much since April 19, 1995.

We all remember the symbols—the ribbons, the angels, the shining lighted cross that looked down from tall buildings at night, the many-colored flags that guarded the rescue workers by day.

We remember the fence, with its thousands of offerings of love.

We remember that moment that is framed forever by these twin gates. Most of all, we remember our neighbors.

Our place of remembrance is filled with those symbols. It is also filled with love—the love of countless Americans whose ideas and support and contributions helped create this beautiful memorial.

I remember so many times in the days after the bombing when those who had come to Oklahoma to help would tell me how wonderful Oklahomans are. I knew what they meant. We came through together. We built this memorial together. And we are together again today.

On April 19 five years ago—another spring Wednesday like today—the flag of our nation was flying over the Murrah building. It is flying over our memorial today, and I know it flies proudly in our hearts.

For those who perpetrated this act, we have one message: In America you can speak and vote and complain, but there is no right to maim and bomb and kill...and if you think you'll bring that flag down, there is your answer.

We have so many special guests today. It is a homecoming for many of you who came to Oklahoma in 1995 and gave us your sweat and your tears and your support. Welcome home to all of you—and this is your home. We are all Oklahomans today, and we are all Americans. May God continue to bless our beloved land.

At the Oklahoma City National Memorial Children's Area, chalkboards give younger visitors an opportunity to express their feelings.

HOW FAR WE'VE COME

January 2005

A blanket of fresh snow covers the chairs at the Oklahoma City National Memorial.

AFTER THE HORROR of September 11, one thing strikes me most about the aftermath of the murderous bombing at the Alfred P. Murrah Federal Building. Oklahoma City, however unintentionally, became an extraordinary leader for national and international communities on how to respond to mayhem and grief. Although the terror of April 19, 1995, would prove to be just a sampling of what the world would later see, at that time no other city in America had endured what we in Oklahoma City became all too familiar with. No instruction manuals existed for this kind of human warfare and its emotional fallout.

Three components of Oklahoma City's reaction to April 19 distinguished our community, making the event a pivotal one in American history beyond the obvious terror it struck in our hearts and the heart of our nation.

First, the decision to memorialize the site with the active and meaningful involvement of the community has brought great recognition to Oklahoma City and the Oklahoma City National Memorial. The process of selecting Hans and Torrey Butzer's architectural plans now has become the standard for design competitions worldwide. The couple's singular vision, too, can be seen in similar memorials built around the country, from a field of evening-lit benches at the Pentagon to reflecting pools in upstate New York and Texas. The memorial's beauty and originality continues to inspire on many levels.

Second, the swift handling of the Murrah site rescue and recovery efforts by first responders from around the city and the country also placed Oklahoma City on the vanguard. As former fire chief Gary Marrs says, "That's just us. That's what we do." And yes, to the credit of fire and police departments who train relentlessly around the country, they, too, we understood, would have responded with similar agility and resolve. But it was Oklahoma City's recruits who would be tested.

Third, perhaps the least understood but most visionary of Oklahoma City's reactions was rooted in a deeply felt desire to be proactive and future-oriented. That responsibility fell to the National Memorial Institute for the Prevention of Terrorism, a lofty creation of victims' families, survivors, and leaders who felt strongly that the important step of memorialization wasn't enough. Leadership, the intangible but critical component that defines a true servant's life, means moving forward. The MIPT does precisely that.

In this 2005 edition, the continued presence of our national leaders—here represented by comments from Bill Clinton, essays from Rudy Giuliani and Tom Brokaw, and official transcripts from the Oklahoma City appearances of George W. Bush and John Ashcroft—underscores how important Oklahoma City is in the national psyche.

For these and countless other individuals, the events put in motion here on April 19, 1995, are as important as those at Yorktown or Gettysburg or Normandy. Oklahoma City, our home, will forever be an American leader.

—**Louisa McCune**, *Editor in Chief*

WITHIN THESE WALLS

At the Journal Record Building, the Oklahoma City National Memorial Center Museum ensures we will never forget.

By Steffie Corcoran

EIGHT YEARS HAVE passed since the world first associated Oklahoma City with a day on a calendar. Time has marched relentlessly forward, gradually but inevitably adding to the divide between the bombing of the Alfred P. Murrah Federal Building in downtown Oklahoma City and the present. That distance has provided a space for healing, and for remembering.

"We will never forget" is no longer a phrase in shoe polish scribbled on a police car's rear windshield. These four words now signify a national impulse to erect monuments honoring the senseless deaths of brothers and sisters, husbands and wives, sons and daughters. Consider the Vietnam Veterans Memorial and the United States Holocaust Memorial Museum in Washington, D.C.

Consider Oklahoma City.

Here, the processes of grief, healing, and remembrance have been soothed, at least in part, by the site on which the tragedy occurred, a place considered by many hallowed ground. Today, the Oklahoma City National Memorial's symbolic gardens and museum occupy that sacred space.

A short walk from the pastoral outdoor grounds to the west entry of the memorial center museum gives visitors scant preparation for the contrast they will experience between one and the other.

The center, inside the Journal Record Building—itself heavily damaged by the massive ammonium nitrate cocktail—rests directly north of the gardens. Proximity and a shared mission statement are among the few things the facilities, two of the three arms of the tri-partite $29.1 million complex, share.

OKLAHOMA CITY ATTORNEY Bob Johnson is widely considered the visionary of the Oklahoma City National Memorial effort. Polly Nichols, seriously injured while working inside the Journal Record Building and today chair of the memorial foundation, says, "Early on, Bob told [then-mayor] Ron Norick that he wanted to do something, that he felt compelled to do something. And Ron, to his everlasting credit, realized what an asset Bob would be in a leadership position."

On November 14, 1995, the Oklahoma City

We come here to remember those who were killed, those who survived, and those changed forever. May all who leave here know the impact of violence. May this memorial offer comfort, strength, peace, hope, and serenity.

OKLAHOMA CITY NATIONAL MEMORIAL MISSION STATEMENT

The Oklahoma City National Memorial Center Museum in the former Journal Record Building sits north of the outdoor symbolic memorial. The grounds, designed by Butzer Design Partnership, incorporate several elements, including a field of 168 chairs, a reflecting pool, and the Gates of Time.

Memorial Task Force, chaired by Johnson, passed a resolution stating that one of the components of the permanent memorial be an information center, to include photos and biographies of the 168 victims.

Over the next four years, thousands became involved in the memorial effort, what Johnson refers to as a "very open, consensus-based process." Memorial trustee Richard Williams, a survivor from the General Services Administration, says, "The process itself of consideration for consensus was absolutely unbelievable. It had to be a consensus to determine that we were making the right decisions."

Consensus, anyone will tell you, is rarely easy—or fast. Those hundreds involved in various parts of the project—fundraising, selecting a designer for the outdoor site, construction—labored on. By early 2000, work on the outdoor memorial was nearly complete. Lippert Brothers, an Oklahoma City construction firm, was already at work on the rehabilitation of the Journal Record Building for the city when, in February 2000, they won the bid to do general contracting on the memorial center. The company had already worked extensively on the outdoor site.

Tom Lippert, senior vice president and project manager for all three jobs, says despite the building's hard hit in 1995, "there were only some select areas that received major damage. That was primarily on the south side of the Journal Record Building. Other than that, the building was quite stout."

Interior design work completed and with just a few loose ends of construction work remaining elsewhere in the building, the $10 million, 30,000-square-foot Oklahoma City National Memorial Center Museum opened to the public on President's Day, February 19, 2001.

THE OKLAHOMA CITY NATIONAL Memorial Center Museum is a unique entity. Receiving no state or federal appropriations for daily operations—but Oklahoma City, the state of Oklahoma, and the federal government made sizable donations during the memorial's construction phase—it is self-funded through admission fees, memorial store profits, museum memberships, funds from the Oklahoma City Memorial Marathon, and endowment earnings.

With a staff of eighteen, the museum operates under the jurisdiction of the nine-member Oklahoma City National Memorial Trust, whose members—including chairman Luke Corbett, CEO of Kerr-McGee, and vice-chair Linda Lambert, who owns an independent oil and gas exploration company—are presidential appointees. The forty-eight-member Oklahoma City National Memorial Foundation manages the endowment and is its fundraising arm. Both boards include survivors, family members of the deceased, and civic leaders.

Unique, too, is the memorial's relationship with the National Park Service, which operates at the request of the trust in cooperation with the memorial's staff and is reimbursed annually for its service. The six park rangers who work at the memorial are responsible for interpretation of the outdoor site and help coordinate security.

Facing page, This portion of the museum's ten-chapter story line depicts 'chaos'. Above, President Bush speaks with Richard Williams, Major Ed Hill, and Bob Johnson at the museum dedication on February 19, 2001; flags recovered from the Alfred P. Murrah Federal Building debris are displayed within the center.

Before the dedication ceremony, President and Mrs. Bush took a private tour of the museum. "It is a really well-done place," the president said in his public comments. "It's powerful."

The president's visit brought the national press, and reporters from the *Washington Post* and elsewhere described the museum with the same adjective, "powerful." An ABC news report said, "The center depicts the frenzied panic after the bomb exploded, a short distance from the building's day-care center." In the *Dallas Morning News*, Arnold Hamilton said, "From display to display, the faces, names, and places become familiar again."

The three-level complex on the west side of the Journal Record Building begins with a subdued, granite-walled lobby and tasteful gift store. Security is tight for the fifth-floor administrative offices, and precautionary measures include a sign-in process, badges, escorts, and photo ID.

The second and third floors, filled with media and artifact exhibits, constitute the museum proper. A ten-chapter story line, scripted by a group of key staff members and volunteers who called themselves the "Wednesday Night Prayer Group," begins on the third floor with a typical morning in Oklahoma City, followed by a journey through the chaos and hysteria of the event and concluding on the second floor with the hope and healing that arose in its aftermath.

The memorial center is an interactive, multimedia experience. Exhibits include glassed-in displays, television monitors with oral histories of the people executive director Kari Watkins calls "walking, talking artifacts," and computerized kiosks. The path through the center twists and turns, something new around every corner.

The images within the memorial center were installed by Hillmann & Carr, an award-winning motion picture and video production company from Washington, D.C., whose clients include the Smithsonian Institution, the National Civil War Museum, and the U.S. Holocaust Memorial Museum, the model to which the Oklahoma City National Memorial Center Museum is frequently compared.

A CTING AS VISUAL PARTNERS to the many competing voices inside the museum are artifacts upon artifacts, the province of collections manager Jane Thomas of Guthrie. Thomas, a historian, began her salvage operation as a task force volunteer in the months following the bombing.

"You have to understand," she says, "people thought I was kind of a nut. You know, I'm over at the First United Methodist Church, and I'm saying, 'Can I have your window?'"

Thomas and other early organizers suspected the items that would resonate most with visitors would be the ones they could easily identify with. A dress, a plastic photo ID badge, and a men's restroom, for instance.

In a case on the third floor hangs a pretty long-sleeved dress with a belt, its only visible damage a small tear on the skirt. Florence Rogers, CEO of the Federal Employees Credit Union, lost eighteen colleagues in the bombing. She had worn the dress to work on April 19.

Once she finally made it home that day, Rogers shook out the dress, dusted with debris from the blast, and stuck it in a shelf in her laundry room, out of sight and out of mind. Four years later,

'You have to understand,' she says, 'people thought I was kind of a nut. You know, I'm over at the First United Methodist Church, and I'm saying, "Can I have your window?"'

she stumbled upon it. "I pressed it up, and I took it to Jane at the archives—I could not throw it away—and I said, 'Jane, do something with this; get it out of my way.'" She pauses. "I didn't know it was going to be displayed in the museum until the board members toured through there. I'm not a person who cries easily, but I stood there and sobbed when I saw it standing there."

In the corner of the same display, the shards of another dress, worn by survivor Nancy Ingram, an IRS secretary inside the credit

Many attended ceremonies at the memorial to remember September 11.

Ties That Bind
At the Oklahoma City National Memorial, a decade of healing comes from hope.

By Kari Watkins

For most of us, it is hard to believe that ten years have transpired since that beautiful spring morning in 1995 turned tragic. For others, it has been an unshakable moment in time. When terrorists sought to strike fear in our home, our community united. Today, ten years later, Oklahoma City can look around to see a city changed, a stronger community and a place of remembrance and education as its hallmark to healing and rebuilding.

Our city and state have made remarkable progress since April 19, 1995. Oklahomans will always remember what happened, but they also have moved forward to rebuild a progressive city torn apart by terrorists.

Maybe some have forgotten how hard it was to move on with their lives, but not the 168 families who lost loved ones or the hundreds of survivors who have spent their last decade adjusting to their "new normal." Maybe some have forgotten how dozens of businesses and agencies had to find new homes, but not the businessman who invested his life savings in what became known as Ground Zero. Maybe some have forgotten how hard the city would struggle with its new image, but not those who worked hard to promote Oklahoma City as a safe and vibrant place to work and call home.

Today, we look back at this decade of hope and see how vital the guiding document of our mission statement has become. We see how developing an international design competition resulted in one of the most beautiful and inspired memorials the world over. Although owned by a private foundation, this place belongs to the people and is maintained to a standard that many around the world admire.

Over the past ten years, businesses and churches have rebuilt around the memorial. Surely it would have been easier

continued on page 158

union at the time of the bombing, fit inside a Ziploc bag.

Thomas envisioned another exhibit filled with ID badges representing the various agencies that worked in rescue and recovery. One badge volunteered from a member of each group—FBI, FEMA, the medical examiner's office, and police department—would do. And of course one badge from the Oklahoma City Fire Department.

Thomas had already procured then-Chief Gary Marrs's helmet for a rescuer's display, and now, she thought, what better badge to represent the fire department than the chief's? "I thought his heart was going to break," she says. "It was so hard to give it up. I said, 'Chief Marrs, another one is okay, but this is just special.'"

"Jane can do that," Marrs, a memorial trustee, says of her powers of persuasion. "I thought long and hard about it. She convinced me that it would be better used there than it would be sitting in my drawer somewhere."

It's difficult to imagine a productive use for a bombed-out men's restroom. But the one on the second-floor landing of the Journal Record Building forever records the devastation of the bomb blast. "One of the things we wanted people to see is how cavities could form—where people survived—because nobody died in this building," says Thomas.

After separating construction residue from that which occurred naturally after the bombing, the room had to be shored up so its destruction could be preserved in perpetuity. The east wall, for example, was reinforced with netting, then tied to supports.

"It's pretty firm up there," Thomas says, noting the room's hidden monitors that help her keep an eye out for pests and changes in the interior that might require attention.

An adjoining closet contains an old typewriter Thomas had long craved, because, as she believes, it's the everyday items visitors most identify with.

"Before I knew the Memorial Center Committee was going to preserve this, I had coveted that typewriter and yet had never gotten it. When the construction crew came in and closed this off, I realized it was forever going to live here."

IF YOU PRESERVE IT, they will come. And come they have. More than 400,000 visitors thus far have journeyed through the museum.

"Of the myriad ways the bombing has transformed this place," said *New York Times* writer Jim Yardley in 2001, "perhaps one of the most unexpected and surprising is that Oklahoma City is now a tourist attraction....Before the bombing, Oklahoma City barely registered on the national consciousness....The worst thing that ever happened to the state became the best thing for its image and, oddly, its self-esteem."

That renewed confidence continues to have national impact.

"That's what the memorial effort is all about," Bob Johnson

The bronze origami cranes suspended from the museum's second-floor ceiling represent the more than 10,000 paper cranes sent to the Oklahoma City mayor's office after the bombing. According to Japanese legend, cranes are a symbol of healing.

continued from page 156

In 2003, nine-year-old P.J. Allen, one of the youngest survivors of the Oklahoma City bombing, takes a music lesson.

and less expensive to move to the suburbs, but then the terrorists would have won by running us out of our downtown. I remember meeting with the memorial's neighbors in 1996 and telling them we could build the most beautiful memorial in the world. But if we didn't bring life back to this site, it would not be the living memorial that we deserve. The people's resilience was evident as they chose to rebuild in the midst of a war zone, one business, one building, and one church at a time.

This was the beginning of our collective healing.

People in Oklahoma have made some tough choices over the past decade. Closing Fifth Street and building a national memorial that forces commemoration is only the beginning. Rather than turning away from this act of terrorism and ignoring April 19, 1995, we took a stand to become a place where people can learn about the senselessness of violence.

Congress also funded the new Oklahoma City Federal Building that now bookends the memorial to the north. Many survivors work there today. For some, it was not easy returning, but they worked to find healing and now are just one block from where they were a decade ago.

Others healed by participating in the legislative process and by changing laws that made a difference. Some healed by never missing a day of the trials. Many more worked on rebuilding their lives by participating in the memorial process or on a museum committee. Still others established scholarships in the names of their lost loved ones. One family established a Head Start program in their daughter's name.

The site has become a pilgrimage for Americans and people from around the world. Often, our staff hears, 'Thank you for building this.' Visitors to the memorial tell us it is one of the most powerful and healing places they have ever been. Indeed, the memorial and museum are more relevant now than ever.

Kari Watkins is the executive director of the Oklahoma City National Memorial and Museum.

says. "It's the effect it had on the people who were touched by it, and I don't think that's just confined to the people of Oklahoma City. I think there were concentric rings of impact that radiated out across the world."

"If you go back and look at television history, the Oklahoma City bombing was one of the first things Americans watched from beginning to end," says Watkins. "That's why people can relate to this site, people who knew nobody and nothing about it. It is sad what happened, but it is incredible what rose out of this tragedy. And that is a global story, an international story that continues to be told."

Continuing to tell the story is one of the memorial center's most critical missions. Immediately after the attacks of September 11, 2001, the staff mobilized to help, placing a full-page expression of sympathy in the *New York Times* and conceiving an exhibit to highlight the common events. Since April 19, 2002, the museum has hosted the award-winning special exhibit, *A Shared Experience: 04.19.95-09.11.01*, also developed by Hillmann & Carr and containing five sections focusing on the experiences Oklahomans shared with New York City, Washington, D.C., and Shanksville, Pennsylvania. Some New York residents have

'I am deeply proud of what the museum represents. It's difficult. We understand that. And yet it is tastefully done.'

made pilgrimages to Oklahoma City to see the exhibit, and the memorial center, for themselves.

Another pilgrim, Mark Andersen of San Diego, California, was captain of the Torrance, California, fire department at the time of the bombing, his unit one of many nationwide to support the rescue and recovery efforts. He returned to Oklahoma City for the first time in April.

"The memorial is exquisite, very tastefully done. I am really impressed with it," he says. "Of course it brought back a lot of memories, some painful, some very good."

Pennsylvanian John Blair also visited in April, for the third time. "I was here shortly after it happened," he says. "They were just erecting the fence. The next time I was here, they were thinking about building a memorial. It was all rubble. So we decided to come see the memorial, and it is just spectacular." The gravity of the moment brings tears. "It is one of the saddest places I have been in the world. I have been to a lot of them, and this one really hurts because it is on our territory."

Like Blair, most visitors experience a range of emotions after going through the memorial center. Volunteer Sue Craig of Midwest City says, "I enjoy volunteering on the second floor, because it is near the end. People are ready to express their feelings. Many of them want to reach out, even hug me or touch me, and they'll say, 'Oh, thank you for volunteering here,' and 'This

Above, from left: The Gallery of Honor features individual shadow boxes for each bombing victim containing personal objects chosen by their families; A Shared Experience: 04.19.95-09.11.01 was installed at the museum on April 19, 2002, and is designed to highlight common experiences of domestic terrorism victims; one of the final stops within the museum is a wall for visitors to share thoughts.

museum is beautiful; you've done such a wonderful job.'"

Family members and survivors feel the impact of the center even more acutely. Kerry Van Ess of Oklahoma City lost her father, HUD appraiser John Van Ess III, in the bombing. "I think the museum is incredibly nice," she says. "The room where they play the tape [the only known recording of the bomb, from a Water Resources Board hearing] is beyond shocking. I will say this, it's very effective."

A customer in the credit union that morning was among the most severely injured. "Being on that third floor, it all hits you," says Susan Walton. "You're just bombarded by everything that was going on that day. I could stand it for fifteen, twenty minutes, and then I had to get out of there. But the second floor is more calming. I love the children's part and where you write on the wall."

Richard Williams, a trustee who has been active in the memorial process since the earliest days, says, "I am deeply proud of what that museum represents. It tells a story, a story of a struggle, a story of loss of life, a story of survivorship, a story of what happened here and how people responded to this city and this state in a manner no one had ever experienced before. It's difficult. We understand that. And yet it is tastefully done. It is accurate. It is historical."

ALTHOUGH WELL AWARE of the importance of the past, the Oklahoma City National Memorial staff looks toward the future, a future they believe begins with children.

"There's still a great deal to be done, particularly in the arena of education," says Bob Johnson. "The most important thing we can do is reach out and touch the lives of children. We can change the mindset among children about how issues are to be resolved and the senselessness of violence as a means of issue resolution."

To that end, the memorial center continuously strengthens its educational offerings. School groups receive discounted admission, and affordable curriculum materials including videos and books on nonviolence and conflict resolution are available to teachers upon request. Each spring, students are invited to compete for cash prizes in an essay competition divided into several grade categories, the prize-winners announced at the April anniversary ceremony.

Watkins is most excited, though, about a distance learning program to be launched in late 2003. "We'll be able to connect with a DSL, computer, or fiber-optic line to a classroom in Baghdad or Tel Aviv and teach a class from the Oklahoma City National Memorial. We can have firemen here talking to firemen in New York City. We can have rescuers here talking to rescuers at the Pentagon."

From the earliest days following April 19, 2001, getting people connected and helping others is, and indeed always has been, what the Oklahoma City National Memorial represents best.

That, and remembering.

Kari Watkins says, "We built this place to last, so it's critical that we maintain it in the manner in which we built it. Our people know that, and they understand that mediocrity isn't acceptable."

She pauses.

"I think back to those 168 chairs. They died in a capacity for their country. I don't think mediocre would serve them."

. . . .

Steffie Corcoran is senior editor at Oklahoma Today.

THE BEST DEFENSE

The Memorial Institute for the Prevention of Terrorism goes on

the offensive to protect Americans.

By Chad Love

The MIPT library is one of the largest public terrorism resource collections in the nation.

IN EVERY JOB, however menial or monumental, there are those unavoidable moments when enthusiasm flags, focus is lost, and tedium sets in. In those moments, we may search for a renewed sense of purpose to sharpen our focus and remind us of the intrinsic worth of the work we do. When General Dennis Reimer starts feeling that way, a quick glance out his office window is all the bolstering he needs.

As director of Oklahoma City's National Memorial Institute for the Prevention of Terrorism (MIPT), Reimer is confronted by those personal motivations every day: His organization's offices are located in the Journal Record Building right next door to the Oklahoma City National Memorial.

"When you can look out the window and see the physical memorial, it really focuses you on what we're doing here," says Reimer, a Medford native who retired in 1999 after a thirty-seven-year career in the army. He returned to Oklahoma to direct the institute, often described as the third part of the Oklahoma City National Memorial, but one whose history and mission many Oklahomans aren't familiar with.

Reimer says, "After the bombing, the family members and survivors felt very strongly about having an organization that looked to the future, one that would try to prevent what happened here from happening again and to help mitigate its effects when it does occur."

And that, says Reimer, is the institute's primary mission and charter. How the MIPT accomplishes those goals is a reflection of how much the organization has evolved and grown, from the kernel of an idea in the minds of a few far-thinking individuals to an important cog in the national homeland defense machinery.

Oklahoma is a relatively small, interconnected state, and the intimacy of our collective suffering in the wake of the bombing certainly reflected that connectedness. It also played a large part in determining the future role of the institute. Personal relationships forged between rescue workers, survivors, and family members was a powerful motivation for the original idea of taking on a project that looked to the future.

"It was extremely impressive that people who had lost so much wanted to work toward something that helped others," says Oklahoma City attorney Cheryl Vaught, who serves as the vice-chair of the MIPT's board of directors. "But that's Oklahoma for you. A rescue worker pulls a wife or husband out of the building, and there's an opportunity to personally get to know

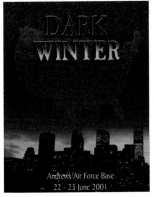

those people and respect the fact of what they did. People made that connection."

Those relationships eventually led to the merging of two not entirely disparate ideas: a desire among survivors and family members for a proactive institute to combat terrorism, and the Alliance for Public Policy, a state organization working to bring more research dollars into Oklahoma. The two groups came together, and the result was the genesis of the National Memorial Institute for the Prevention of Terrorism.

"It was a terrific process," says Vaught. "Some of the best minds in the state were saying, 'We want this to be something meaningful, with longevity.'"

The two groups met with the U.S. Department of Justice Science and Technology Division to work on legislation and funding. "It's amazing what this has turned into," says Vaught. "It's really important that people understand what has been accomplished in Oklahoma in such a short time."

Initially, the institute was heavily involved in research projects, but, in addition to a continuing focus on first responders, the organization has moved more into the field of content management for online terrorism databases.

"September 11 showed us that the line between domestic terrorism and international terrorism is really blurred," says Reimer. "Although the Murrah bombing was domestic terrorism and 9/11 was international, the mitigation is the same. We talk about combating terrorism on U.S. soil."

Reimer also categorizes the institute as an "honest broker" that tries to facilitate coordination between the various agencies charged with responding to terrorism.

"If you're going to have a national system that deals with terrorist attacks, you've got to have the federal, state, and local governments cooperating in a focused and coherent manner," Reimer says. "All of them have separate responsibilities, so you really need some entity to tie this all together, and that is the purpose we serve."

Some of the Institute's programs have had far-reaching national consequences. In 2001, it hosted an exercise dubbed Dark Winter, in which the MIPT and several other organizations hypothesized what would happen if smallpox were reintroduced into the population. "Because of that," says Reimer, "the government changed its policy and provided enough smallpox shots for every man, woman, and child in the country."

The Institute is also starting to play a key role in designing and implementing national terrorism policy.

"We're heavily involved with writing the implementation plan for what's known as Homeland Security Presidential Directive 8," says Reimer. "That requires the Department of Homeland Security to come up with a national preparedness system."

WHILE REIMER'S DEVOTION to the institute is rooted in duty, Don Ferrell's is rooted in loss. His daughter, thirty-seven-year-old Susan Ferrell, was an attorney for the United States Department of Housing and Urban Development who died in the Murrah building bombing.

Ferrell has been involved with the institute from the initial idea to its current status as one of the premier sources of terrorism information in the world. He also has served as the chair of the institute's board of directors since the organization was officially chartered on September 23, 1999.

"In the beginning, it was just an idea," he says. "The memorial and the museum look backward to tell us what happened, and everyone involved thought we needed to have something looking forward, an activist part that tries to do something about the future."

The institute operates under a nine-member board that oversees the organization's charter while giving the staff the flexibility to expand its original mission, and Ferrell believes the original vision of the survivors and family members has been successfully met.

"The MIPT has been a well-kept secret, but it has great potential," says Ferrell. "We have a fantastic board and an exceptional staff under General Reimer."

Today, the institute is involved in a dizzying number of projects, but from the beginning, one of its key missions has been helping first responders, those emergency personnel who risk their lives in the immediate aftermath of a terrorist attack.

"We've always had a focus on emergency responders across the nation, not just in Oklahoma," says Reimer. "We're not a think tank; we're more of an action agency. We do a lot of thinking, but what we do most is listen to emergency responders, figure out what they need, and then try to best help them." In essence, the institute acts as a clearing-house and database for a wealth of technical information for first responder agencies.

"Definitely one of the most important projects we have going is what we call our Lessons Learned Information Sharing database," Reimer says. The Lessons Learned program is an online

Dennis J. Reimer, director of the National Memorial Institute for the Prevention of Terrorism, discusses the MIPT-produced book, Oklahoma City, Seven Years Later.

In May 2004, crews worked on the ceiling of the MIPT library. The library, which opened in November 2004, is a research repository containing thousands of terrorism-related documents, books, and articles.

network allowing emergency responders across the nation to share good ideas and lessons learned from real-world training exercises. According to Reimer, the program has become "the national system" for emergency responders.

Another successful component of the institute, says Reimer, was its effort to put together a "responder knowledge base" which emergency agencies can access to get the latest information on specialized equipment.

"Responders have to purchase and use equipment in any disaster, and they don't really have a good way to determine if the equipment they're buying is the right equipment," he says. "The responder knowledge base lists all of the authorized equipment federal funds can be used to purchase and gives a link on how to get federal funding to purchase the equipment."

Major Brian Stanaland of the Oklahoma City Fire Department says the institute is an invaluable resource for agencies nationwide. "A fire department may experience something that's never happened before, and if another department has had a similar incident, they can get with the MIPT and utilize that information," he says.

In 2002, the institute sponsored a report entitled *Oklahoma City: Seven Years Later.*

"The project went back and looked at the main decision-makers—the governor, mayor, police chief, fire chief, and all of the others who participated," says Reimer. "We basically said, with seven years of hindsight, tell us what you think you did right, what you think you could have done better. The book provides a summary analysis of that."

The document, which was started prior to September 11, 2001, has been widely distributed around the country.

As important as the institute's work prior to September 11, its aftermath vaulted the MIPT to the forefront of the nascent homeland defense movement. It is a testament to the foresight of the institute's vision that many of its projects became even more important in a post-September 11 world.

That prescience is the reason why the institute is now playing a prominent role in the U.S. Department of Homeland Security. Most of the institute's funding flows through the Office of Domestic Preparedness, directed by Suzanne Mencer.

"Homeland Security has many partners across the country," she says, "but the MIPT is our lead in providing first responders with lessons learned. We are in constant contact with the MIPT on a variety of issues, including the implementation of Homeland Security Presidential Directive 8."

Edwin Corr, an MIPT board member and associate director of international programs at the University of Oklahoma, concurs. "Because of the superb work that's been done by the staff, the excellence of the institute has come to be recognized by people all over, particularly in the Department of Homeland Security."

Corr, a former United States ambassador and career diplomat with twenty-nine years in some of the most terrorism-wracked regions of the world, believes many of the things Reimer and his staff have focused on have begun paying off.

"Although we're still a semiautonomous group, we are becoming more and more an integral part of that whole mission of trying to deal with terrorism," says Corr. "There's a sense in Washington that here [in Oklahoma City] we have this superbly led staff of very competent people. They know that with the brainpower and experience and focus we bring to a subject, we can produce high-quality studies and proposals in a very short time."

Like everyone associated with the institute, Reimer is justifiably proud of what the MIPT has accomplished in its relatively short life. But he's even more proud of what and whom the institute represents.

"It truly is a living memorial," says Reimer. "One of the things that always impresses me is that Oklahoma City in 1995 was really at a crossroads. We could have felt sorry for ourselves, and no one would have blamed us. We had suffered a great and unexpected tragedy, and it affected everyone in the city to some extent. But Oklahoma City chose to make things better for others. That's why this mission and charter is so very important to all of us."

A COMMUNITY CHANGED

In December 1993, Oklahoma City voters approved the most ambitious public works project in the nation's history, the Metropolitan Area Projects (MAPS). The visionary plan, combined with the construction of the memorial on the Alfred P. Murrah Federal Building site, resulted in Oklahoma City's emergence as a progressive metropolis.

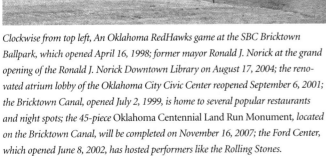

Clockwise from top left, An Oklahoma RedHawks game at the SBC Bricktown Ballpark, which opened April 16, 1998; former mayor Ronald J. Norick at the grand opening of the Ronald J. Norick Downtown Library on August 17, 2004; the renovated atrium lobby of the Oklahoma City Civic Center reopened September 6, 2001; the Bricktown Canal, opened July 2, 1999, is home to several popular restaurants and night spots; the 45-piece Oklahoma Centennial Land Run Monument, located on the Bricktown Canal, will be completed on November 16, 2007; the Ford Center, which opened June 8, 2002, has hosted performers like the Rolling Stones.

TIMOTHY McVEIGH RECEIVES THE DEATH PENALTY

By Julie DelCour

IN A YEAR THAT saw a record-setting number of Oklahoma executions, the one most closely identified with our state did not even happen here.

On June 11, 2001, an hour after sunrise, Oklahoma City bomber Timothy James McVeigh was put to death by the government he despised at the U.S. Penitentiary in Terre Haute, Indiana.

The first federal execution in thirty-eight years was carried out six years, one month, and twenty-three days after the deadliest crime in Oklahoma history. The April 19, 1995, bombing of the Alfred P. Murrah Federal Building killed 168 people, including 19 children. Until eclipsed by the September 11 attacks on the World Trade Center and Pentagon, the bombing ranked as the worst act of terrorism on American soil.

"This is a completion of justice," Kathleen Treanor, who lost her four-year-old daughter and in-laws in the bombing, told the *Dallas Morning News*. "From my family's standpoint, we have gathered no joy from seeing a person die. I don't think anything can bring me peace....When I die and they lay me in my grave is when I'll have closure."

From the nation's capital, President Bush issued a statement: "Today every living person who was hurt by the evil done in Oklahoma City can rest in the knowledge that there has been a reckoning."

Originally set for May 16, the execution was delayed one month after the FBI revealed it had withheld more than 4,400 pages of material from the defense. McVeigh's attorneys frantically battled for more time to investigate.

But at a June 6 hearing in Denver, U.S. district judge Richard P. Matsch denied a request for a stay of execution, calling McVeigh an "instrument of death and destruction." The next day, after a panel of the U.S. Court of Appeals, Tenth Circuit, also rejected a stay, McVeigh ordered his attorneys to abandon further appeals.

Four days later, the life of the man who took so many lives ended quietly. The first federal execution since the Kennedy administration went off like clockwork inside the never-used $500,000 federal execution facility, completed five years previously.

Unlike his cruel and unusual crime, which ripped apart bodies and shredded a nine-story building in a mangle of chaos and terror, the execution of McVeigh was an exhaustively scripted, seemingly painless process following a fifty-four-page U.S. Bureau of Prisons' protocol.

"There was no sign of suffering," said reporter Crocker Stephenson of the *Milwaukee Journal Sentinel*, one of ten media witnesses who viewed the execution. "The most remarkable thing to me was how...subtle the process was in which he slipped from life to death."

McVeigh made no final statement at the execution. Instead, he earlier had given Warden Harley Lappin a poem to release as his last words. In his own handwriting, McVeigh had carefully printed the 1875 poem "Invictus," by William Ernest Henley, which read in part, "I am the master of my fate; I am the captain of my soul."

Before the execution began, McVeigh, an agnostic raised in a Catholic family, received the last rites, which ask for forgiveness from God in the event of death. Viewing the execution from Oklahoma City, Larry Whicher, whose brother, Alan, died in the bombing, described McVeigh as having a look of defiance. "I don't think he gave himself to the Lord. I don't think he repented, and personally I think he's in hell."

Media witness Kevin Johnson of *USA Today* saw something else: "There was no sense of defiance." Johnson added that the thirty-three-year-old McVeigh had aged considerably from April 21, 1995, when, outfitted in an orange jail-issue jumpsuit and handcuffs, he emerged from the Noble County Courthouse in Perry, Oklahoma.

McVeigh never apologized for his crimes.

Strapped to a gurney, he died with his piercing blue eyes open, staring straight into an overhead closed-circuit television camera that beamed his execution to 232 victims and survivors gathered at an Oklahoma City auditorium.

Lappin pronounced McVeigh dead at 7:14 a.m. (CDT), only minutes after lethal chemicals, coursing into his right leg through gray and yellow IV tubes, put him to sleep, halted his breathing, and stopped his heart.

According to McVeigh's wishes, his body was cremated. His attorney, Rob Nigh Jr. of Tulsa, said the ashes would be strewn at a secret location that Nigh promised would not be in Oklahoma.

"Of course, we can say it was Tim himself [who] caused their pain, and we would be half right. It would be a lie to say that we are not responsible for doubling their pain, because there is a reasonable way to deal with crime that doesn't involve killing one more human being," Nigh said.

The ten victim witnesses, selected by lottery to view the execution, embraced each other afterwards. Witness Paul Howell, whose daughter Karan Shepherd died in the blast, said: "I was looking directly at him...I thought, this man can never hurt us again in any form or fashion."

With his demise, McVeigh undid the last wish of Victor Harry Feguer, who, in 1963, was the last federal inmate executed. Feguer's dying words were: "I sure hope I'm the last one to go."

Journalists from around the world gather at the U.S. Penitentiary in Terre Haute, Indiana; on the morning of Timothy McVeigh's execution, Aren Almon Kok, mother of Baylee Almon, visits her daughter's chair with husband Stanley Kok at the Oklahoma City National Memorial; death penalty opponent Bud Welch, who lost daughter Julie Welch in the bombing, in Terre Haute

JUSTICE REVISITED

Federally convicted conspirator Terry Nichols receives a

second trial, this time on state soil.

By Rod Walton

*On August 9, 2004, Terry Nichols enters the Pittsburg County
Courthouse for sentencing on state charges of murdering 161
people in the Oklahoma City bombing.*

WHATEVER TERRY NICHOLS'S state trial achieved, most of all, it seemed to give many Oklahoma City bombing survivors and victims' families a long-sought sense of justice. That gnawing pain most of them still felt in the pits of their stomachs, that groaning in the heart, finally had expression in 2004. Nichols was forced to sit in a McAlester courtroom nearly every day from March to mid-June to face charges of murdering 161 people. He will serve life in prison for each of those deaths.

It wasn't the type of penalty many survivors and victims' families had hoped for, but they believed it was at least Nichols's comeuppance for his role in killing all of those people—168 altogether—on an April morning nearly ten years ago.

"Terry Nichols, for the first time now, is a convicted mass murderer, a term and title he's never had before and a responsibility he's always had," Oklahoma County district attorney Wes Lane said during a press conference after the trial.

Nichols's state trial ended in June in much the same way his federal trial for killing eight federal agents ended in 1997: He was convicted of counts that could have brought the death penalty, but once again, a jury agonized over the decision. Their deadlock meant that Oklahoma district judge Steven Taylor would have to make the decision. By law, he could not give the death penalty without a jury's recommendation.

And just as in 1997, Nichols received a sentence of life in prison without parole. "It's my judgment that you have a long time to think about what you've done," Judge Taylor said at Nichols's sentencing in August. But the real news at sentencing was that Nichols finally decided to face the people most aggrieved over his plot. In a thin, shaky voice, the previously silent coconspirator apologized for the bombing—while not exactly taking responsibility—and warned his audience to get closer to God.

It was the Almighty, after all, who had spared Nichols himself, he pointed out. "The reason death was not given is for the simple and abundantly clear fact that God is in control," he said. "And it was God who, through the Holy Spirit, worked in the hearts of those jurors who refused to vote for death."

His audience was unmoved. "I don't appreciate being preached to by him," Darlene Welch told the *Tulsa World*. Welch lost her four-year-old niece, Ashley M. Eckles, in the Murrah

Clockwise from top left, Witness Michael Fortier enters the Pittsburg County Courthouse; sisters Peggie Pietrowicz and Lynne Gist, who lost their sister Karen Gist Carr in the bombing, hug during a break; Oklahoma County district attorney Wes Lane and former district attorney Bob Macy leave the courthouse; Timothy McVeigh's sister, Jennifer McVeigh, is escorted out of the courthouse under a jacket; district judge Steven W. Taylor presided over the state trial.

bombing. "The sad thing to me is that even today, Mr. Nichols couldn't stand here and say, 'I did it,'" Welch said.

From day one of the trial, his defense team, led by Ponca City attorney Brian Hermanson, focused on Timothy McVeigh and asked both judge and jury to consider the possibility that numerous other people, not Nichols, were responsible for the crime.

The prosecution, led by assistant Oklahoma County district attorney Sandra Elliott, meanwhile, was centered on much of the same evidence used at Nichols's federal trial. Jurors learned about using fertilizer and fuel to make bombs and about Nichols and McVeigh's joint hatred of the federal government. They also heard that Nichols drove to Oklahoma City on Easter Sunday 1995 to drop off the getaway car.

The first day of testimony began with Taylor removing three jurors because of their family relationship to an Oklahoma County prosecutor not involved in the trial. Another juror eventually left during the trial due to health problems, while two more were dismissed between the verdict and sentencing phases. It seemed Taylor was proved right in his decision to seat eighteen total jurors early on. By final deliberations, he was left with no extras.

The jury took only four hours to cut through three months of testimony and find Nichols guilty on all counts. Many onlookers publicly guessed that Nichols would surely die by lethal injection someday.

It wasn't to be. The deadlock encouraged various trial critics, who complained that the case wasn't worth the multimillion-dollar expense because Nichols already was spending life in prison. But, some survivors replied, those critics hadn't lost a loved one in the Oklahoma City blast.

"What I realized is that it was not about the death penalty," Wes Lane told reporters afterward. "What I realized that day was that this was about all these families believing they had never had their day in court."

A RACE TO REMEMBER

The Oklahoma City Memorial Marathon inspires athletes from around the world.

By Evan Jensen

Norman resident Conor Holt wins the 2004 race with a time of two hours, 22 minutes, and 54 seconds, a course record.

ON A SUNDAY morning in late April, they wait silently in darkness. The seconds tick by on an illuminated digital clock. A light wind travels down Robinson Avenue, stirring the leaves of a stalwart American elm, familiarly known as the Survivor Tree. The nearly 1,700 runners have been prepared with iron will and months of training, but none edges toward the starting line or speaks a single word. A solemn 168 silent seconds elapse.

Honoring the victims who perished in the April 19, 1995, bombing of the Alfred P. Murrah building, the 26.2-mile Oklahoma City Memorial Marathon begins. The annual race is a celebration of life and the premier endurance event in Oklahoma. It is also a rare opportunity to unite the entire community.

"Virtually everyone in the state was touched somehow by the bombing," says Mark Bravo, Oklahoma City running coach and KFOR-TV color commentator for the marathon. "This race is an inclusive event that gives us a way to remember the tragedy, honor the victims who died, and enjoy the sport of running."

Thanks to the inspiration and efforts of runners Chet Collier and Thomas Hill of Oklahoma City, the inaugural marathon began in 2001 and quickly became the most renowned marathon in the region. Keeping the entire community in mind, race organizers encouraged volunteer support and included relay events, a kids' marathon, shorter runs, and an event expo.

Three years later, boasting marathon participants from forty-seven states and several foreign countries, the Oklahoma City Memorial Marathon was ranked among the twelve top marathons in the world by *Runner's World* race and event promotion director Bart Yasso, a veteran of 150 marathons, who called it his "most memorable."

Showcasing Oklahoma City highlights including Bricktown, the State Capitol, Automobile Alley, the shorelines of Lake Hefner, and historic neighborhoods, spectators and runners like Norman resident Adam Cohen return to challenge personal limits and honor the victims and survivors of one of the

Hundreds of runners at the 26.2-mile 2004 Oklahoma City Memorial Marathon

worst terrorist attacks in United States history.

"Standing in the shadow of the memorial and looking out at the field of empty chairs at the start of the race really puts the marathon in a different perspective," says Cohen, who has competed in twenty-three marathons, including the New York and Boston marathons. "I keep coming back to this race because of its purpose and support from the entire city."

With crowd support, runners charge through challenging miles of the marathon known as "the wall," a point of physical exhaustion often compared to hitting a brick wall and occurring around the eighteen- to twenty-two-mile mark. The finish line is marked by bleachers filled with cheering fans and postrace amenities like massage, cold drinks, and energy foods.

Says 2004 women's champion Tracy Evans of Woodward, "I really like this race because it is an emotional event tied to remembering what happened here. Even after running the last four years, I still cry a little when I cross the finish line."

Paul and Linda Lekawski have participated in the marathon each year, but that's just the beginning of their involvement. The two also stuff race packets, work at the event expo merchandise store, and man the expo booth for the Oklahoma City Running Club. While they share a love of running, the Oklahoma City Memorial Marathon also provides a way for them to honor their nephew, Scott Williams of Tuttle, who died in the bombing.

"We ran the first marathon together with a picture of our nephew on our shirts," says Paul Lekawski. "Overcoming thoughts of quitting at twenty-two miles and finally crossing the finish line really gave me a sense of accomplishment. I think this marathon helps take the sadness out of the tragedy by honoring the victims and lifting the spirits of the survivors."

An enduring hallmark of human compassion and personal achievement, thousands of runners each year will accept the challenge of the Oklahoma City Memorial Marathon. Beginning with 168 seconds of reverent silence, each step of the race will honor the memory of those lost, celebrate the gift of life, and move forward to a better future.

FROM THE GROUND UP

A new federal building symbolizes the future and an indomitable spirit.

By Mike Brake

Colonel Sheila Scanlon speaks at the May 3, 2004, dedication of the Oklahoma City Federal Building. The new facility houses 12 federal agencies.

FOR DIANNE DOOLEY, moving into Oklahoma City's new downtown federal office building in spring 2004 was "like coming home."

With hundreds of others who survived the 1995 bombing of the Alfred P. Murrah building, Dooley had endured a nine-year diaspora. The displaced agencies and the shaken, often injured survivors who made up their staffs had faced unimaginable obstacles as they tried to reconstitute their work homes.

In the bombing, files had been damaged or destroyed. Computers and office furniture, along with the typical desktop keepsakes so many had brought to work, lay buried in rubble. Most of all, there were missing coworkers, human voids that never could be filled.

But those agencies existed to serve the public. They had to rebuild. In the early days after the bombing, they found new temporary office space at a variety of locations, and over the years, agencies like the Department of Housing and Urban Development, the Social Security Administration, and Dooley's own Department of Veterans Affairs settled into what many called a "new normal."

Still, it was clear that the city needed a new, centrally located federal building. U.S. representative Ernest Istook secured congressional funding for the structure as long ago as late 1995, and soon after, a site was selected: directly across the street to the northwest from the former Murrah building location, now occupied by the Oklahoma City National Memorial.

Carol Ross Barney of Ross Barney and Jankowski, a Chicago architectural firm, was selected to design the new building. For her, the project was a unique challenge, since new federal buildings were required to adopt certain security features implemented in the wake of the Oklahoma City bombing. Those additions ultimately drove the building's cost to $33 million.

"It has a lot of significance to the people of Oklahoma City and the people of our country," says Ross Barney of the new three-and-a-half-story Oklahoma City Federal Building, which essentially replaces, in its 180,000 square feet, the office space once provided by the Murrah building.

Ross Barney's design was for a structure encompassing a full city block with two main entrances and sturdy concrete barriers to prevent future attacks. The building's glass is blast-resistant, and entry and exit points are closely guarded.

Those features reassured Dooley and many other bombing survivors, but a group of HUD workers repeatedly petitioned the government to allow them to work elsewhere. Many said they were concerned about returning to work so close to the place where they had lost friends and coworkers. HUD ultimately permitted eighteen employees to continue working at another location downtown or from their homes.

But for Dooley and most other former Murrah building workers, restoring their federal offices to downtown was right and proper.

"I feel like we've come full circle," she says. "They didn't keep us down. We built a bigger, better, safer building."

A FATEFUL DAY

A decade later, Oklahoma's governor looks back on the Alfred

P. Murrah building bombing and its impact. By Brad Henry

INCREDIBLY, I WITNESSED the explosion on April 19, 1995. It happened during my ordinarily mundane commute from Shawnee to the State Capitol building, where I was serving in the Oklahoma State Senate. I was traveling north on the Centennial Expressway, approaching the downtown exit. I was talking to a constituent on my cell phone when something caused me to glance west.

Suddenly, a tremendous orange fireball burst above the cityscape. I put the phone down, wondering what was happening. Then I saw thick, dark smoke, great billowing clouds blanketing the sky.

My immediate thought was that someone had ventured to start a fire on top of the old YMCA building. But as I watched the black smoke engulf the skyline, I had a strange, sickening feeling. Seconds later, I heard the din of police and ambulance sirens speeding toward downtown. Only then did I begin to realize the magnitude of what had occurred.

You can experience something and still not fully comprehend its impact. Indeed, the bombing wounded Oklahoma City and the entire state and nation in immeasurable ways that the national media, despite comprehensive coverage, was unable to capture in TV images and newspaper headlines. The scars were deep and enduring.

When we talk about the Oklahoma family, it is without irony or rhetorical flourish. Oklahomans are a close-knit people, and collectively we weathered the agony of April 19, 1995.

There were 168 of our friends and loved ones murdered for the sole transgression of going about their daily routine. They went to work that morning, visited a federal office, were dropped off at daycare—and they died for it. The numbers were staggering: 168 people dead, 850 others injured, more than 300 buildings damaged or destroyed. Some estimated that nearly 400,000 Oklahoma City residents knew at least one person who died in the explosion.

But Oklahomans are strong and resilient. We rise from adversity with a renewed commitment to persevere and learn. From the Dust Bowl of the 1930s to the oil bust and subsequent economic crisis of the 1980s to the despicable act of violence on April 19, 1995, our struggles do not conquer us. When Will Rogers remarked that the best way out of difficulty was to go through it, he summed up a key characteristic of Oklahoma.

The bombing stemmed from the flames of white-hot hatred, but from that furnace emerged a steely resolve. Our faith and spirit would not be defeated. The world witnessed an extraordinary phenomenon in Oklahoma, a unity of purpose that came to be called the Oklahoma Standard.

Firefighters and other rescuers worked around the clock. Law enforcement proved tireless. Medical professionals performed miracles. Residents lined up to donate blood, clothing, bottled water—anything that was needed. It was an exceptional display of people coming together, and it predated by six years the goodwill that America would see again in the wake of September 11, 2001.

When we talk about tragedies such as the federal building bombing or 9/11, we often use the phrase "forever changed" so much that we nearly sap it of any meaning. But it remains an accurate description of the bombing's aftermath. A beautiful memorial and poignant museum are where the Alfred P. Murrah Federal Building once stood. Our federal laws reflect that the attack raised awareness of victims' rights and highlighted the need for vigilance in combating terrorists, whether foreign or homegrown. Oklahoma has moved on, but we are not the same state that existed prior to 9:02 a.m. on that ill-fated day.

The Oklahoma City National Memorial is truly astonishing. I have visited it and its museum on a number of occasions, and each time I find myself deeply moved. It evokes so many emotions—anger, grief, sadness, resolve, hope, love.

As a lifelong Oklahoman who is privileged to serve as governor of this great state, I sometimes feel as if I am still seeing the explosion without fully comprehending its impact. Scholars can discuss its role in United States and world history. Psychologists and sociologists can examine the emotional residue left in its wake. All I know with certainty is that I love this great state; Oklahomans are strong, compassionate people; and the bombing forever changed us—in ways that are still unfolding.

God bless us all.

The Heartland Chapel is located at the First United Methodist Church, across the street from the Oklahoma City National Memorial.

FROM APRIL 19 TO SEPTEMBER 11: THE LASTING CONNECTION BETWEEN OKLAHOMA CITY AND NEW YORK CITY.

By Rudolph W. Giuliani

THE TERRORIST BOMBING at the Alfred P. Murrah building in Oklahoma City sent a shock throughout the nation. We learned that no city is immune from the horrors of those who kill innocent Americans. The 168 people killed on April 19, 1995, made the attack the deadliest act of terrorism on American soil in our country's history—until September 11, 2001.

In fact, those two terrorist attacks link New York City and Oklahoma City, and many of the memories are eerily similar: a shocking blast in the morning of a beautiful day; a building collapsing with innocent people inside it; the shriek of sirens; rescue workers bravely rushing to the scene in a desperate search for survivors; the collapsed façade of an office building.

Images from both days still haunt us. In Oklahoma, the picture of Baylee Almon's lifeless body in the tender grasp of a firefighter is one Americans will never forget. In New York, the image of Father Mychal Judge's lifeless body being carried out of the devastation by New York City emergency responders stays with us.

AP/WIDE WORLD PHOTOS

Rudy Giuliani at the December 2001 dedication of the World Trade Center's Ground Zero public viewing platform

And just as September 11, 2001, produced countless acts of bravery and heroism, so too did the rescue efforts in Oklahoma City. It bore witness to the inspiring selflessness of the American spirit. In fact, I'm proud to say that the Urban Search and Rescue team sent to Oklahoma to assist in the recovery operation included dozens of New York City firefighters and police officers.

Tragically, several of the people who led that effort were killed in the attack on the World Trade Center. Men like Ray Downey, Terry Hatton, Michael Curtin, William Lake, and several others were among those who helped in Oklahoma City and then died on September 11, 2001. They were the exact people I would have relied on to lead the recovery effort in New York City, had they not been murdered by the terrorists who perpetrated the attacks on September 11, 2001.

Terrorists cannot invade and conquer our country. They cannot take over American cities. Their most effective weapon is to do the unexpected. We must not focus therefore exclusively on the tactics or source of terror from the last attack. The next may well be different.

For example, the first bombing of the World Trade Center in 1993 might have raised national consciousness about the threat of radical Islamicists. But someone focused exclusively on radical Islam might have ignored the threat of Timothy McVeigh and Terry Nichols.

We must not underestimate the ingenuity of terrorists. No amount of preparation can anticipate every attack. But preparing for all of the attacks you can envision inevitably leaves you better prepared for the attacks you cannot. Our goal must be relentless preparation. For example, no one anticipated that passenger jet airliners would be hijacked and used as intercontinental ballistic missiles. However, the rescue teams in New York City constantly prepared and drilled for building collapses, high-rise fires, mass evacuations, plane crashes, and hospital triage. Therefore, they were able to handle the attacks, even though the precise nature of the attack had not been predicted.

It might not appear that Oklahoma City, in the heart of the Midwest, would have much in common with the metropolis of New York City. But that would be an uninformed conclusion. In their respective times of crisis, the cities demonstrated their similarities. Both cities were so resilient because both cities are American.

The tragedy of the Oklahoma City bombing reminds us that terrorists can live close to home. And it reminds us that heroes live here, too.

Rudy Giuliani is chairman and chief executive officer of Giuliani Partners, which he founded in January 2002. He served New York City as mayor for two terms, from 1993 to 2001.

In the Days Following the Bombing, One Network Anchor Found the Heartland

By Tom Brokaw

WHEN THE INITIAL news bulletins about a massive explosion in the heart of Oklahoma City first began to cross my desk, I was as puzzled as everyone else. Was it some kind of natural gas malfunction? Terrorism was not yet America's first reaction to a sudden catastrophic event.

When it became clear that in fact the Murrah federal building was the deliberate target of a huge truck bomb and as the television images of dead children and battered adults being carried out of the wreckage began to emerge, I wondered aloud, "My God, why would anyone do such a thing?"

Ten years later, after all the trials, the execution of Timothy McVeigh, and the lifelong imprisonment of Terry Nichols, that remains an enduring question. The rage of McVeigh and Nichols against the federal government was a deeply irrational response to distortions and delusional conclusions about the place of government in the lives of ordinary Americans. That they believed they could somehow advance their cause by destroying lives and inducing physical, psychological, and emotional terror in the American heartland defies any explanation or understanding.

Indeed, as I learned when I arrived in Oklahoma City the morning after the bombing and in subsequent visits, the response of the people of this great heartland state was a profound and powerful rebuttal to the despicable actions of these homegrown terrorists.

Oklahoma City's first responders—the fire and police departments, emergency medical teams and doctors, nurses and aides in the hospitals—performed heroically under the most difficult possible conditions. Strangers quickly became family for the victims, providing emotional, financial, and everyday assistance. Political adversaries set aside their differences and joined in the common cause of healing the wounds of the city and the state.

For those of us who arrived from out of town to cover the tragedy, it was a welcome lesson in Oklahoma hospitality. NBC News set up shop in a family printing business that had been badly damaged by the explosion, and the owners were there every day to make sure we had what we needed.

In the days, months, and years that followed, the people of Oklahoma, through their courage, compassion, and memorials, have provided us all with lasting lessons on the real meaning of the American experience. We have our differences, large and small, but we are bound together more by what joins us than what divides us.

Tom Brokaw, former anchor and managing editor of NBC Nightly News, *was the first network anchor to report from the site of the Oklahoma City bombing. He retired on December 1, 2004.*

A DECADE LATER, THE WORLD TOOK NOTE

Family, victims, the community, and national leaders—all were touched by the Oklahoma City bombing. Here, a few remark on the event and the passage of time. As former attorney general Janet Reno said in fall 2004, "The strength of the people of Oklahoma City will shine through the years."

BILL CLINTON, *president of the United States of America, 1993-2001*

As we approach the tenth anniversary of the Oklahoma City bombing, our thoughts are once again with those who lost their lives and their loved ones.

Because of them, and those we have lost since, we can never forget our responsibility to protect America from terrorism. Because of them, we can never forget to respect public servants, honor their contributions to our lives, and remain on guard against the kind of hate speech that encourages a climate of violence. Because of them, we can never forget that while our differences make life interesting, our common humanity matters more.

On this anniversary, we must also remember and honor the powerful example the people of Oklahoma City have set for the rest of us. I said in my remarks at the dedication of the memorial in 2000, "We may never have all the answers for what happened here. But as we continue our journey toward understanding, one truth is clear: What was meant to break has made you stronger." In the ten years since the attack, the people of Oklahoma City have shown America and the world the true meaning of strength and the healing power of community and faith.

Hillary and I offer our prayers for all the families who suffered such a grievous loss in 1995 and our thanks for the lives of those they loved. The memories of husbands, wives, parents, and children who went to work or daycare and did not come home will never dim. May the power of their spirits and their sacrifice inspire us to do all we can to build a more peaceful future for our country and the world.

FRANK KEATING, *Oklahoma governor, 1995-2003*

When Reverend Billy Graham walked to the podium at the nationally televised prayer service four days after the 1995

The image of an Oklahoma City firefighter holding Baylee Almon is recalled in a Slate.com cartoon about the 2004 Russian school hostage crisis.

bombing, I wondered what he could say to heal this terrible wound. What he said was this: God didn't do this, man did—but God can redeem us.

If there is one feeling that returns whenever I think of what our city and state endured ten years ago, it is the overwhelming sense of spirituality embodied in Billy Graham's words. We clogged the churches in those days and weeks in 1995, even when some of those churches had been damaged by the bomb. We prayed. We looked to something larger than ourselves. And in that seeking, we found a closer connection to God. May we never lose that gift.

CATHY KEATING, *first lady of Oklahoma, 1995-2003*

I'll never forget one of the first things I saw at the Murrah building site in April 1995. It was a teddy bear, propped lovingly against a makeshift fence—a sign of hope.

Teddy bears and toys began appearing within hours after the bombing. Soon they were followed by lapel pins signifying the agencies that had lost members in the blast, and then by multicolored ribbons. We didn't know it at the time, but we were creating a new national tradition.

Since 1995, wherever tragedy has come from—natural disasters or man-made violence—those ribbons and pins and bears have appeared once again, symbols of a special strength that began in Oklahoma. That's a legacy that emphasized the good, not the bad. I am proud to say it was Oklahoma's gift to the nation.

RONALD J. NORICK, *Oklahoma City mayor, 1987-1998*

It's hard to imagine the tragic bombing of the Murrah building was ten years ago. Anytime I think about that day, it is still so vivid in my mind—not just the destroyed building, but also all of the rescue workers trying to find some reason why this happened.

I remember talking to every team of rescue workers who came from all parts of this great land to help us. They all asked the same questions: Why Oklahoma City? Why were innocent peoples' lives taken, regardless of their age? Since that time, Oklahoma City has rebuilt itself physically, but that tragic time will never be forgotten. I witnessed a great nation come together to help their fellow man like never before. God bless America.

JAMES LEE WITT, *director of the Federal Emergency Management Agency, 1993-2001*

It's hard to believe that so much time has passed since that horrible day. It seems just like yesterday. The images are still so vivid in my mind, images of people who were suffering and images of all of the rescue and law enforcement teams we worked with so long and hard. I'll always remember when I was there with President Clinton and we visited with the little boy who had undergone so many surgeries. His dad was so proud of his strength and courage. These are memories I will always carry with me, particularly of the hope and spirit of the survivors and families. I pray they will remember the good things about their loved ones and that those memories will carry them through in peace for the rest of their lives.

SALLY FERRELL, *mother of bombing victim Susan Ferrell*

Ten years later, the pain of Susan's death subsides but remains like a lingering, chronic illness. Helping keep this illness of grief at bay and giving us courage and strength has been the meaningful, ongoing work of compassionate Oklahomans. We shall never forget the leadership of Bob Johnson and all the others to establish the Oklahoma City Memorial. It not only records and archives the history but actively educates the public, especially the children. How else can we have hope our grandchildren will not be faced with such horror?

Many good works and remembrances of 168 victims have been accomplished far and wide, from educational scholarships to the laying of bricks. Susan's name appears on a brick in a Sand Springs downtown garden, as do others. At a Tennessee roadside stop, we found a moving remembrance of April 19 carved in stone.

Some New York family members and rescue workers came to Oklahoma City and found comfort and understanding at the memorial. I gave them each a packet of flower seeds in memory of Susan and all the others. It was my way of sharing the joy that Susan spoke of that beautiful morning ten years ago when she said, "I'm so happy it's spring and I can plant my flowers."

ROBERT M. JOHNSON, *founding chairman, Oklahoma City National Memorial*

The Oklahoma City bombing and 9/11 broke our hearts and dampened our spirits. Although our hearts and spirits have healed, all of us have been diminished, and scars will remain. I believe our experience in Oklahoma has confirmed that memorialization is an effective means of soothing those scars.

Without the Oklahoma City National Memorial and Museum, we would have shortchanged future generations. Without it, they could not learn of the horror of the tragedy and the innocence we lost. Without it, they could not go to the memorial and learn and resolve to do what they can in their own lives to help prevent violence.

As a state, we could have responded to the forces of hate with more hate, but we did not. Rather, the museum captures our response, consisting of thousands of acts of virtue—a selfless response known to the world as the Oklahoma Standard. As we are judged by future generations, in the museum, they will see that in April 1995, evil did not triumph.

The Oklahoma City National Memorial, in all its power and beautiful grandeur, is not about the monumental or the spectacular: It is about people. The memorial will forever remember our losses and the erosion of our senses of innocence and security, and, for the generations, it will represent the commitment of the people of the United States to the preservation of peace and the sanctity of life.

CHRISTOPHER GROSS, *senior financial analyst for Applied Materials in Santa Clara, California, who donated his salary to a special fund for scholarships for victims' children in 1995*

After the bombing, all I could think about was what it would have been like to grow up without a parent. I knew immediately that many children who lost their mother or father were going to need extra help, especially after the day-to-day media attention waned. Giving up my salary was a way to motivate others to offer what they could to make certain that these children would have one less thing to worry about as they moved forward with their lives. My folks paid for my college education, and finishing college without debt helped me save enough money to enable me to work for the year without receiving a paycheck. I have never looked back on the financial implications of donating $54,000, and the experience was the most rewarding thing I have ever done. In 1996, I entered Harvard Business School, and today I work for OQO, a start-up computer company in San Francisco.

GARY MARRS, *chief of the Oklahoma City Fire Department, 1993-2002*

In some ways, it's hard to believe it has been ten years since the Oklahoma City bombing, but in some ways it seems like recent history. I still think about our community and how we took care of our own. That's just the way we do things here in Oklahoma, period. The community showed its respect and continues to show support through the Oklahoma City National Memorial and Museum. I find it a little humbling that people still want me involved in things because they think I bring something to the table as an expert. But we just did the best job we could. The recognition of Oklahoma values brought awareness to what is good about us. In my travels after the bombing, people always remarked on how well we came together. And I told them, "That's just us. That's what we do."

REMARKS BY THE PRESIDENT

George W. Bush's comments at the dedication of the Oklahoma

City National Memorial Museum

February 19, 2001

President George W. Bush laughs during his speech at the 2001 dedication of the Oklahoma City National Memorial Museum. Don Ferrell, who lost his daughter Susan in the bombing, applauds.

THANK YOU FOR your kind words. Thank you all very much. Thank you very much. Mr. Governor, thank you very much. The picture was a better picture.

Laura and I are honored to be here. I want to thank the choirs for their beautiful music. I want to thank the congressional delegation for your hospitality. Mr. Mayor, thank you very much; it's good to see you again, sir.

I appreciate so very much the tour of the Memorial Center we just took. It is a really well done place. It's powerful. And, Bob Johnson, you and your board deserve a lot of credit.

I particularly want to thank our tour guides, Jeannine Gist and Richard Williams and Major Ed Hill. A lot of Americans are going to come and be better people for having walked through this center.

I want to thank the families of the victims, the survivors and the fine citizens of the great state of Oklahoma for your welcome.

One of the things that we remember of that day in 1995 is the conduct of the leaders of Oklahoma—Oklahoma City and of your state, particularly your governor and his great wife, Cathy. You had just taken office, Frank—and, yet, in the aftermath of the awful moment you showed such character and strength. America came to admire that, and the people of Oklahoma will never forget it.

Americans found a lot to admire in Oklahoma during those days. You suffered so much and you responded with courage. Your loss was great and your pain was deep; but far greater and deeper was your care for one another. That is what lasts and that's what brings us back to this place on this day.

MEMORIALS DO NOT take away the pain. They cannot fill the emptiness. But they can mark a place in time and tell the value of what was lost. The debris is gone and the building is no more. Now, this is a place of peace and remembrance and life.

A mother who lost her daughter here will be working in the new museum. She said, when I come down here to the memorial I've always felt a very good feeling—this is where she was happy, and this is where she was last. The time for mourning may pass, but the time for remembering never does.

Here, we remember one act of malice. The Gates of Time record the very moment of it. Yet, we also remember many acts of human kindness and heroism and love. Some are recorded, some not. But by 9:03 a.m. on that morning, a new and hopeful story was already being written. The truth of Oklahoma City is the courage and comfort you found in one another. It began with the rescue. It continues with this memorial. It is recorded in this museum.

Together, you endured. You chose to live out the words of St. Paul, "Be not overcome of evil, but overcome evil with good."

Because of this spirit, your memorial belongs to all America. People from all over our country come here every day, and will always come to look and remember and say a prayer. Oklahoma City will always be one of those places in our national memory where the worst and the best both came to pass.

The presence of evil always reminds us of the need for vigilance. All of us have an obligation to confront evil, wherever and whenever it manifests itself. We must enforce laws and reject hatred and bigotry. And we have a duty to watch for warning signs.

Last year the United States Secret Service conducted a study of targeted violence in our nation's schools. They found that most of the time, the person who planned the violence told someone before the attack. In almost every case, the individual displayed some behavior that caused others to be concerned. We all have a duty to watch for and report troubling signs.

The evil that destroys and the good that saves are equally real. Both can be taught. Both can be learned. All order in our society begins in the souls of citizens. Character is often shaped or bent early in life. In every family, and in every school, we must teach our children to know and choose the good, to teach values that defeat violence, to teach good kids—kids to respect one another, to do unto others, the meaning of love.

Our first response to evil must be justice, yet a part of us is never satisfied by justice alone. We must search for more—for understanding and healing, beyond punishment. Faith tells us that all wrongs are righted, and all suffering redeemed. But that faith is tested, especially for those of you with empty chairs at home. Hardest of all is the loss of the children, of the lives taken so soon after they were given.

Hundreds of people gathered for the 2001 dedication of the museum.

I hope it helps to remember that we are never closer to God than when we grieve. Faith is tested in suffering. And faith is often born in suffering, for that is when we seek the hope we most need. That is when we awaken to the greatest hope there is, that is when we look beyond our lives to the hour when God will wipe away every tear, and death will be swallowed up in victory.

On this earth, tragedy may come even on a warm spring day, but tragedy can never touch eternity. This is where they were last; but beyond the gates of time lie a life eternal and a love everlasting. You in Oklahoma City are victims of tragedy and witnesses to hope. You have overcome evil, and you have suffered with courage. And for that, your nation is grateful.

God bless.

ATTORNEY GENERAL

JOHN ASHCROFT'S

remarks at the dedication of the Oklahoma

City Federal Building

May 3, 2004

THANK YOU, [CONGRESSMAN] Ernie [Istook], for that introduction. I thank Carl Truscott, the new director of the ATF, for joining me.

Distinguished friends, family, and honored guests, I am grateful for the opportunity to be here with you to share in this day of hope and healing.

Each morning, I begin my day reviewing the continuing terrorist plots and threats against the United States. I see in daily dispatches and reports the ceaseless efforts of terrorists to attack America. Day after day, I see evidence of their insatiable desire for revenge and death.

Today, I am reminded why terrorists will never succeed in fulfilling their desire to defeat America with acts of terror. This gathering, this building, and this city show that men and women —allowed to breathe the bracing air of freedom—will always come together to defeat the tyranny of fear and hatred.

The people of Oklahoma City know the terrible cost of terrorism. You have seen firsthand the death and carnage that terrorists seek. You have felt the loss of loved ones. You have lived in the aftermath of man-made destruction. Long before September 11, 2001, you had to grapple with the cost of hate and the price of extremism.

Yet today, we are brought together by noble and enduring values—values that were expressed in the lives of those who were taken here.

As Abraham Lincoln surveyed the battlefield at Gettysburg,

he said, quote, "[W]e cannot dedicate...we cannot consecrate ...we cannot hallow this ground....The world will little note, nor long remember what we say here, but it can never forget what they did here. It is for us the living, rather, to be dedicated here to the unfinished work...."

We face the same challenge that confronted Lincoln and his listeners at Gettysburg.

We gather to dedicate more than a building. We gather to dedicate ourselves to "the unfinished work" of freedom. We dedicate ourselves to liberty and to the rule of law that will be defended by those who work each day in this new federal building.

Real dedications are found in lives lived, days devoted. With each act of service, governance, education, law enforcement, prevention and prosecution, this building will be rededicated.

AP/WIDE WORLD PHOTOS

This facility will be dedicated as lives are here dedicated to serve others.

We cannot forget the past.

We will never forget. One hundred sixty-eight lives were lost that bright, sunny morning more than nine years ago. Children lost moms and dads; brothers lost sisters; mothers and fathers lost innocent, irreplaceable children, including unborn children.

We will not forget because, in this nation, we are dedicated to the fundamental belief that every life is precious. We remember the achievements, the dreams, and the potential of those who were lost. And it is because we hold every life precious that this nation will never bow to terror.

I am grateful to the people of Oklahoma and Oklahoma City. The response to the attacks here is an example of leadership for America, and it is an example for the world. Pain and bloodshed were turned into action and resolution.

Shortly after September 11, President Bush said, "Terrorist attacks can shake the foundations of our biggest buildings, but they cannot touch the foundation of America."

That foundation is secure as long as citizens dedicate themselves to the enduring vision that founded this nation.

We saw that dedication in the aftermath of this attack. Thanks to the help of courageous citizens, local law enforcement, and the justice community, those responsible for this craven act of murder were hunted down and caught. They were prosecuted. And they were imprisoned. One murderer has met his final end.

We will not rest until those who commit terror are brought to justice.

The first priority of government is to protect the lives and liberties of the people. Over the last three years, the world—and the networks of terror—have seen and felt our nation's tireless commitment to justice.

It is especially fitting that this new building links the business districts with downtown neighborhoods. It stands at the crossroads of the community we defend—a culture of life and liberty, free trade and security. This federal building is a reminder of that precious rule of law that binds us together in equality and links our liberties at home with our freedoms in the marketplace.

Today we remember, and we continue in sorrow. But we also dedicate ourselves, and this facility, to continuing the unfinished work Lincoln spoke of—the unfinished work of freedom.

We look to the future. This building challenges us profoundly to endurance and resilience. It is a reminder to every terrorist that this nation will not be beaten by murderous acts. It is a shining symbol that in America we will rebuild: Stronger... Higher...And ever more hopeful.

Thank you. God bless you. And God bless America.

United States Attorney General John Ashcroft during the Pledge of Allegiance at the 2004 dedication of the Oklahoma City Federal Building

AP/WIDE WORLD PHOTOS

*Governor Frank Keating presents the Ray Downey Courage and Valor Award to
Ray Downey's wife, Rosalie Downey, and son, New York firefighter Joe Downey.
Ray Downey oversaw the Oklahoma City rescue and died on September 11, 2001.*

GOVERNOR FRANK KEATING'S

remarks about Ray Downey,

originally published in state newspapers

September 13, 2001

I FIRST MET Ray Downey late on the night of April 19, 1995, in front of the bleak, bombed-out skeleton of the Murrah building in Oklahoma City. It was rainy and cold, and we were just beginning the awful work of bringing out the dead from the scene of what was, until Tuesday, the worst domestic terror attack in American history.

For the next two weeks, as a member of New York's Urban Search and Rescue team and as site operations chief for the Federal Emergency Management Agency, Chief Downey was far more than a helping hand. He was an inspiration of unrivaled expertise. He was also a man whose beaming smile lightened some dark hours. I was honored to say he became my friend.

Tuesday, Downey rode the collapsing World Trade Center down to his death. We in Oklahoma fear that many more of our friends from New York gave their lives in Tuesday's rescue effort. If our prayers weigh a bit more heavily than those from other states, it's because we came to know so many New York firefighters and police officers in 1995. The New York search and rescue team was one of the first FEMA groups deployed to Oklahoma City after the bombing.

Some of those who survived the 1995 bombing are having an especially difficult time with the events in New York,

Washington, and Pennsylvania. It's a nightmare replayed, on a much larger scale, and our wounds are still raw. But our grief is tempered by memories of the good men and women who stood with us six years ago. Tuesday, as I watched the endless replays of those tall towers collapsing, I couldn't help but think of Ray Downey.

Ray had been a firefighter for thirty-nine years. He was the most decorated member of the New York Fire Department, perhaps the nation's top expert in what firefighters call "collapse rescue." In Oklahoma City, he diagnosed the tottering Murrah building with a practiced eye and worked with us to shore up the structure so rescue and recovery operations could proceed.

Ray named the huge concrete slab that hung ominously overhead. "That 'Mother,'" he said simply, as if it had no power to fall on him. He worked with local firefighters and other FEMA teams to place support beams that prevented the rubble from shifting. I have no doubt that he saved lives in Oklahoma City.

I looked forward to seeing Ray each day at the bomb site, and I hope he felt the same. We bantered about our shared Catholic religion, and when some nuns from Germany sent some rosaries to my office, I went in search of Ray to give one to him. A year later, when I visited New York to pin yet another decoration on Ray Downey and his fellow fire and police heroes, he was still wearing the rosary. I hope he had it with him Tuesday.

When the New York team filed its report after its tour of duty in Oklahoma City, it ended with four words: "God Bless You All." Today, Oklahoma returns that sentiment to New York, and to all those members of the police and fire services who died, were injured, or who remain missing.

Not long ago, Ray attended the funeral of another New York firefighter who died in the line of duty. "Sometimes," he told a reporter, "goodbye is really goodbye."

I refuse to believe that, Ray. You and those who so proudly wore the badge and principles for which you died will always be with us in Oklahoma.

GOVERNOR BRAD HENRY'S

remarks on the sentencing of federal building

bombing conspirator Terry Nichols

August 9, 2004

ALTHOUGH THIS HAS been a difficult and sometimes frustrating process, I hope today's sentencing brings a sense of closure to the thousands of Oklahomans who were changed forever by the tragedy of April 19, 1995. The sentence by Judge Taylor ensures that Terry Nichols will spend the rest of his life behind prison bars.

The Official Record

179

The Survivor Tree, located on the circular promontory at the Oklahoma City National Memorial

The Oklahoma City bombing will go down in history books as one of the worst terrorist attacks on United States soil in American history: 168 people—most of them civilians, nineteen of them children—lost their lives. In the days following, as the magnitude of the tragedy made itself clear, handmade declarations appeared on police cars, in store windows, on billboards, and in epistles attached to the chainlink fence that encircled the bombing site. Ultimately, that we not forget the victims was the one request family members asked of us.

ACKNOWLEDGMENTS

SPECIAL THANKS TO the following individuals who worked so hard to create the three editions of *The Official Record of the Oklahoma City Bombing*: Joan Henderson, Louisa McCune, Steven Walker, Steffie Corcoran, Brooke Adcox, Colleen McIntyre, Lisa Breckenridge, Kathy Hehnly, Kim Ryan, Laura Beam, Jeanne Devlin, Nancy Woodard, Anne M. Barajas, Renae Romans, Aimée Winneberger, Priscilla Mohnkern, Andrea Walker, Brian Brown, Melanie Breeden, Becky Isaac, Jane Leonard, Pam Poston, Melanie Holt, Walt Disney, Carole A. Lee, *and* Roger Johnson

Additional thanks to the State of Oklahoma, the Oklahoma Tourism and Recreation Department, the Oklahoma Tourism and Recreation Commission, the Oklahoma State Legislature, Governor Frank Keating, Governor Brad Henry, *and* Lieutenant Governor Mary Fallin